D0179705

☆ ☆ ☆ ☆ ☆ ☆ ☆ ☆ ☆ ☆

WHO'S COUNTING?

HOW FRAUDSTERS AND BUREAUCRATS PUT YOUR VOTE AT RISK

John Fund and Hans von Spakovsky

Encounter Books 𝑒 New York • London

© 2012 by John Fund and Hans von Spakovsky

All rights reserved. No part of this publication may be reproduced, stored in a retrieval system, or transmitted, in any form or by any means, electronic, mechanical, photocopying, recording, or otherwise, without the prior written permission of Encounter Books, 900 Broadway, Suite 601, New York, New York, 10003.

First American edition published in 2012 by Encounter Books, an activity of Encounter for Culture and Education, Inc., a nonprofit, tax exempt corporation. Encounter Books website address: www.encounterbooks.com

Manufactured in the United States and printed on acid-free paper. The paper used in this publication meets the minimum requirements of ANSI/NISO Z39.48 1992 (R 1997) (*Permanence of Paper*).

FIRST AMERICAN EDITION

LIBRARY OF CONGRESS CATALOGING-IN-PUBLICATION DATA
Fund, John H., 1957–
Who's counting?: how fraudsters and bureaucrats put your vote at risk / by John Fund and Hans von Spakovsky.
p. cm.
Includes bibliographical references and index.
ISBN 978-1-59403-618-7 (pbk.: alk. paper)—
ISBN 978-1-59403-619-4 (ebook) 1. Elections—Corrupt practices—United States. 2. Political corruption—United States.
I. Von Spakovsky, Hans. II. Title.
JK1994.F87 2012
364.1'324—dc23
2012017926

☆ ☆ ☆ ☆ ☆ ☆ ☆ ☆

*To my family, the source
for my curiosity and strength.
—John Fund*

*This book is dedicated to my parents,
Anatol and Traudel von Spakovsky, immigrants to
the United States who were true Americans.
—Hans von Spakovsky*

Contents

Contents

☆ ☆ ☆ ☆ ☆ ☆ ☆ ☆ ☆

Introduction

Come November 2012 we may be on the brink of repeating the 2000 Florida election debacle—but this time in several states—with allegations of voter fraud, intimidation, and manipulation of voting machines added to the generalized chaos that sent the Bush–Gore race into overtime.

There is still time to reduce the chance of another electoral meltdown, both this year and in future years. But this will not happen unless we acknowledge that the United States has a haphazard, fraud-prone election system more befitting an emerging Third World country than the world's leading democracy.

With its hanging chads, butterfly ballots, and Supreme Court intervention, the Florida fiasco compelled this country to confront an ugly reality: that we have been making do with what noted political scientist Walter Dean Burnham has called "the modern world's sloppiest electoral systems."

Just how sloppy was demonstrated in February 2012, when the Pew Center on the States found 1.8 million names of deceased persons still registered to vote on state rolls. Roughly 2.75 million people are registered to vote in more than one state. The study found altogether that 24 million voter registrations—13 percent of the nation's total—contained major inaccuracies or were otherwise invalid. That's a lot of room for confusion or mischief.

With the demise of most big-city political machines and the rise of election supervision by nonpartisan civil service employees, concerns about honest and accurate election counts receded. But Dr. Larry J. Sabato, the director of the University of Virginia's Center for Politics, who cowrote a pioneering book on the subject, *Dirty Little Secrets: The Persistence of Corruption in American Politics*, warned as early as the 1990s that "voter fraud is making a comeback." As he testified before Congress after the Florida debacle: "When we look at the registration system and voting process we have to balance two conflicting values; one, the goal of full and informed participation of the electorate, and two, the integrity of the system. To the extent that we keep expanding the participation rate and make it easier and easier for people to register and vote, we almost certainly increase the chances for voter fraud. So, in a sense it is a tradeoff. To move completely in the direction of one value as opposed to the other is foolhardy."

"My strong suspicion—based on scores of investigated and unexplored tips from political observers and interviewees over the years—is that some degree of vote fraud can be found almost everywhere, and serious outbreaks can and do occur in every region of the country. Whether fraud is Democratic or Republican, or located in the North or the South or the West, the effect on American democracy is similar. While electoral hanky-panky affects the outcome in only a small proportion of elections [mainly in very tight races], one fraudulent ballot is one too many for the integrity of the system and the confidence that the people have in the system. The need for reform is urgent and clear. Voter turnout in the United States is traditionally too low, and cynicism among citizens too high, to permit the malodorous malady of election fraud to continue unchecked—or to spread."[1]

The 2000 recount was more than merely a national embarrassment; it left a lasting scar on the American electoral psyche. A Zogby poll a few years ago found that 38 percent of Americans still regarded the 2000 election outcome as questionable. Many Republicans believe that Democratic judges on the Florida Supreme Court tried to hand their state to Al Gore via selective partisan recounts and the illegal votes of felons and aliens. Many Democrats feel that the justices of the U.S. Supreme Court tilted toward George Bush, and they refuse to accept his victory as valid. But this issue transcends red-state-versus-blue-state partisan grievances. Many Americans are convinced that politicians can't be trusted to play by the rules, and either will commit fraud or intimidate voters at the slightest opportunity.

Indeed, the level of suspicion has grown so dramatically that it threatens to undermine our political system. A Fox News poll taken in April 2012 reported that 34 percent of voters believe supporters of voter ID laws are trying to "steal" elections by keeping eligible voters away from the polls. But more people—50 percent—think opponents of the laws are acting in bad faith by trying to increase participation from ineligible or illegal voters.[2]

Such attitudes can create a toxic brew. The United States ranks 139th out of 163 democracies in the rate of voter participation. "If this escalates, we're in horrendous shape as a country," says Curtis Gans, who runs the Center for the Study of the American Electorate at American University. "If election results are followed by lawsuits, appeals, fire, and counterfire, many people who are already saying to hell with the process are going to exit." The more that voting is left to the zealous or self-interested few, the more we see harshly personal campaigns that dispense with any positive vision of our national future.[3]

A Rasmussen Reports poll taken for this book found that both interest in and concern about voter fraud is high. Nearly two-thirds of Americans reported they were following news reports about voter fraud closely or somewhat closely. When asked how serious a problem it is, 64 percent said "very serious" or "somewhat serious." Interestingly, the highest levels of concern came from African Americans (64 percent) , conservatives (85 percent), and those earning under $20,000 a year (71 percent). When it came to remedies, an astonishing 82 percent of respondents supported requiring that voters prove their identity before voting. The lowest support across demographic groups was still sky-high: 67 percent of African Americans, 67 percent of Democrats, and 58 percent of professed liberals all backed having people prove who they say they are as a condition of voting.[4]

The Supreme Court is in agreement with the majority. In a unanimous decision reinstating Arizona's voter identification law in 2006, it stated:

> Confidence in the integrity of our electoral processes is essential to the functioning of our participatory democracy. Voter fraud drives honest citizens out of the democratic process and breeds distrust of our government. Voters who fear their legitimate votes will be outweighed by fraudulent ones will feel disenfranchised.[5]

Confusion and claims of fraud are again likely this time around, especially if the election is as close as it was in 2000. Can the nation take another Florida-style controversy?

Indeed, we may be on the way to turning Election Day into Election Month (or Election Year) through a new legal quagmire: election by litigation. Every close race now carries with it the prospect of demands for recounts, lawsuits, and seating challenges in Congress. "We're waiting for the day that pols can just cut out the middleman and settle all elections in court," jokes Chuck Todd, former editor of the political tip sheet *The Hotline*. Such gallows humor may be entirely appropriate, given the predicament we face. Much as the battle over the Supreme Court nomination of Robert Bork changed, apparently forever, the politics of judicial appointments, the 2000 election may have marked a permanent change in how elections can be decided: the number of election-related lawsuits has skyrocketed since 2000.

Democrats plan to have more than ten thousand lawyers on the ground in every state in November 2012, ready for action if the election is close, and they see a way to contest it. "If you think of election problems as akin to forest fires, the woods are no drier than they were in 2000, but many more people have matches," says Doug Chapin, founder of Electionline.org, an Internet clearinghouse of election news. If the trend toward litigation continues, winners in the future may have to hope not only that they win, but that their leads are beyond "the margin of litigation."

Some of the sloppiness that makes fraud and foul-ups in election counts possible seems to be built into the system by design. The "Motor Voter Law"—the National Voter Registration Act of 1993—the first piece of legislation signed into law by President Clinton upon entering office, imposed fraud-friendly rules on the states by requiring driver's license bureaus and welfare agencies to register anyone applying for a license, and to offer mail-in registration with no identification needed, while making it difficult to purge "deadwood" voters (those who have died or moved). In 2012, the voter rolls in many American cities include more names than the U.S. Census listed as the total number of residents over age 18. Philadelphia's voter rolls, for instance, have increased dramatically as the city's population has declined. CBS's *60 Minutes* created a stir in 1999 when it found people in California using mail-in forms to register fictitious people, or even pets, and then obtaining absentee ballots in those names. By this means, the illegal alien who assassinated the Mexican presidential candidate Luis Donaldo Colosio was registered to vote in San Pedro, California—twice.

Ironically, Mexico and many other countries have election systems that are far more secure than ours. To obtain voter credentials in Mexico, a citizen must present a photo, write a signature, and give a thumbprint. To guard against tampering, the voter card includes a picture with a hologram covering it, a magnetic strip, and a serial number. To cast a ballot, voters must present the card and be certified by a thumbprint scanner. This system was instrumental in allowing the 2000 election of Vicente Fox, the first opposition-party candidate to be elected president in 70 years.

But in the United States, at a time of heightened security and mundane rules that require citizens to show identification to travel or even rent a video, only 17 states require some form of documentation in order to vote. "Why should the important process of voting be the one exception to this rule?" asks Karen Saranita, a former fraud investigator for a Democratic state senator in California. Americans agree. Polls have consistently shown that people should be required to show a driver's license or some other form of photo ID before they are allowed to vote.

The reason is because citizens instinctively realize that some people will be tempted to cut corners in the cutthroat world of politics. "Some of the world's most clever people are attracted to politics, because that's where the power is," says Larry Sabato, the University of Virginia political scientist. "So they're always going to be one step ahead of the law."

Election fraud, whether it's phony voter registrations, illegal absentee ballots, vote-buying, shady recounts, or old-fashioned ballot-box stuffing, can be found in every part of the United States, although it is probably spreading because of the ever-so-tight red state/blue state divisions that have polarized the country and created so many close elections lately. Although most fraud is found in urban areas, there are recent scandals in rural Kentucky and Minnesota; St. Louis, Detroit, New Orleans, and Memphis have all had election-related scandals. Wisconsin officials convicted a New York heiress working for Al Gore of giving homeless people cigarettes if they rode in a van to the polls and voted. *The Miami Herald* won a Pulitzer Prize in 1999 for uncovering how "vote brokers" employed by mayoral candidate Xavier Suarez stole the 1997 election by tampering with 4,740 absentee ballots. Many were cast by homeless people from outside Miami who were paid $10 apiece and shuttled to the elections office in vans. All of the absentee ballots were thrown out by a court four months later, and Mr. Suarez's opponent was installed as mayor.

But such interventions are rare, even when fraud is proven. In 1997, the House of Representatives voted along partisan lines to demand that the Justice Department prosecute Hermandad Mexicana Nacional, a group that investigators for the House Administration Committee said registered hundreds of illegal voters who were not citizens in a razor-thin congressional race in Orange County, California. But federal immigration officials refused to cooperate, citing "privacy" concerns, and nothing was done beyond yanking a federal contract that paid Hermandad to conduct citizenship classes. The same year, a Senate probe of fraud in a Louisiana Senate race found more than 1,500 cases in which two voters provided the same Social Security number. But further investigations collapsed after Democratic senators abandoned the probe, calling it unfair; Attorney General Janet Reno then removed FBI agents from the case because the probe wasn't "bipartisan."

A note about partisanship: Since Democrats figure prominently in the vast majority of examples of election fraud described in this book, some readers will jump to the conclusion that this is a one-sided attack on a single party. The authors do not maintain that Republicans are inherently more virtuous or honest than anyone else in politics. Voter fraud occurs both in Republican strongholds such as Kentucky hollows and Democratic bastions such as south Texas. When Republicans operated political machines (such as Philadelphia's Meehan dynasty, up until 1951, or the patronage mill of Nassau County, New York, until the 1990s), they were fully capable of bending—and breaking—the rules. Earl Mazo, the journalist who exhaustively documented the election fraud in Richard Daley's Chicago that may have handed Illinois to John F. Kennedy in the photo-finish 1960 election, says there was "definitely fraud" in downstate Republican counties, "but they didn't have the votes to counterbalance Chicago."[6]

While they have not had the control of local and administrative offices necessary to tilt the rules improperly in their favor, Republicans have at times been guilty of improper tactics. In December 2011, Maryland political consultant Paul Schurick was convicted of authorizing robocalls on Election Day that used false information to discourage 112,000 registered Democrats in largely black Baltimore and in Prince George's County from voting in 2010. Schurick was sentenced to 500 hours of community service and a probation period of four years.

Schurick was the campaign manager for ultimately unsuccessful Republican gubernatorial candidate Robert L. Ehrlich

Jr., and paid Julius Henson, a black Democratic consultant who was a gun for hire, to write the robocall script. It implied that the call came from Democrats who had already won, and read: "Our goals have been met. The polls are correct, and we took it back. We're OK. Relax. Everything's fine. The only thing left is to watch it on TV tonight."

Henson, who was convicted in May 2012 on one of four counts in the incident, has used sleazy tactics on behalf of many candidates in Maryland, usually Democrats. In 1998 he was behind an effort to portray Republican gubernatorial candidate Ellen R. Sauerbrey as a racist. And in 2002, while working for Democrats, he vowed to portray Ehrlich, who was running his first race for governor that year, as a "Nazi." By 2010, he was working for Ehrlich as a campaign consultant.[7]

In their book *Dirty Little Secrets*, Larry Sabato and coauthor Glenn Simpson, formerly of *The Wall Street Journal*, noted another factor as to why Republican election fraud is less common. Republican-base voters are middle-class, and not easily induced to commit fraud, while "the pool of people who appear to be available and more vulnerable to an invitation to participate in vote fraud tend to lean Democratic." Some liberal activists that Sabato and Simpson interviewed even partly justified fraudulent electoral behavior on the grounds that because the poor and dispossessed have so little political clout, "extraordinary measures [for example, stretching the absentee ballot or registration rules] are required to compensate." Paul Herrison, director of the Center for American Politics at the University of Maryland, agrees that "most incidents of wide-scale voter fraud reportedly occur in inner cities, which are largely populated by minority groups."

Democrats are far more skilled at encouraging poor people—who need money—to participate in vote-buying schemes. "I had no choice. I was hungry that day," Thomas Felder told *The Miami*

Herald in explaining why he illegally voted in a mayoral election. "You wanted the money, you were told who to vote for." Sometimes it's not just food that vote stealers are hungry for. A former Democratic congressman gave one of the authors this explanation of why voting irregularities more often crop up in his party's backyard: "When many Republicans lose an election, they go back into what they call the private sector. When many Democrats lose an election, they lose power and money. They need to eat, and people will do an awful lot in order to eat."

Investigations of voter fraud are inherently political; and because they often involve race, they often are not zealously pursued or prosecuted. Many federal and state prosecutors remain leery of tackling fraud or intimidation, and sentences imposed for convictions are often far too light. While voting irregularities are common, the number of people who have spent hard time in jail in the last few years as a result of a conviction for voter fraud can be counted on your fingers.

The former U.S. Attorney for the western district of Louisiana, Donald Washington, admits that "most of the time, we can't do much of anything [about ballot-box improprieties] until the election is over. And the closer we get to the election, the less willing we are to get involved because of just the appearance of impropriety, just the appearance of the federal government somehow shading how this election ought to occur."[8] Several prosecutors told the authors they fear charges of racism or of a return to Jim Crow vote-suppression tactics if they pursue fraud cases. Hilary Shelton of the NAACP had the following exchange with Eric Shawn of Fox News in 2012:

Shawn: "You talk about Jim Crow. Is voter ID similar?" Shelton: "Absolutely." Shawn: "Even to murder? Even to lynchings?" Shelton: "It's the same thing in many ways.

Now look, we can argue that it's not as violent. It's not as bloody. Bottom line is, what kind of effect does it have?"

Artur Davis, the former Democratic congressman from Alabama who seconded Barack Obama's nomination for president at the 2008 Democratic convention, finds that analogy preposterous. "I never heard a single voter in my 68 percent African American district complain to me about ID being something that was onerous or burdensome or difficult."

He went on to say: "The idea that people in low-income African American communities are bothered or intimidated or burdened by attaching just a few responsibilities to their all-important core right of voting—it's a condescending idea. It's a patronizing idea. If the law works the same with respect to everybody, it's free and clear of whatever history or bigotry or racial animus [exists]."[9]

And when voters are disenfranchised by the counting of improperly cast ballots or outright fraud, their civil rights are violated just as surely as if they were prevented from voting. The integrity of the ballot box is just as important to the credibility of elections as is access to it. Voting irregularities have a long pedigree in America, stretching back to the founding of the nation—though most people thought the "bad old days" had ended in 1948, after pistol-packing Texas sheriffs helped stuff Ballot Box 13, stealing a U.S. senate seat and setting Lyndon Johnson on his road to the White House. Then came the 2004 primary election, when Representative Ciro Rodriguez, a Democrat, charged that during a recount, a missing ballot box reappeared in south Texas with enough votes to make his opponent the Democratic nominee by 58 votes.

Even after the events in Florida in 2000, the media tend to downplay or ignore stories of election incompetence, manipulation, or theft. Allowing such abuses to vanish into an informational black hole in effect legitimates them. The refusal to insist on simple procedural changes like requiring a photo ID to vote, secure technology, and more vigorous prosecutions accelerates our drift toward banana-republic elections.

Scrutinizing our own elections the way we have traditionally scrutinized voting in developing countries is a sad, but necessary, step in the right direction.

☆ ☆ ☆ ☆ ☆ ☆ ☆ ☆ ☆

CHAPTER ONE

A Crisis of Voting Confidence

WOULD OBAMACARE HAVE PASSED
WITHOUT VOTER FRAUD?

Minnesota's 2008 Senate race wasn't just an ordinary election. Disputes over the razor-thin margin held the Senate seat vacant for eight months, until early July 2009. That was when Democrat Al Franken was declared the winner by 312 votes by Minnesota's Supreme Court.

Franken's seating gave the Democrats the critical 60 votes they needed to overcome Republican filibusters, and proved vital to the passage of ObamaCare. They quickly lost their 60-seat majority in January 2010, when Scott Brown won the Senate seat of the late Ted Kennedy in a special election. But in the preceding six months, Democrats rammed ObamaCare through the Senate, wrapping up the process with a late-night Christmas Eve vote in which they had no margin for error.

"ObamaCare doesn't pass if the result of the Minnesota election is different," says former Senator Norm Coleman, whom Franken defeated.[1] Most observers agree with him that ObamaCare in its final form wouldn't have passed without Senator Franken's vote; the process by which he was seated is thus worth reexamining.

Minnesota Majority, a conservative watchdog group, has come up with compelling evidence that at least 1,099 ineligible felons voted illegally in the Franken *v.* Coleman contest. That's more than three times the victory margin Franken eventually achieved through litigation.

Minnesota Majority compared criminal apprehension data to voter history files, and then examined court records to verify matches, convictions, and probation records. The group's conclusions are bolstered by the fact that since 2009, courts in Minnesota have convicted 177 felons for voting illegally in the Senate race; another 66 felons are awaiting trial. The numbers aren't greater because the standard for convicting someone of voter fraud in Minnesota is that they must have both been ineligible, and "knowingly" voted unlawfully.[2]

Rick Hodsdon, the assistant prosecutor in charge of voter fraud for the Washington County Attorney's office, openly admits that a person can get off scot-free for voting illegally if he admits the crime and simply says he didn't intend to vote. "That's why some of our counties in Minnesota have received hundreds of referrals, and yet have prosecuted a relatively small number of cases."

Of course, no one can be certain how the felon votes uncovered by Minnesota Majority were cast. "I am highly skeptical that felons voted for one candidate or another en masse,"[3] says Sue Gaertner, the former Ramsey County Attorney who has convicted 27 felons for voting illegally. But there are clues to prove her wrong. In a 2003 study, sociologists Christopher Uggen and Jeff Manza found that an overwhelming majority of felons lean toward voting Democratic. They estimated that in 1992, Bill Clinton received 86 percent of votes cast by felons, and in 1996 a whopping 93 percent.[4] Statistician John Lott's own work in Washington State found that felons were 37 percent more likely to be registered Democrats even when accounting for race, gender, education level, religious habits, employment, age, and county of residence.

Indeed, in Minnesota, when Fox News went door-to-door to interview some of the felons who were convicted of voting illegally in 2008, nine of the 10 people interviewed said they had voted for Franken. When asked if she thought her vote helped Al Franken get into office, Sabrina Ruth Hall was blunt: "I don't know, but I hope it did."

Dan McGrath, the investigator who supervised Minnesota Majority's work, is distressed that so few convictions have been obtained despite the data he compiled and sent to prosecutors. "First, felon voting is wrong for a reason. We don't want gangsters and drug dealers electing county sheriffs and county attorneys and others ultimately in charge of the law." With that as a given, he says, it's "a shame we as private citizens had to compile the data ourselves before anything happened. I believe a far greater number of convictions could have been obtained if some prosecutors hadn't slow-walked the process. And the statute of limitations has run out on election-related crimes from the 2008 election, so we will never know all the facts or see many more people brought to justice."[5]

It is especially galling to McGrath that so many prosecutors resisted filing felon voting charges for so long. John Kingery, the head of the Minnesota County Attorneys Association, displayed his dismissive attitude toward voter fraud when he publicly complained that investigating the Minnesota Majority findings "diverted resources from the job that we want to do," and that felon voter investigations are not only time-consuming but costly.[6] Luckily, in Minnesota, failure to investigate voter-fraud allegations in affidavit form is a misdemeanor offense, and any county attorney found guilty must forfeit office.

The county attorneys association unsuccessfully lobbied the Minnesota legislature in 2012 to have that law changed.

EARLY-WARNING SIGNALS IGNORED

It's not as if Minnesota Majority hadn't issued early warnings that there were problems brewing with the November 2008 election. On October 16 of that year, the group sent Minnesota Secretary of State Mark Ritchie a letter expressing serious concerns about discrepancies in the voter rolls. Ritchie responded the next day by calling a press conference, assuring voters that Minnesota had the best election system in the country.

On October 31, Minnesota Majority forwarded evidence of its concerns to 30 county attorneys and 30 county auditors. Several failed to respond, and two flatly refused to initiate any probes, contrary to their obligation under Minnesota law.

After the election, Minnesota Majority found that the number of voters recorded as having cast a ballot did not match the number of ballots certified by the election canvassing board. There were approximately 40,000 more ballots counted than voter histories to account for them. It discovered a host of other anomalies:[7]

- Duplicate voter registrations: The group uncovered thousands of voter records having an exact match on the criteria of first name, middle name, last name, and birth year. The federal Help America Vote Act (HAVA) requires removing duplicate registrations from state election rolls.

- Double voting: It found evidence of nearly 100 cases in which voter registration and voter history records strongly indicated that a registrant may have voted more than once in a single election, and flagged thousands of additional voter records that merited more scrutiny.

- Vacant and nondeliverable addresses: The United States Postal Service flagged the recorded addresses of nearly 100,000 voters as being either "vacant" or "undeliverable." Minnesota Majority visited about two dozen of these undeliverable addresses to verify the USPS results, and discovered that approximately half of the addresses did not exist.

- Deceased voters: Using a standard deceased matching service commonly utilized by mailing houses, Minnesota Majority discovered thousands of individuals flagged as deceased but still on the active voter rolls. Following the 2008 election, it compared the state's voter history to a list of deceased voters and found thousands of potential matches. Further investigation into a small sampling turned up death records showing that several voters had died before someone apparently had voted in their name in the 2008 election.

- Voting by ineligible, mentally incapacitated wards: In October 2010 a number of mentally disabled individuals were observed being led into the Crow Wing County Courthouse to vote early by in-person absentee ballot. Witnesses described what amounts to the exploitation of mentally incapacitated, vulnerable adults, an all-too-common occurrence in too many states.

- Noncitizen voters: Prior to the 2008 election, then state Representative Laura Brod brought a list of possibly noncitizen voters to the attention of Secretary of State Ritchie. He gave her assurances that noncitizens would be cleaned from the voter rolls, and that checks would be made regularly going forward. After the election, a check of voter histories showed that not only were some of the same apparent noncitizens still registered, some had cast ballots.

- Bizarre voter registration records: Minnesota Majority turned up several thousand voters registered after August 1, 1983 whose birth years suggesting they were 108 years of age or older. The group also found nearly two thousand individuals who appear to have registered and voted *before* the age of 18.

FIXING THE PROBLEM

Despite the lengthy delays and lack of action on many cases, Minnesota Majority won praise in many quarters for its dogged work. Phil Carruthers of the Ramsey County district attorney's office found that the group "had done a good job in their review." The St. Paul *Pioneer Press*, the major newspaper in Ramsey County, editorialized that Minnesota Majority had "done important and constructive work" and "called attention to a weakness that needs repair."

The new Republican legislature Minnesotans elected in 2010 decided to tackle many of the shortcomings in the election process, and began its "repair." But efforts to pass a bill requiring that a photo ID be presented in order to vote were vetoed by Democratic Governor Mark Dayton, who claimed it was an overkill approach for problems that barely existed. In March 2012, after months of contentious argument, both houses of the state legislature passed a Constitutional amendment mandating photo ID. It will go before voters in November 2012.

Republican state senator Scott Newman says the bill makes very modest changes in the election law. The state's controversial same-day registration provisions will remain intact, but the curious practice of "vouching," by which a voter at a polling place can vouch for the identity of up to 15 people who lack a printed ID, would be ended.

Minnesota Majority contends that vouching is ripe for abuse, and McGrath cited examples.

In 1990, a Minneapolis poll watcher observed a person loitering in front of a Tenth Ward polling place wearing a "Wellstone green" button—it resembled U.S. senator Paul Wellstone's campaign buttons, but had no other text. The watcher saw people arriving in vans and looking for the person with the green button—they had been told that individual would vouch for everyone at registration, so they could vote.

In 2004, an organization called America Coming Together created a sophisticated vouching-fraud campaign that included preprinted name badges; as an e-mail to its Minnesota volunteers explained, these made it "easier to find a volunteer to vouch for a voter at the polls."

In 2010, eyewitnesses (including an election judge at a Minneapolis polling place) submitted sworn affidavits claiming that Organizing for America, a Democratic get-out-the-vote group, was systematically vouching for people registering on Election Day, even though the people doing the vouching clearly didn't personally know anyone. At least one volunteer admitted to vouching for someone she didn't know, but said she was just doing what she had been told to do.

"This issue has been a bitter bone of contention in this state for too long," says Senator Newman. "It's time the voters themselves settle the argument, and I'm convinced they will approve this Main Street, common-sense reform."

MORE MINNESOTA FUNNY BUSINESS

Leaving aside felon voting and all of the other irregularities Minnesota Majority found, the recount of the Minnesota vote showed a pattern of double standards in counting, and absentee balloting problems throughout, throwing the fairness and completeness of the entire process into doubt.

After the initial count on Election Night, Al Franken trailed Norm Coleman by 725 votes out of 2.9 million cast, including approximately 300,000 absentee ballots. After the initial canvass, which is the process by which counties resubmit to the secretary of state the vote totals of local precincts from Election Day, Coleman's lead shrank to only 206 votes.[8] So the Democratic strategy focused on how to conduct the recount so that votes could be added to Franken's total. The Franken legal team swarmed the recount, aggressively demanding that votes that had been disqualified for failing to meet state legal requirements be added to his count, while others be denied to Coleman.

The team's goldmine was the thousands of absentee ballots the Franken team claimed had been mistakenly rejected. While Coleman's lawyers demanded a uniform standard for how counties should reevaluate these rejected ballots, the Franken legal team ginned up an additional 1,350 absentees from Franken-leaning Democratic counties. By the time this treasure hunt ended, Franken was 312 votes up, and Coleman was left to file legal briefs to overturn that result.

Under Minnesota law, the *only* absentee ballots that should have been included in the recount were those that were actually cast in the election. As the state's Assistant Attorney General

Kenneth E. Raschke Jr. wrote to Democratic Secretary of State Ritchie on November 17, 2008, rejected absentee ballots are not considered as "cast" in an election.[9] "Only the ballots cast in the election and the summary statements certified by the election judges may be considered in the recount process," the Minnesota Code specifies in Section 204C.35, subd. 3.

In fact, Ritchie's own administrative rules (which he conveniently ignored for the benefit of Al Franken), as outlined in the Hand Count instructions of his 2008 Recount Guide (issued prior to the election), explained that:

> . . . an *administrative* recount . . . is *not* to determine who was eligible to vote. It is *not* to determine if campaign laws were violated. It is *not* to determine if absentee ballots were properly accepted. It is *not*—except for recounting the ballots—to determine if [election] judges did things right. It is simply to physically recount the ballots *for this race!*

As Assistant Attorney General Raschke said, the proper forum to remedy the claimed wrongful rejection of any absentee ballots is "a judicial election contest." However, a second letter, submitted to the Canvassing Board in December and this time from the Minnesota solicitor general, took the opposite view. He asserted that "a reviewing court would likely uphold a determination by the State Canvassing Board to accept amended reports . . . that include absentee ballots of voters . . . whose votes were improperly rejected by election officials due to administrative errors" even though such actions are "not necessarily contemplated under a strict reading of the statutes."[10]

Despite Minnesota law, the pre-election instructions for recounts issued by the secretary of state, and the conflicting opinions from the office of the state's attorney general, both the

Minnesota Canvassing Board and Mark Ritchie recommended that counties sort and count absentee ballots that were "mistakenly" rejected on election day. When Senator Coleman filed a petition with the Minnesota Supreme Court to stop this procedure, the court inexplicably ruled that such absentee ballots could be counted if "local election officials and the parties agree that an absentee ballot envelope was improperly rejected."[11]

Minnesota law does provide that obvious errors by election judges and county canvassing boards in the *counting or recording* of votes can be corrected if the candidates for that office unanimously agree in writing that an error occurred.[12] However, the Minnesota Supreme Court specifically held that the "improper rejection of an absentee ballot envelope is not within the scope of errors subject to correction" under this law.[13] Despite that determination, the court allowed local election officials to waive the applicable law established by the Minnesota legislature on absentee ballots, and make their own decisions on which previously rejected ballots should count.

Minnesota law also stipulates that a "ballot shall not be rejected for a technical error that does not make it impossible to determine the voter's intent."[14] Specific rules governing how to determine a voter's intent are defined by law. One of those rules is that if "the names of two candidates have been marked, and an attempt has been made to erase or obliterate one of the marks, a vote shall be counted for the remaining marked candidate."[15]

Yet the Minnesota Canvassing Board applied those rules inconsistently when it was determining voter intent on ballots with such technical errors. For example:

- It has been reported that on some ballots where voters had completely filled in the oval for Coleman and then put an "x" through the oval, the board determined that there was no vote for Coleman.

- On other ballots where the exact same type of markings were made for Franken, the board determined that they were valid votes for Franken.
- On a ballot where the voter had placed an "x" next to the Constitution Party candidate but had filled in the oval for Coleman, the board determined that there was no vote for anyone.
- On a ballot where the oval next to Coleman was filled in but an "x" had been placed next to Franken, the board determined this was a vote for Franken. [16]

There was no consistency in the board's determinations of intent other than that their inconsistent decisions overall seemed to benefit Al Franken.

What Franken understood was that courts would later be hostile to overruling decisions made by the canvassing board and local election officials, however arbitrary those decisions were. He was right. The three-judge panel overseeing the Coleman legal challenge and the Supreme Court that reviewed the panel's findings in essence found that Coleman hadn't demonstrated there was a willful or malicious attempt on behalf of officials to deny him the election. And so they refused to reopen what had become a forbidding tangle of irregularities, including reports of precincts where "ballots may have been double-counted during the manual recount" and returns "from one Minneapolis precinct in which some ballots were lost before the manual recount."[17] One of the members of the Minnesota Canvassing Board admitted there was "a very good likelihood" that there was double counting, but dismissed it as a problem "because there was very little of it."[18] The board allowed those double votes to be included in the recount, and the courts refused to question that dubious decision. Coleman didn't lose the election so much as he lost the fight to stop the state canvassing board from changing the vote-counting rules after ballots had been cast. The recount cost to both campaigns for legal fees, fund-raising, staff, and associated expenses was upwards of $20 million, an enormous sum.

Coleman's lawyers not only lost the legal battle, they lost the technology battle. The system implemented by the Franken campaign's lawyers to record and track all of the disputed ballots was quite extensive, far beyond what the Coleman campaign did, or what had been done in 2000 in Florida. According to Franken's lead attorney, Marc Elias, scanners, laptops, and other mobile devices were used to record and keep track of every single disputed ballot in every county in Minnesota. Decisions made by local election boards on each ballot were immediately uploaded to a "cloud" database set up by the campaign so that Elias and his legal team knew exactly what vote totals were for each candidate across the state at every point in time. This gave them a tactical advantage over Coleman's legal team by providing them with information on when to object or not object in individual ballot disputes.

As *The Wall Street Journal* editorialized after Franken's seating: "Modern elections don't end when voters cast their ballots. They only end after the lawyers count them."[19]

DEMOCRACY IN DANGER

The long litigation fight in Minnesota and the reversal of the results after the election did not help to inspire the public's confidence in our electoral process. Pollster John Zogby has spent a lot of time analyzing Americans' attitudes toward our election system, particularly in the wake of the bitterly contested elections we've seen recently. The picture his polls draw is one of suspicion and cynicism.

A 2006 Zogby poll found that at the stunning rate of 92 percent, Americans insist on the right to watch their votes being counted. And 80 percent strongly object to the use of secret computer software to tabulate votes without citizen access to that software. An earlier Zogby poll from 2004 found that nine percent of Americans don't believe their votes are counted accurately, and another eight percent aren't sure. Among African Americans, fully 18 percent are skeptical, and among Hispanics the figure is 13 percent.

The percentages are up sharply from November 2000, *after* what was arguably the most contentious vote count in our history, when only three percent of those surveyed said they didn't think their vote was counted. "There is a worrying element of paranoia that is eroding public confidence in the fairness of results," Zogby says.

Zogby has found that there certainly are lapses in the proper conduct of elections. He recalls doing a study of local election practices for the League of Women Voters in the 1980s and visiting a precinct in his hometown of Utica, New York. After the polls closed at 9 p.m., workers spent seven minutes writing down the tallies from the lever machines. "Then one of the workers brought out this big cardboard box filled with absentee ballots," Zogby remembers. "The chief worker said, 'To hell with the absentee ballots. We've been working for fifteen hours straight. Let's go home.' They then called in the final results to the elections office and left."[20]

FUNDAMENTAL DISAGREEMENT

It's clear that Americans are separated not just by political disagreements but by a basic difference in how we regard voting.

Democrats gravitate to the view that the most important value is empowering people to exercise their democratic rights, and they worry about people being denied that right. The Democratic National Committee's Voting Rights Institute emphasizes the need "to remove every barrier that impedes or denies an eligible vote." High in the Democratic Party's pantheon of heroes (unlike 40 years ago, when the party had many segregationist leaders) are "activists from all over America who converged on Mississippi in the summer of 1964 to help educate and register tens of thousands of previously disenfranchised American citizens."

While Republicans also want to ensure that eligible Americans are able to vote, they tend to pay more attention to the rule of law, and the standards and procedures that govern elections. Conservative legal scholars have noted that voters as well as election officials have an obligation to ensure that democracy works. Republicans worry publicly about the upcoming presidential election, but not for the same reason as Democrats. "Illegal aliens, homeless people, and vote brokers who bus people from place to polling place will all figure in this election," said Rush Limbaugh on his national radio show. Republicans have their own legal team to combat fake voter registrations, absentee-ballot fraud, and residents of nursing homes being improperly "assisted" in casting votes. The former House majority leader Tom DeLay has been openly dismissive of Democratic claims to want clean elections: "It's their stock in trade to say one thing, and while you're not looking, do something shady with the ballots and then cry racism if anyone complains."

On the other side of the aisle, Terry McAuliffe, former DNC chairman, says that while his party "opposes any fraudulent behavior or activity at polling places," the real issue is having the Justice Department ensure that no voter is harassed or intimidated. In 2004 he rejected GOP calls for a joint bipartisan task force that would have paired a Republican and a Democratic volunteer on visits to problem precincts, calling it a "public relations gambit."[21]

Some Democratic Party allies have had even harsher things to say about Republican efforts to police the polls. Wade Henderson of the Leadership Conference on Civil and Human Rights contends that such actions "serve no useful purpose other than to prevent people from voting." Liberal legal groups are suing to set aside laws in some of the states that aim to tighten antifraud protections.

Clearly the nature and conduct of our elections has become a highly polarized political issue. Getting the parties to agree on anything in the heat of a rancorous election season is well-nigh impossible. Al Gore's decision to contest the Florida election in 2000 until the bitter end may have permanently changed the way close elections are handled.

If the 2012 election and future contests are close, the doubts that have collected around the way we vote (and count our votes) could guarantee endless lawsuits and recriminations that will poison public opinion and create a climate of illegitimacy around any ultimate winner.

CONFLICT OF VISIONS

In his classic 1988 book *A Conflict of Visions: Ideological Origins of Political Struggles*, the economist Thomas Sowell outlined the important role that social "visions" play in our thinking. By "vision" he meant a fundamental sense of how the world works.

Competing visions or worldviews are particularly powerful in determining how people regard issues because, unlike "class interests" or other motivating forces, they are largely invisible, even—or especially—to those who harbor them. They explain how so often in life the same people continually line up on the same sides of different issues. For decades, public-opinion researchers sought the perfect polling question, one that best correlated with whether someone considered himself a Republican or a Democrat. In the 1960s, Gallup finally came up with the question that has had the most consistent predictive power over the last 40 years: "In your opinion, which is more often to blame if a person is poor? Lack of effort on his own part, or circumstances beyond his control?" Today, as might be expected of a divided nation, these competing views on what creates poverty are equally strong in their hold on American public opinion.

Sowell maintains that conflicts of visions dominate history. "We will do almost anything for our visions, except think about them," he concludes. Sowell identifies two distinct visions that shape the debate on controversial issues. The first he calls the "unconstrained" vision of human nature, and the second he terms the "constrained" vision.

Those with an unconstrained vision think that if we want a society where people are enlightened, prosperous, and equal, we must develop programs to accomplish those goals and work to implement them. The focus is on results or outcomes. That would include making sure that as many people as possible vote, thus animating the ideals of democracy. But sometimes the desire to expand voting opportunities takes on unrealistic qualities. Before he became New York's governor, David Paterson sponsored a bill to allow noncitizen residents to vote in local elections. He now has backed off "active" support of that idea. Electorates in San Francisco and in Portland, Maine have voted down proposals that would have allowed noncitizens to vote in school board races.

But that hasn't prevented other civic leaders from proposing the idea.

In 2011, Mayor John DeStefano of New Haven, Connecticut pushed for allowing all noncitizens in his city—whether legal or not—to vote in municipal elections. DeStefano planned to ask a state legislative committee to introduce a bill that would allow New Haven to offer noncitizen residents that vote.

DeStefano told reporters that some ten thousand to twelve thousand undocumented immigrants live in New Haven, along with five thousand noncitizens who teach and study at Yale University. "I'm just saying if you live here, you work here, you pay taxes here—I think it's reasonable that you have a say about what goes on," DeStefano said. His idea was quickly shot down by Governor Dan Milloy, a Democrat.[22]

Those with a "constrained" vision of human nature believe that the goal of reason should not be to remodel society, but rather to identify "natural laws," and work within them. Such people focus on general rules and processes. In regard to elections, the constrained vision would favor setting up procedures ensuring that votes are counted accurately and fairly, but not bending those procedures to increase voter participation by ineligible individuals.

During the 2000 Florida recount many key players represented each of these conflicting visions. At a Jesse Jackson rally one of the authors attended, the crowd chanted "Count every vote!" and "One ballot is one vote." Meanwhile, many Republicans carried a brochure from the Florida Department of Law Enforcement that outlined "Voter Responsibilities." It read in part:

Each registered voter in this state should: Familiarize himself or herself with the candidates and issues. Maintain with the supervisor of elections a current address. Know the location of his or her polling place and its hours. Bring proper identification to the polls. Familiarize himself or herself with the voting equipment in his or her precinct. Make sure that his or her completed ballot is correct.[23]

"I run into two kinds of people," says Mischelle Townsend, the former registrar of Riverside County, California. "The first is focused on making sure everything is geared to increasing turnout and making sure no one is disenfranchised. The other is more interested in making sure things get done right, are secure, and the law is followed." She vividly remembers the 2003 recall that put Arnold Schwarzenegger in office as governor of California. The ACLU, the NAACP, and other liberal groups convinced a three-judge panel of the U.S. Court of Appeals for the Ninth Circuit to cancel the election because six counties still used punch-card ballots, which according to the anti-recall plaintiffs had a higher error rate than other forms of voting. The argument was that some minority voters would thus be disenfranchised. But an 11-member panel of the Ninth Circuit unanimously rejected that view, contending that postponing a recall election was tantamount to disenfranchising all voters.

According to the pollster Scott Rasmussen, it used to be that the kinds of people who thought elections were not fair would fluctuate depending on who had won the most recent close national election. "During the Clinton years my surveys showed more Democrats thought elections were fair to voters, while Republicans were less convinced," he says. "I guess attitudes depend in part on whether your side won or not."[24] Regardless of how the views of some people might shift, whoever holds to extreme versions of either vision isn't helping our electoral system.

An excessively cramped view of elections, holding that rules and procedures must be interpreted in such a way as to guarantee that absolutely no improper vote is cast, may be regarded as unfairly denying some people the right to vote. Antifraud efforts that cross the line, like stationing off-duty cops at polling places (as some Republican campaigns did in the 1980s), invite a response such as that of Steven Hill, a senior analyst for the Center for Voting and Democracy: "There must be something about certain types of voters that Republicans don't trust."

At the other extreme, a loose and lax approach toward the law can lead to unacceptable attempts to cheat the system, such as the one that created thousands of suspect voter registrations during South Dakota's photo-finish Senate race in 2002. Maka Duta, the woman at the heart of that scandal, admitted duplicating signatures on both registration forms and applications for absentee ballots. But she asked for understanding: "If I erred in doing so, I pray that Attorney General [Mark] Barnett will agree with me that I erred on the side of angels."[25] In other words, doing the devil's work of forging voter signatures is somehow understandable given her angelic goal of increasing voter turnout.

Despite the passionate opinions on each side as to what undermines the electoral process, there are potential points of agreement that should have clarity for both "visions." Donna Brazile, who served as Al Gore's campaign manager in 2000, shares his outrage over the Florida outcome. But she also says, "Both parties should want every voter having information and training to cast a ballot that counts. And if that's done, both parties should support steps to ensure every vote cast is a valid and proper one."[26] Mary Kiffmeyer, a past president of the National Association of Secretaries of State, also endorses having both governmental units and political parties do more to make sure that voters understand how to vote, and what is involved. Both women agree that high school curricula, which might teach students what to eat, how to balance a checkbook, and other mundane tasks, should include instruction on voting. Many high schools already invite seniors to volunteer to work at polling places on Election Day; they earn academic credit in their civics classes as well as a small stipend for the day's work.

Still, it will be some time before voter education contributes to a reduction in tension between those who hold so firmly their competing visions of what's important in an election. Meanwhile, we have national elections taking place every two years in an atmosphere of mistrust and bitter division that makes governance increasingly difficult.

CHAPTER TWO

What Voter Fraud?

The campaign to deny the existence of voter fraud knows no bounds.

The Brennan Center for Justice says "voter fraud is essentially irrational" because the risk of getting caught is so high. It claims fraud "happens 0.0009 percent of the time," a statistical nullity. Howard Simon, executive director of the Florida ACLU, insists there "are probably a larger number of shark attacks in Florida than there are cases of voter fraud." Josh Marshall of Talking Points Memo sniffs that "it seems like the main source of voter fraud in the USA is James O'Keefe's pranks," referring to the conservative provocateur who has filmed how easily someone can vote in the name of another in sting operations ranging from New Hampshire to Washington, D.C.

Voter fraud is so rare "you're more likely to get hit by lightning than find a case of prosecutorial voter fraud," asserts Judith Browne-Dianis, co-director of the Advancement Project, a liberal voting group. Alex Wagner, an MSNBC host, ups the ante, claiming there is "more likelihood of you getting hit by lightning twice." Some pundits even downplay the seriousness of the issue. Lawrence O'Donnell, a former U.S. Senate staff director and current MSNBC host, stated on air that it is "perfectly reasonable" to commit voter fraud once. He went on to repeat his assertion.[1]

But how does such hyperbole stack up with reality? According to the National Weather Service, the last reported death from a lightning strike in the state of New York was in 2009. But in August 2011, William McInerney, the former city clerk of Troy, N.Y., pleaded guilty to forging a signature on an absentee ballot, for which he was sentenced to 90 days in a work program.[2] McInerney's cooperation with prosecutors led to four more elected officials and political operatives pleading guilty to felony charges. One of the defendants told police that "faking absentee ballots was a commonplace and accepted practice in political circles, all intended to swing an election." The ballot-fraud trial of two others, Democratic Elections Commissioner Edward McDonough and former City Councilman Michael LoPorto, ended in a mistrial in March 2012; separate retrials are upcoming.

Voters told Fox News they were "stunned" to learn their ballots had been stolen. Eric Shawn of Fox reported on court testimony by voters whose ballots had been faked. Prosecutors produced evidence of at least "38 forged or fraudulent ballots," enough to have "likely tipped the city council and county elections" to the Democrats. So at least 38 voters had their votes stolen, and five of seven defendants pleaded guilty. That is a lot more fraud than one terminal lightning strike in three years.

In West Virginia, the National Weather Service reports that the last death from a lightning strike was in 2005. In Lincoln County, West Virginia, former Sheriff Jerry Bowen and former County Clerk Donald Whitten pleaded guilty to stealing the May 2010 Democratic primary by stuffing ballot boxes with illegal absentee ballots. Bowen admitted "to falsifying more than 100" absentee ballots while in office.

The investigation proved harrowing at times. In February 2012, James Matheny was arrested and accused of threatening to kill an FBI agent and an investigator from the secretary of state's office when they visited him with questions about his role in the plot. When his account was challenged, Matheny said, "Are you calling me a liar? I will kill you." He then brandished a handgun.[3] Matheny apparently was trying to cover up a scheme in which one candidate for county clerk was ahead by 235 votes on election night until additional batches of absentee ballots "started mysteriously appearing, repeatedly, throughout the evening," giving the win to Whitten. The losing candidate went to court; the judge threw out more than 300 ballots and overturned the results of the election, ousting Whitten from office.

So anywhere from 100 to 300 voters in Lincoln County had their ballots stolen through fraud in 2010 (and that's not counting the 2005 conviction of the former Lincoln County auditor for felony voter-fraud conspiracy). That means that there was at least ten thousand percent more voter fraud in just one county in West Virginia than terminal lightning strikes in the state over the past seven years—and potentially as much as thirty thousand percent more.

Remember: According to liberals, there essentially is no such thing as voter fraud. So pay no attention to the vote stealers behind the voting-booth curtain.

But there's a lot going on behind that curtain. In Texas, Attorney General Greg Abbott has convicted more than 50 people of voter fraud, including a woman who voted in the name of her dead mother, a campaign worker who voted for two people, and a city councilmember who registered foreigners to vote in an election decided by 19 votes.[4]

In Oregon, where all voting is conducted by mail and no one has to present themselves to election officials, Lafayette Frederick Keaton was convicted in 2011 of voting in the names of both his deceased son and his deceased brother. He also collected Social Security, food stamps, and Medicare benefits in his brother's name. He was sentenced to 12 months in prison and a $5,000 fine.[5]

In Indiana, the state's highest election official, Republican Secretary of State Charlie White, was convicted in 2012 of voter fraud and perjury for using his former wife's address on his voter registration form in the May 2010 primary, in an attempt to continue drawing a salary as a local official after he moved out of the area. White was forced to resign his office. And the mayor of Austin, Indiana was charged in May 2012 with tampering with absentee ballots in a 2011 election in which almost half of the early ballots cast were absentee, compared to the state average of only 15 percent.[6]

In rural and Republican Clay County, Kentucky, a jury convicted eight of the county's most powerful political players of election fraud in March 2010. Former circuit judge R. Cletus Maricle and former school superintendent Douglas Adams were found guilty of rigging a series of elections over many years. Maricle was sentenced to 320 months in prison, with prosecutors accusing him of creating a culture of lawlessness in the county that persisted for three decades. He is thought to have used $400,000 to bribe eight thousand voters in the course of his efforts.

The conspiracy bloomed in 2002, when Maricle began heading the Clay County Board of Elections. Candidates who agreed to participate in buying votes (mostly in the Republican primary) first compiled lists of voters who had agreed to be bribed, then provided cars to drive those voters to the polls. Precinct workers in on the fraud made sure the voters cast ballots as they had been told and handed them a ticket to redeem for cash later. Investigators first became suspicious when they noted a high incidence of election officials going into polling booths to assist people with their ballots. Nearly 40 people who had said they were blind and needed help with voting turned out to have licenses to drive.

Those who stole their way into office rigged contracts for their friends, accepted bribes, and perverted justice. Kenneth Day, a convicted drug dealer, got Judge Maricle's help in fixing a jury to return a multimillion-dollar verdict in Day's favor. "In Clay County, if you're not in politics or in with the clique, you don't get nothing," Day testified at Maricle's trial. Another convicted drug dealer, Eugene "Mutton" Lewis, testified at the trial that one candidate gave him $1,000 and a request for help in rigging the election. When Lewis was asked if there were not other ways to help a candidate besides buying votes, he replied "Not that I know of."

Carmen Webb Lewis, former mayor of Manchester in Clay County, says the epidemic of vote-buying caused many people to become so cynical about politics that they stopped voting. But with the convictions, she said, people are now running for office who would never have considered the idea before. "That is kind of uplifting. I think it's wonderful," she said.[7]

Sometimes it takes years for the law to catch up with fraudsters. Former Santa Ana, California school board member Nativo Lopez pleaded guilty in 2011 to a felony count of voter registration fraud. He was sentenced to three years of probation and 400 hours of community service; seven other felony counts, including perjury and fraudulent voting, were dropped.[8]

Lopez, president of the Mexican-American Political Association, had been infamous in Southern California politics for years through his leadership of the Hermandad Mexicana Nacional (now the Hermandad Mexicana Latinoamericana), a group accused of registering hundreds of illegal aliens in a close 1996 Orange County congressional race between GOP Representative Bob Dornan and Democrat Loretta Sanchez. Final returns showed Sanchez winning by 984 votes, but evidence turned up by a House investigating committee found that at least 748 illegal votes had been cast, with 624 of them coming from noncitizens. More than half of those were registered by Hermandad. Despite serious concerns about Lopez's role, local prosecutors and the Clinton Justice Department declined to press charges. In its report, the House committee expressed the strong belief that hundreds of other illegal votes had been cast in the Dornan–Sanchez race, but federal immigration officials declined to cooperate further with the probe, citing "privacy" concerns.

Sometimes those who dismiss vote fraud will reconsider when presented with evidence. In April 2012, the *Richmond Times-Dispatch* printed a remarkable editorial that began: "We'd like our helping of crow medium rare, please." It acknowledged that it had recently trashed a bill in the Virginia legislature requiring ID at the polls as "a solution in search of a problem," while there was "not even apocryphal evidence" supporting the sponsors of the bill. "Oops," it went on to say, noting that a Richmond grand jury had indicted 10 convicted felons of lying on voter registration forms.[9] Donald Palmer, secretary of the Virginia State Board of Elections, noted that a total of 38 people had been charged that month with voter fraud across the state. "Unfortunately, fraud does exist in Virginia's elections," he told the *Times-Dispatch*. Some of those indicted had actually cast ballots, he said.

Apparently, many of the felons had been urged to register by voter advocacy groups that told them their rights had been restored, or would be soon. This subterfuge recalled the tactics of the infamous voter registration and liberal activist group

ACORN, which saw its operatives indicted in 15 states in 2008, and went bankrupt in 2010. "At least among certain groups, there is [still] an active effort to subvert the laws," says GOP state senator Thomas Garrett, a former prosecutor.

It frustrates Garrett that even evidence such as this will have little impact on colleagues who opposed voter ID: "[I would] relate with specificity actual investigations, charges, and convictions for voter fraud, and then have someone on the other side of the aisle suggest that it didn't exist and it didn't happen—and we were more likely to find the Loch Ness monster," he sighs. State senator Henry Marsh of Richmond fits that category. The data, he told the *Times-Dispatch*, "doesn't convince me of anything other than the fact that somebody is trying to create an impression that doesn't exist."[10]

At least 54 individuals who worked for ACORN have been convicted of voter fraud or related activities. One of the biggest cases was in Las Vegas, where Nevada Attorney General Catherine Cortez Masto and Secretary of State Ross Miller, both Democrats, filed fraud charges against two ACORN senior employees in 2009. ACORN itself was also charged with election fraud. ACORN's Las Vegas field director, Christopher Edwards, pleaded guilty and turned state's evidence, implicating his boss, ACORN's deputy regional director Amy Busefink.

The two had engaged in a conspiracy to provide illegal bonuses to voter registration workers for exceeding daily quotas. Nevada makes the practice illegal, because it creates an incentive to flood the system with bogus registrations. Las Vegas registrar of voters Larry Lomax told reporters his office was inundated with suspect registrations, and soon discovered that ACORN had hired 59 inmates from a nearby prison work-release program to collect registrations. Several who had been convicted of identity theft were made ACORN supervisors: the group was hiring specialists to do its work.

In January 2011 Busefink entered a plea of no contest and was sentenced to two years in jail. The sentence was suspended provided she abided by the terms of her probation, paid a fine of $4,000, and did 100 hours of community service. Amazingly, in the months before she was sentenced Busefink continued to run the 2010 national voter drive for Project Vote, the ACORN affiliate that hired Barack Obama as an organizer in 1992.[11]

An investigative report by WBBH-TV in Fort Myers, Florida found there were no effective measures preventing noncitizens from registering to vote. In just two counties, Lee and Manatee, it discovered 87 people who had filled out jury excusal forms, saying they were noncitizens, yet who had also voted.

WBBH found that county election supervisors have no way to track noncitizens who vote. Under the 1993 Motor Voter Law, proof of citizenship is not required. "We have no policing authority. We don't have any way of bouncing that information off any other database that would give us that information," said Lee County supervisor of elections Sharon Harrington. "It could be very serious. It could change the whole complexion of an election."

Because of the WBBH investigation, both counties' election officials say they will now request copies of all jury excusal forms on which residents report they can't serve because they aren't a citizen. That doesn't mean that other Florida counties will automatically follow suit—but they should. "This absolutely affects other counties in the state," the WBBH report concluded.[12]

Sometimes it's election officials who actively encourage voter fraud. Jada Woods Williams, the supervisor of elections in Madison County, Florida, was indicted in November 2011 on 17 counts of neglect of duty and corrupt practices, for allowing distribution of illegal absentee ballots in a 2010 school board race. Williams was one of nine people involved in the scheme. Its ringleaders were a candidate for the school board race, Abra "Tina"

Hill Johnson, and her husband Ernest. They would approach voters and ask them to sign an "Absentee Ballot Request Form." They would then put an alternate address on the ballots, which were mailed to a third party rather than the purported voter. The Johnsons collected the ballots from the mail drops they had set up, brought the ballots to the voters to sign, and then delivered them to the supervisor of elections. In some instances they watched while people filled out the ballots; at other times they voted for them.[13]

Despite the extensive evidence trail laid out in the indictments, the "Madison Nine" fought back. Benjamin Crump, a local attorney from nearby Tallahassee, filed suit against the Florida Department of Law Enforcement. "The FDLE has launched a voter-suppression campaign to intimidate minorities from going to the polls in this upcoming election," he declared at a news conference in January 2012. Ernest Rains, president of the Madison County NAACP, said the indictments had meant "a lot of people" are now "afraid to vote absentee or any other type of way because they're afraid they'll have the same treatment done to them."[14]

The indictments certainly haven't slowed down Jada Woods Williams, the county supervisor of elections. Despite being suspended from her duties by state authorities, she announced she will run for re-election in 2012.

Four Democratic party officials in Indiana, including St. Joseph County chairman Butch Morgan, were charged in February 2012 with conspiracy, forgery, and official misconduct in the 2008 presidential primary election. Morgan allegedly ordered three county officials to duplicate signatures from a 2008 petition for Democratic gubernatorial candidate Jim Schellinger onto petitions for then presidential candidates Hillary Clinton and Barack Obama. The signature of the Republican member of the Board of Voter Registration, which is required for final authorization of all petitions, was apparently rubber-stamped without her knowledge. In Indiana, a candidate must secure 500 signatures from each of the state's nine congressional districts in order to qualify for the ballot. Then senator Barack Obama barely made it, with 534 signatures.

The *South Bend Tribune* collaborated with an independent political newsletter, *Howey Politics Indiana*, to investigate the allegedly faked petitions. Erich Speckin, an expert forensic document analyst, told the paper that up to 270 of the ballot signatures for candidate Obama were fraudulent. "It's obvious. It's just terribly obvious" that various signatures were written by the same hand, Speckin said after reviewing the documents. Previous investigations had already found no fewer than 150 fraudulent signatures on the petitions.

The fraud was uncovered when a source from inside the county Democratic party who had personal knowledge of the scheme approached local investigators: Lucas Burkett, who had attended meetings where Morgan had ordered the forgeries. Investigators then compared signatures on the Obama and Clinton petitions to signatures on file for registered voters, and contacted voters whose names appeared on the forms to confirm that the signatures were forgeries. There exists the real possibility, then, that systematic voter fraud led to Barack Obama's name appearing on a ballot in a state where he would not otherwise have qualified to run.

Many common citizens were shocked and dismayed to see their name and personal information on a petition they had supposedly signed four years earlier. "It's scary. A lot of people have already lost faith in politics . . . and that solidifies our worries and concerns," Mishawaka resident Charity Rorie told Fox News.[15] Morgan was a veteran county party official, working for a political party that has dominated northern Indiana for nearly two decades. The exact extent of the corruption is unknown; as Dr. Deb Fleming, St. Joseph County's Republican chairwoman, pointed out to the *South Bend Tribune*, "I'm sure there are other things. They've just never gotten caught. Because they've been in control of St. Joseph County for so long, they felt they could get away with it."

Morgan and the other Democratic officials could face several years in prison and tens of thousands of dollars in fines. In a twist that would be comical if it weren't so serious, the court had to appoint a special prosecutor to handle the case after the county prosecutor's own forged signature appeared on a petition.

Indiana's voter ID requirement for in-person voting would not have stopped this type of petition fraud. But it illustrates that there are people—including party activists—who are willing to cheat and defraud the public in order to win elections. Local party officials in Indiana apparently forged voter signatures to make sure their candidates were on the ballot. If this had been detected in 2008, and Barack Obama had been disqualified from the Indiana ballot, what would that have done to his presidential campaign?

Despite all of these examples, those who would dismiss voter fraud as a serious issue plow on undeterred. "No credible evidence suggests a voter-fraud epidemic," insists the Brennan Center. "There is no documented wave or trend of individuals voting multiple times, voting as someone else, or voting despite knowing that they are ineligible." But as many voter-fraud cases show, it doesn't take an epidemic to change the results of an election, or to get a candidate on the ballot through fraud.

None of this surprises former Alabama congressman Artur Davis, a Democrat-turned-independent who says he regrets having opposed laws cracking down on voter fraud even though he knew it occurred in his district; as a reformer challenging an entrenched machine, he had to calculate how many phony votes he would have to overcome to win. "I took the path of least resistance as an African American official," he says. "I regret that. But

43

partisan and ideological pressures were great."[16] Still, he thinks no amount of evidence of voter fraud will sway most opponents. "Most people would not change their opinion on voter ID if someone walked in front of them and admitted they committed voter ID fraud yesterday," he says. "They have their heels dug in. A number of people opposed to voter ID are opposed for political reasons, for reasons that don't have substance. People plead guilty to fraud, and that doesn't seem to move the opinions of some of those opposed."[17]

CHAPTER THREE

The Battle Over Voter ID and the Myth of the Disenfranchised Voter

In recent years, the biggest battle in election reform has been over voter ID—requiring voters to present a government-issued photographic identification when they vote at their polling places on Election Day. This is a common-sense requirement passed by legislatures in states such as Georgia, Indiana, Texas, Rhode Island, South Carolina, Tennessee, Alabama, and Kansas.[1] In Mississippi, voters overwhelmingly approved a referendum in November 2011 that amends the state constitution to implement voter ID; Missouri voters will decide on a similar measure in November 2012.

These efforts have been blasted by leftist advocacy groups, which claim this is solely an effort to suppress the vote of minorities and the poor—who tend to vote for Democrats. Despite America's unfortunate and long history of voter fraud and the fact that claims about "suppression" have been disproved in the polling place and in the courtroom, Benjamin Jealous, the president and CEO of the NAACP, asserted that "This is the greatest assault on voting rights, happening right now, that we have seen since the dawn of Jim Crow"—a historically preposterous claim. Jealous joined Al Sharpton and Representative Charles Rangel on the steps of New York City Hall in November 2011 to call for nationwide protests, decrying what they described as a voter-suppression effort.

The NAACP has gone so far as to complain to the United Nations that voter ID requirements are a human rights violation. This silly claim would be laughable if it were not so embarrassing for that formerly respected organization, which has morphed from its beginnings as a champion for civil rights to being a subordinate arm of the Democratic Party and an advocate for the racial-spoils system of racial preferences (discrimination) in employment, contracting, and college admissions. Its tolerance for voter fraud, as described in the chapter on absentee ballots, is disturbing.

Rhode Island Governor Lincoln Chafee, an independent, certainly disagreed with the NAACP's assessment when he signed into law the voter ID bill passed by the Democrat-controlled state legislature in 2011. Chafee said that "requiring identification at the polling place is a reasonable request to ensure the accuracy and integrity of our elections."[2] State representative Jon Brien, a Democratic sponsor of the bill, said it was wrong for party leaders to "make this a Republican-versus-Democrat issue. It's not. It's simply a good-government issue." Brien added that "we as representatives have a duty to the citizenry to ensure the integrity of our elections, and the requirement to show an ID will ensure that integrity."

THE NEED FOR VOTER ID

There is no question that every individual who is eligible to vote should have the opportunity to do so. It is equally important, however, that the votes of eligible voters are not stolen or diluted by a fraudulent or bogus ballot cast by an ineligible or imaginary voter. The evidence from academic studies and actual turnout in elections is overwhelming that—contrary to the shrill claims of opponents—voter ID does *not* depress turnout, including among the ranks of minority, poor, and elderly voters. The real myth in this debate is not the existence of voter fraud, which exists; the real myth is the claim that voters are disenfranchised because of voter ID requirements.

Voter ID can deter not just impersonation fraud at the polls, but also voting under fictitious voter registrations, double-voting by individuals registered in more than one state or locality, and voting by illegal aliens. There are examples of all of these types of fraud that could have been prevented with voter ID requirements. As the Commission on Federal Election Reform, headed by former president Jimmy Carter and former secretary of state James Baker, reported in 2005:

> The electoral system cannot inspire public confidence if no safeguards exist to deter or detect fraud or to confirm the identity of voters. Photo IDs currently are needed to board a plane, enter federal buildings, and cash a check. Voting is equally important.[3]

Jimmy Carter knows the issue of voter fraud well. His first run for office, in a Democratic primary in Quitman County,

Georgia in 1962, was stolen by voter fraud that local residents said "had been going on on election days as long as most people could remember."[4] He went to court and got the election overturned, and ended up winning the general election. Newly minted state senator Carter helped sponsor a comprehensive reform of the state's election code; the culprit responsible for stealing the primary election was later convicted of voter fraud in a previous congressional election.[5]

As Jimmy Carter learned, fraudulent voting does exist, and criminal penalties imposed after the fact are an insufficient deterrent. In *Crawford v. Marion County Election Board*, the 2008 case upholding Indiana's voter ID law, the Supreme Court said that, despite criminal penalties:

> It remains true . . . that flagrant examples of such fraud in other parts of the country have been documented throughout this Nation's history by respected historians and journalists, that occasional examples have surfaced in recent years . . . that . . . demonstrate that not only is the risk of voter fraud real but that it could affect the outcome of a close election.[6]

Voter ID opponents were surprised that the majority opinion in *Crawford* was written by Justice John Paul Stevens, a stalwart liberal, rather than one of the conservative justices. But the ACLU's cries that voter fraud is a myth did not resonate with a justice who practiced law in Chicago, a city with one of the worst records of electoral malfeasance in American history. Years after Democratic boss and longtime mayor Richard J. Daley died, his political machine was still stealing elections in the city. The Department of Justice prosecuted its largest voter fraud case ever in Chicago—prosecutors estimated that 100,000 fraudulent ballots were cast in the 1982 gubernatorial election. The conspirators came within five thousand votes of throwing the race to the losing Democratic candidate, and a federal grand jury found that "similar fraudulent activities" had occurred in prior elections.[7] Tens of thousands of individuals had voted twice; thousands of other bogus votes had been cast in the names of individuals who were dead, in prison, or whose registered addresses were vacant lots. Absent voters were impersonated, voters' signatures on ballot applications "had been forged wholesale in many precincts," and votes were fraudulently cast under fictitious voter registrations and in the names of transients, the incapacitated, and senior citizens.

If liberals couldn't convince Justice Stevens, they may also have a hard time with Chris Matthews, a former Tip O'Neill staffer and reliable liberal cheerleader in most circumstances. When the topic came up on *Hardball*, Matthews admitted that this type of impersonation fraud has "gone on since the Fifties." He explained the scheme: Someone calls to enquire whether you voted or are going to vote, and "then all of a sudden somebody does come and vote for you." Matthews says this is an old strategy in big-city politics: "I know all about it in North Philly—it's what went on, and I believe it still goes on."

For those trying to defend America's electoral integrity, the stakes are high. The relative rarity of prosecutions for voter-impersonation fraud, as the Seventh Circuit Court of Appeals pointed out in the Indiana case, can be "explained by the endemic underenforcement" of voter-fraud cases and "the extreme difficulty of apprehending a voter impersonator" without the tools—a voter identification card—needed to detect such fraud.[8] This nation should not tolerate even one election being stolen, but without the tools to detect these illegal schemes, it is hard to know just how many close elections are being affected.

In 1984, a dramatic example of such fraud was revealed in a New York State grand jury report released by Kings County district attorney and former Democratic congresswoman Elizabeth

Holtzman.[9] When *The New York Times* railed against the Supreme Court's *Crawford* decision and claimed voter fraud is a myth, it should have checked its own archives. It would have found a news story headlined "Boss Tweed Is Gone, But Not His Vote." [10] The article detailed the findings of that grand jury, reporting that "cemetery voting and other forms of stuffing the ballot box were not buried with Tammany Hall."

According to the grand jury, a widespread conspiracy had operated without detection for 14 years in Brooklyn, involving not only impersonation of legitimate voters at the polls, but also voting under fictitious names. For all those years, the conspirators engaged in practices that included:

> . . . the forgery of voter registration cards with the names of fictitious persons, the filing of these cards with the Board of Elections [without detection], [and] the recruitment of people to cast multiple votes on behalf of specified candidates using these forged cards or the cards of deceased and other persons.

To register fictitious voters, registration cards were filled out with fictitious first names and real last names taken from party enrollment books within the targeted voting precinct:

> For example, if a John Brown actually lived at 1 Park Place, Brooklyn, New York, the application would be completed in the name of Mary Brown, 1 Park Place, Brooklyn, New York. It was anticipated that when the mail for the fictitious Mary Brown was delivered to John Brown at his address, John Brown would discard the notice rather than return it to the post office. This plan reduced the likelihood that the voter registration notice card would be

returned to the Board of Elections, thereby minimizing the possibility that the fraud would be detected.

This process was also successful because of the way the U.S. Postal Service handles mail. The normal procedure in all election jurisdictions across the United States is to mail a voter registration card to a newly registered voter. Although the primary purpose is to provide the new voter with the voter registration card, it is also intended to ensure that a real person has registered and provided an accurate address. The New York Board of Elections thus relied on the Postal Service to return any cards that were undeliverable because the registrant was fictitious or did not live at the address on the application (election jurisdictions today still rely on the Postal Service for this validation). But the grand jury found that "mail carriers did not return these cards particularly where the address on the card was that of a large multiple dwelling . . . [and] would frequently leave the undeliverable voter registration cards in a common area of the building." To take advantage of this, the conspirators used the addresses of large apartment buildings in which members of their crews lived, which allowed them to collect the bogus cards.

In addition to voting in the names of fictitious people, the crews used several other methods of casting fraudulent votes involving voting under the names of legitimate voters.

By reviewing voter registration records at the Board of Elections prior to Election Day, conspirators were able to identify newly registered voters. Crews would go to the appropriate polling places as soon as polls opened in the morning to vote under those names:

The reasoning behind this method, according to the experience of one witness, was that newly registered voters often do not vote. By arriving at the polling sites early, the bogus voter would not need to worry about the possibility that the real voter had actually voted.

Another method entailed collecting, during nominating petition drives, the names of registered voters who had died or moved—deadwood voters. Crews were then sent to vote under those names. The requirement that New Yorkers provide a signature when voting did not deter the fraudsters; this emphasizes the inadequacy of signature matching (a highly trained skill that cannot be taught in a matter of hours to the average poll worker) in preventing this type of fraud, similar to credit card theft, where the signature requirement does not prevent a significant volume of fraud.

Database technology is a tool of the trade that was not available in 1984, but is widespread now. Voter registration lists are public information in most states, and databases containing detailed information on voters are available from a wide array of commercial vendors, and usually are much more up to date than the voter registration databases maintained by election officials. This makes it easy for anyone to determine the names of voters who are still registered, but who have died or moved out of a jurisdiction. As the Supreme Court pointed out in the Indiana voter ID case, litigation records showed that 41.4 percent of the names on Indiana's voter registration rolls were bad entries, representing tens of thousands of ineligible voters—a trove of potential fraudulent votes.

One of the witnesses before the New York grand jury described how he led a crew of eight individuals from polling place to polling place to vote. Each member of his crew voted in excess of 20 times, and there were approximately 20 other such crews operating during that election. This extensive fraud could have been stopped if New York required voters to authenticate their identity at the polls, and there had been poll watchers making sure that election officials were verifying voters' IDs. The grand jury explained that "the ease and boldness with which these fraudulent schemes were carried out shows the vulnerability of our entire electoral process to unscrupulous and fraudulent manipulation." As a result, thousands of fraudulent votes were cast in New York legislative and congressional elections.

According to the grand jury in the Brooklyn case, the advent of mail-in registration in New York—a form of registration that was implemented nationally with the passage of the National Voter Registration Act of 1993—was a key factor in perpetrating the fraud. In recent years officials have detected numerous fraudulent forms, many submitted by ACORN, the ethically challenged organization responsible for tens of thousands of invalid voter registration forms in multiple jurisdictions. In states without identification requirements, election officials have no means for preventing the casting of fraudulent votes. Given that most election jurisdictions engage in minimal-to-nonexistent screening efforts, there is no way of knowing how many invalid registrations have slipped through.

This was illustrated dramatically by filmmaker James O'Keefe in the January 2012 GOP primary in New Hampshire, a state with no voter ID law. His operatives, equipped with hidden cameras, visited multiple New Hampshire polling places on Election Day. They had identified from published obituaries the names of registered voters who were deceased, but who had not been removed from the voter registration rolls.[11] O'Keefe's revealing footage shows local election officials giving the operatives ballots in the names of deceased voters; when election officials were asked if they wanted to see an ID, they answered that none was required. The undercover operatives then returned their ballots to the election officials and did not actually cast votes—but they could have easily done so, without detection. In only one instance did a poll worker realize there was a problem—and that was only because the worker knew the dead voter.

And what was the reaction of leftist groups that oppose voter ID, such as People for the American Way? They presented a petition to state Attorney General Michael Delaney urging him to prosecute O'Keefe! They want state authorities to go after the messenger who showed how vulnerable New Hampshire's "honor" system is, *instead* of improving the state's election procedures to ensure the integrity of the vote.[12]

Despite the difficulty of detecting impersonation fraud, there are other examples. Dr. Robert Pastor, who was the executive director of the Baker-Carter Commission on Federal Election Reform and now heads the Center for Democracy and Election Management at American University, testified before the U.S. Commission on Civil Rights in 2006 that he was once unable to vote because someone had already cast a ballot in his name at his polling place.[13]

In a 2007 city council election in Hoboken, New Jersey, former zoning board president John Branciforte noticed a group of men and women near his polling place being given index cards by another man. One of those men later entered the polling place and attempted to vote in the name of a registered voter who, it turned out, no longer lived in the ward. The imposter was caught only because he was challenged by Branciforte *after* the imposter signed the voter roll book and was headed for a polling booth. When he was challenged and asked for ID, the imposter left, but was followed by Branciforte:

> "I followed him outside where he crossed the street and joined the same group of men and women I saw him with earlier. The group quickly dispersed north and I followed [him]. While we were in a foot chase I called the police on my cell phone and reported the possible voter fraud. The chase continued for seven or eight blocks until the police

stopped him, coincidentally in front of another polling place."[14]

The imposter admitted to the police that the group was from a homeless shelter, and each person was paid $10 to vote using others' names.[15]

The Hoboken case illustrates a curious problem with voter fraud—the all too frequent reluctance of election officials and local prosecutors to investigate and prosecute such fraud. In a letter to Senator Robert Bennett, Branciforte described how local election officials tried to discourage him from pursuing this attempted fraud, telling him nothing would ever come of the arrest, and that the charges would eventually be dropped anyway. That, unfortunately, turned out to be correct. Local authorities released the imposter and refused to charge him because he had never actually voted—despite the fact that he had fraudulently signed in as another registered voter. That "real" registered voter confirmed to a local reporter that he had not voted in the city council election. And both the winning and losing city council candidates in that particular ward reported hearing of other voters who discovered, at the polls, that someone had already voted in their names—an organized effort to shape the outcome of the election.[16]

In 2007, in a case reminiscent of Boss Tweed and that Brooklyn grand jury report, the Department of Justice won a voting rights lawsuit in Noxubee, Mississippi against a defendant named Ike Brown and the county election board.[17] Brown, a convicted felon, was the head of the local Democratic Party. He had set up a political machine that worked to guarantee the election of his approved candidates to local office—essentially his version of Tammany Hall.

One of the contentions in the litigation was that the local election board's "failure to purge the voter registration roll to eliminate persons who have moved or died and who are thus no longer eligible voters" increased the opportunity for voter fraud by creating "the potential for persons to vote under others' names." The court cited the testimony of one government witness, a former deputy sheriff, who said that he "saw Ike Brown outside the door of the precinct talking to a young black lady . . . and heard him tell her to go in there and vote, to use any name, and that no one was going to say anything."[18] Brown is infamous throughout Mississippi, and this case may have been one of the reasons that voters approved a ballot referendum in November 2011 to amend the state constitution to require voter ID.

Voter ID might also help prevent double-voting by someone who is registered in two states.[19] In 2004, a comparison of the voter registration rolls in North and South Carolina by the *Charlotte Observer* found more than 60,000 people who were registered in both states, at least 180 of whom were listed "as having voted in two places in either the 2000 or 2002 general election." Some of these 180 may have been misidentified as errors, including family members with similar names. But the North Carolina Board of Election admitted that it had caught at least a dozen people trying to vote in more than one location, and election officials acknowledged that "it would be hard to catch anyone who intentionally double-voted across state lines, because states don't share their voter databases."[20]

A similar investigation by the *New York Daily News* of voting rolls in New York City and Florida found 46,000 individuals registered in both states, 68 percent of whom were Democrats; 12 percent were Republicans, and 16 percent didn't claim a party. Between 400 and 1,000 individuals voted in both states in at least one election—this in Florida, where the presidential election was decided in 2000 by 537 votes—and some of the registered voters double-voted in multiple elections.[21] Interviewed by the *New York Daily News*, Edwin Peterson, a registered Democrat, admitted he had voted twice in the 2000 election, and attributed his violation of the law to his distrust of the Republican Party: "That was a situation where Florida is so messed up with the Republicans, you don't know if your vote is even going to be counted."[22] There is no indication that he was ever prosecuted.

However, the Department of Justice *has* prosecuted (and obtained convictions in) a number of double-voting cases. The convicted include a man who voted in both Wyandotte County, Kansas and Jackson County, Missouri in 2000 and 2002; and two residents of Kansas who also voted in the 2000 and 2002 elections, in both Johnson County, Kansas and Kansas City, Missouri.[23]

The double-voting problem was illustrated, to the great embarrassment of the League of Women Voters, by an amicus brief the League filed in *Crawford v. Marion County Election Board*, the Indiana voter ID case. One of the Indiana voters highlighted in the League's brief was used as an example of someone who had difficulty voting because of the voter ID requirement. But when an Indiana newspaper interviewed the voter, it discovered that her problems stemmed from her trying to use a Florida driver's license to vote in Indiana. Not only did she have a Florida driver's license, she was also registered to vote in Florida, where she owned a second home and had claimed residency by filing for a homestead exemption on her property taxes, normally only available to state residents.[24] So the Indiana law worked as intended: It prevented someone from voting twice who might otherwise have done so illegally without detection.

As will be discussed in Chapter Five, noncitizen voting is a significant problem that must be dealt with to help ensure the integrity of our elections. Since the vast majority of states (and the federal government) will not issue an official identification card to an illegal alien, making a state- or federally-issued photo ID a voting requirement can prevent noncitizens, particularly illegal aliens, from fraudulently participating in elections.

The potential for abuse and the casting of fraudulent ballots—by ineligible voters (like illegal aliens or persons registered in more than one state), or in the names of fake voters, dead voters, or voters who have moved—is real. As the Supreme Court recognized, there is a "real risk that voter fraud could affect a close election's outcome."[25] There are enough incidents and reported cases of actual voter fraud to make it clear that America must take the steps necessary to make such fraud harder to commit. Requiring voter ID is a simple, common-sense step towards that goal.

THE MYTH OF THE DISENFRANCHISED VOTER

States must protect the security of the election process, but they also must ensure that every eligible individual is able to vote. Where photo-ID requirements have been implemented, it has not reduced turnout. Despite many claims to the contrary, particularly by the NAACP and the Brennan Center for Justice, there is no credible evidence that requiring a voter ID decreases the turnout of voters, or has a disparate impact on minority, poor, or elderly voters.

Rhode Island state senator and African American Democrat Harold Metts, who sponsored the state's voter ID law, dismisses claims of depressed turnouts, saying that "as a minority citizen and a senior citizen, I would not support anything that I thought would present obstacles or limit protections."[26] Numerous studies have borne out this fact. For example:

- A study by the University of Missouri on turnout in Indiana showed that turnout actually *increased* by about two percentage points overall in 2006 in the first election after the voter ID law went into effect. There was no evidence that counties with higher percentages of minority, poor, elderly, or less educated populations suffered any reduction in voter turnout. In fact, "the only consistent and statistically significant impact of photo ID in Indiana is to increase voter turnout in counties with a greater percentage of Democrats relative to other counties."[27]

- In September 2007, The Heritage Foundation released an analysis of 2004 election turnout data for all states, with the findings that voter ID laws do not reduce the turnout of any demographic group, including African Americans and Hispanics. Such voters were just as likely to vote in states requiring ID as in states where only a name was required in order to vote.[28]

- A study by the University of Delaware and the University of Nebraska–Lincoln examined data from elections in 2000, 2002, 2004, and 2006. At both the aggregate and individual levels, the study found that voter ID laws do not affect turnout, including across racial, ethnic, and socioeconomic lines. The study concludes that "concerns about voter identification laws affecting turnout are much ado about nothing."[29]

- Multiple surveys of voters have found that a very small number lack identification. The Center for Democracy and Election Management at American University surveyed registered voters in Maryland, Indiana, and Mississippi to see whether they had photo IDs. Less than half a percentage point of respondents had neither a photo ID nor citizenship documentation. The Center concluded that "showing a photo ID as a requirement of voting does not appear to be a serious problem in any of the states" because "[a]lmost all registered voters have an acceptable form of photo ID."[30] A 2008 election survey of 12,000 registered voters across all 50 states found that fewer than nine people were unable to vote because of voter ID requirements,[31] while a 2006 survey of more than 36,000 voters found only "23 people in the entire sample—less than one-tenth of 1 percent of reported voters" who were unable to vote because of an ID requirement.[32]

- In 2010, a Rasmussen poll of likely voters in the United States showed overwhelming support (82 percent) for requiring a photo ID in order to vote in elections. This support runs across ethnic and racial lines; Rasmussen reported that "[t]his is a sentiment that spans demographics, as majorities in every demographic agree."[33]
- A similar study by John Lott in 2006 also found no effect on voter turnout, and in fact found an indication that reducing voter fraud (through means such as requiring a voter ID) may have a positive impact on voter turnout.[34]

Actual election results in Georgia and Indiana confirm that suppositions about voter ID hurting minority turnout are wrong. In 2008, in the first presidential election after their voter ID laws went into effect, both states saw turnout increase more dramatically in both the presidential preference primary *and* the general election than turnout increased in some states *without* the photo-ID requirement.

There was record turnout in Georgia in the primary election—over two million voters, more than twice as many as in 2004, when the voter photo-ID law was not in effect (the law was first applied to local elections in 2007). The number of African Americans voting in the 2008 primary also doubled from 2004. In fact, there were 100,000 more votes in the Democratic primary than in the Republican primary, and the number of individuals who had to vote by provisional ballot because they had not obtained the free photo ID available from the state was less that 0.01 percent. Since upwards of 90 percent of African Americans vote Democratic, turnout in Democratic primaries is an obvious indicator of black turnout.

In the 2008 general election, when President Barack Obama was elected, Georgia (which has one of the strictest voter ID laws in the nation) had the largest turnout in its history—more than four million voters. Democratic turnout was up an astonishing 6.1 percentage points from the 2004 election (when there was no photo ID requirement)—the fifth-largest increase of any state. Overall turnout in Georgia went up 6.7 percentage points, the second-highest increase in the country and a striking jump, even in an election year when there was a general increase in turnout nationwide over the prior presidential election.[35]

The black share of the statewide vote increased from 25 percent in 2004 to 30 percent in 2008, according to the Joint Center for Political and Economic Studies.[36] And according to Census Bureau surveys, 65 percent of the black voting-age population voted in the 2008 election, compared to only 54.4 percent in 2004—an increase of more than 10 percentage points.[37] Although John McCain won the state with 52.2 percent of the vote, versus Barack Obama's 47 percent, Obama actually outscored Al Gore by almost four percentage points: Gore only won 43.2 percent of the vote in 2000, when there was no photo-ID law in place.

By contrast, the Democratic turnout in nearby Mississippi— also a state with a high percentage of black voters, but without a voter ID requirement—increased by only 2.35 percentage points. Turnout in Georgia, in the 2010 congressional election, was more than 2.6 million voters—an increase of almost 500,000 voters over the 2006 election. While only 42.9 percent of registered black Georgians voted in 2006, 50.4 percent voted in 2010—with the voter ID law in effect—an increase of more than seven percentage points.[38] As Georgia's secretary of state pointed out, when compared to the 2006 election, voter turnout in 2010 "among

African Americans outpaced the growth of that population's pool of registered voters by more than 20 percentage points."[39]

The Georgia voter ID requirement went into effect only after it was challenged, and upheld, in every state and federal court in Georgia that reviewed it, including the Eleventh Circuit Court of Appeals[40] and the Georgia Supreme Court.[41] As these courts ruled, an ID requirement is not discriminatory, and does not violate the Constitution or any federal voting rights laws, including the Voting Rights Act of 1965.

There was a similar ruling in 2005, when Georgia submitted its voter ID law to the Justice Department for review under Section 5 of the Voting Rights Act. Section 5 is a leftover relic of the civil rights era, when official discrimination was widespread. It requires that nine states, including Georgia, get approval from either the Justice Department or a federal court in the District of Columbia before any changes in their voting laws can go into effect. The burden of proof is on those states to show that their new law will not have a discriminatory effect. Amid great criticism from so-called civil rights organizations, the Civil Rights Division of the Bush Justice Department precleared Georgia's voter ID law without objection.[42] The information submitted by the state showed that the ID requirement was not discriminatory; election results since then show that judgment was correct.

The division's Section 5 analysis was based on information received from Georgia's attorney general, including four sets of data on state driver's licenses. As the assistant attorney general of the Office of Legislative Affairs, William Moschella, explained in a letter to Senator Christopher Bond dated October 7, 2005, the data received by the division showed the following:

- Almost 6.5 million Georgians possessed identification from the Department of Motor Vehicles acceptable under the state statute—more than the Census Bureau's total projected voting-age population of Georgia when ineligible individuals, such as noncitizens and felons, are subtracted.

- There were two million more state-issued DMV identification cards than there were registered voters.

- The DMV data indicated that 28 percent of ID holders were African American, slightly higher than the African American percentage of the voting-age population in Georgia.

- Information from the state university system, which issues student identification cards that are acceptable under the law, showed that the number of African American students enrolled, and thus possessing acceptable identification, was slightly higher than the percentage of African American students in the voting-age population.

- Census data showed that about 14.3 percent of Caucasian and 19.4 percent of African American Georgians worked for government at the local, state, or federal level; therefore, a higher percentage of blacks than whites would have access to acceptable government-issued employee identification cards.

- Individuals unable to afford an identification card could receive one without paying a fee, and the state had a mobile licensing program.

- No identification card was needed to vote by absentee ballot.

When Eric Holder's Justice Department objected under Section 5 to South Carolina's voter ID law in December 2011, it very noticeably did not mention its prior approval of Georgia's more restrictive law. South Carolina's law would allow an individual without an ID to vote if he or she has a religious objection or a "reasonable impediment" that prevents them from getting a free photo ID.

The Justice Department was ignoring inconvenient facts and clear legal precedent in claiming that South Carolina's law is discriminatory; given its prior approval of the Georgia law, it should have had a hard time explaining its objection to South Carolina's.

The move was driven by the radical, left-wing ideology that has been behind almost all of the law-enforcement decisions made by the Justice Department during the Obama administration. South Carolina's comparison of its voter registration list to its driver's license records showed that a scant 1.2 percent of registered voters did not already have a DMV identification card, once adjustments were made for the deceased, individuals who had moved to other states, or mismatches. Yet the Justice Department still made the nonsensical claim that minority voters would be less likely to have a photo ID.

In a sign of the hypocrisy that drives the Holder Justice Department, anyone who wants to make an appointment with the attorney general or the head of the Civil Rights Division to discuss their objection to South Carolina's voter ID law as "discriminatory" had better bring their government-issued photo ID. No outsider can enter the main Justice headquarters building, situated between Pennsylvania and Constitution Avenues in Washington, D.C., *without* one. And to those who would argue that voting is a constitutional right, so is speaking to government officials: The First Amendment specifically protects the right of the people to "petition the Government for a redress of grievances."

In another graphic illustration of this hypocrisy, PJTV made an undercover video in which it visited the offices of several liberal groups opposing voter ID laws—the Advancement Project, the Lawyers' Committee for Civil Rights, and the Center for American Progress—*all of which require a photo ID to enter their offices.*[43]

In Georgia, as has happened in every state that has considered voter ID legislation, organizations including the ACLU and the NAACP claimed there were hundreds of thousands of voters who lacked photo IDs, a claim they continue to make today. Yet when their lawsuit against Georgia was dismissed, the federal court pointed out that after two years of litigation, none of the plaintiff organizations had produced a single individual who did not have a photo ID or could not easily obtain one. The district court judge concluded that:

> . . . [this] failure to identify those individuals 'is partic-
> ularly acute' in light of the Plaintiffs' contention that a
> large number of Georgia voters lack acceptable Photo
> ID. . . . [T]he fact that Plaintiffs, in spite of their efforts,
> have failed to uncover anyone 'who can attest to the
> fact that he/she will be prevented from voting' provides
> significant support for a conclusion that the photo ID
> requirement does not unduly burden the right to vote.[44]

The plaintiffs in the Georgia case at one point became so desperate that Daniel Levitas of the ACLU's Voting Rights Project sent an e-mail to his "Key Georgia Contacts" with the subject line "URGENT REQUEST FOR HELP IN THE PHOTO ID CASE." Levitas was forwarding an e-mail from Emmet Bondurant, the principal lawyer representing the plaintiffs, who was trying to find someone—anyone—who couldn't secure an ID. This broad appeal, sent to advocacy groups, churches, and other organizations all over Georgia, failed to turn up anyone who could support the claim made by the plaintiffs that the voter ID law would prevent any Georgian from voting.

In Indiana, which the U.S. Supreme Court said has the strictest voter ID law in the country, turnout in the Democratic presidential preference primary in 2008 quadrupled from the 2004 election, when the law was not in effect—in fact, there were 862,000 more votes cast in the Democratic primary than in the

Republican primary. In the general election that November, the turnout of Democratic voters increased by 8.32 percentage points from 2004, the largest increase in Democratic turnout of any state in the nation. According to Census Bureau surveys, 59.2 percent of the black voting-age population cast ballots in the 2008 election, compared to only 53.8 percent in 2004, an increase of more than 5 percentage points.

The neighboring state of Illinois—President Obama's home state—which had no photo-ID requirement, saw a rise in Democratic turnout of only 4.4 percentage points—only half of Indiana's increase. In Indiana, turnout in the 2010 congressional election was almost 1.75 million voters, an increase of more than 77,000 over the 2006 election. Indiana was one of the states with a "large and impressive" increase in black turnout in the 2010 election: "[T]he black share of the state vote was higher in 2010 than it was in 2008, a banner year for black turnout," an analysis showed.[45] In fact, the black share of the total vote went from only seven percent in 2008 to 12 percent in 2010.[46]

One misleading story, constantly relied on by opponents of Indiana's ID law, is the claim that some elderly nuns in Indiana "were turned away from the polls for lack of picture IDs."[47] The nuns had pointedly refused to obtain photo IDs prior to the election, and were turned away from the polls by another nun who ran the convent precinct, and who violated federal and state law that required her to provide the nuns with provisional ballots. Provisional ballots are counted if the individual casting one visits the county clerk's office within 10 days after the election to show an ID or sign an affidavit testifying to identity. The nuns could have easily obtained a valid ID only two miles from the convent; plus, they all were over 65, automatically entitling them to vote by absentee ballot without an ID.

These nuns could have voted were it not for their refusal, and *not* their inability, to comply with Indiana law, and the refusal of the precinct election official, their fellow sister, to comply with federal and state law.[48] This raises the question of whether the entire incident was trumped up to generate misleading news from gullible reporters and sympathetic activists.

Just as in the federal case in Georgia, the federal court in Indiana noted the complete inability of plaintiffs to produce anyone who could not vote because of the photo-ID law:

> Despite apocalyptic assertions of wholesale voter dis-enfranchisement, Plaintiffs have produced not a single piece of evidence of any identifiable registered voter who would be prevented from voting pursuant to [the photo ID law] because of his or her inability to obtain the necessary photo identification. Similarly, Plaintiffs have failed to produce any evidence of any individual, registered or unregistered, who would have to obtain photo identification in order to vote, let alone anyone who would undergo any appreciable hardship to obtain photo identification in order to be qualified to vote.[49]

Despite all efforts, the opponents of a voter ID requirement have failed to gain traction in any courtroom across the country.

Another gambit is the claim that requiring an ID, even when it is free, is a "poll tax" because of the incidental costs that may be involved, such as transportation to a registrar's office or the need to obtain a birth certificate. The poll-tax claim was raised in the lawsuit filed against Georgia by the NAACP. The federal court, however, dismissed this claim, agreeing with the Indiana federal court that:

> . . . [such an argument] represents a dramatic overstate-ment of what fairly constitutes a 'poll tax.' Thus, the imposition of tangential burdens does not transform a

regulation into a poll tax. Moreover, the cost of time and transportation cannot plausibly qualify as a prohibited poll tax because those same 'costs' also result from voter registration and in-person voting requirements, which one would not reasonably construe as a poll tax.[50]

These absurd cries of "poll tax" are clearly another tactic in the increasingly desperate campaign against voter ID legislation.

About the only thing the Left has had to rely on for its hollow claims against voter photo-ID requirements is a flawed 2006 study by the Brennan Center for Justice at New York University Law School. Titled *Citizens Without Proof*, it supposedly shows that millions of Americans who are eligible to vote lack photo ID. This faulty study is constantly cited for its unsupported claim that 25 percent of blacks do not have a photo ID. The Brennan Center has been vigorous in opposing almost every sensible voter reform, from requiring voter ID to requiring proof of citizenship when registering to vote. The report is dubious in its methodology, and especially suspect in its sweeping conclusions. It is based on a survey of only 987 "voting-age American citizens," although it contains no information on how it was determined whether a respondent was actually an American citizen entitled to vote. The survey uses the responses of these 987 individuals to estimate, based on the 2000 Census, the number of Americans lacking valid documentation. Although the report says it was weighted to account for underrepresentation of race, it does not provide the methodology used.

By neglecting to ask whether respondents were actual or likely voters, registered voters, or even eligible voters, the study ignored the most relevant data: the number of eligible citizens who would have voted, but could not, because of voter ID laws. All pollsters know that the only accurate polls are of likely voters, not of the voting-age population. Surveys of registered voters have shown the exact opposite of the Brennan Center study: that only a tiny percentage of registered voters do not already have some form of government-issued photo ID.

Also, the Brennan Center survey didn't ask whether respondents had IDs; it asked whether IDs were "readily available." And the question about citizenship documentation asked whether respondents had access to this "in a place where you can quickly find it if you had to show it tomorrow," even though elections are not scheduled on such a short-term basis. This question obviously was intended to skew the results. The survey also failed to ask whether respondents had student IDs, which are acceptable under many state laws, or tribal IDs, which are acceptable in some states, including Georgia and Arizona. On one question, 14 percent of respondents were so confused that they indicated they had both a U.S. birth certificate and naturalization papers, an obviously contradictory response.

The Brennan Center, like Henny Penny, has been predicting since 2006 that the sky will fall, and there will be massive disenfranchisement of voters. None of its predictions have ever come true, and it has been unable to prove its claims in court. The findings in *Citizens Without Proof* simply do not match up with the findings of more objective and unbiased research. If we use the same standards that the Brennan Center used, of looking at the voting-age population instead of eligible, registered, or actual voters, then the report's claims contradict even the most obvious evidence, such as the fact that there are millions more government-issued IDs than registered voters across the country. Statistics from the U.S. Department of Transportation show that there are 205,781,457 valid state driver's licenses for individuals 18 years of age or older; the U.S. Election Assistance Commission cites a total of 186,874,157 registered voters. That means there are almost 19 million *more* holders of driver's licenses than there are registered voters nationwide. This does not include the additional three to four percent of individuals who, according to a Federal Election Commission study in 1995, have an identification card issued by state motor vehicle agencies in lieu of a driver's license.

These statistics also do not include the more than 85 million passports issued by the federal government, as reported by the Government Accountability Office. Passports are acceptable forms of identification under state voter ID laws. And we should not forget government employees, be they federal, state, or local, full- or part-time workers. In Georgia, for example, the voter ID requirement can be met by a "valid employee identification card containing a photograph" issued by any entity of federal, state, or local government. The same is true in Indiana. There are 22,632,381 people nationwide who work for public institutions and who would have this type of ID, according to the Census Bureau.

The desperate search by the Left to find a voter who will not be able to vote due to common-sense ID requirements is at times comical. When one of the authors was a guest on a radio show of the Canadian Broadcasting Corporation discussing voter ID, the only voter the CBC could find to interview was an elderly man from Tennessee, which had recently implemented a voter ID requirement. His complaint? He had had to switch his non-photo driver's license to a driver's license with a photo, and did not realize that he could do so free of charge. He was upset that he had paid eight dollars when he went to the state office to change IDs. An appearance on CNN by one of the authors was preceded by an interview with another elderly voter, this time from Missouri, who was a longtime elected Democratic official. She made the not-credible claim that, despite being a former public official, she was unable to obtain a photo ID—apparently also not realizing that she fell within an age exemption under a previously passed Missouri law.

CONCLUSION

With the courts against them, the public against them, and the turnout in actual elections against them, what do liberals have left? Only racial polemics, fear-mongering, and a Justice Department at the beck and call of the ACLU, the Democratic National Committee, and the NAACP. The vitriolic rhetoric is a sign of desperation, and the claims of "suppression" and "intimidation" have been shown to be completely untrue.

Liberals claim that only states with legislatures controlled by Republicans have implemented voter ID requirements, as evidence that this is a sordid plot to suppress Democratic votes. It is true that most of these measures have been sponsored by Republicans, but that is more akin to a sad commentary on the unwillingness of some Democratic politicians to protect the integrity of the election process, and their toleration of voter fraud. Democrats in Rhode Island certainly did not agree when they sponsored and passed that state's voter ID law; nor did Democratic legislators in Kansas: Two-thirds of Democrats in the state House and three-quarters of Democrats in the state Senate voted in favor of Secretary of State Kris Kobach's voter ID bill.

Polls consistently show that Americans of all races and party affiliations support voter ID laws, illustrating how out of touch the leaders of civil rights organizations and the Democratic Party are with their constituents. Americans must produce a photo ID to obtain a library card, drink a beer, cash a check, board an airplane, buy a train ticket, or check in to a hotel. They understand that requiring voter ID is a common-sense reform that helps protect the security and integrity of our election process. Happily, it's a requirement voters can easily meet.

In fact, the federal government places an identification burden on individuals that is similar to what states are implementing for voting. The right to seek employment to support oneself and one's family is fundamental and basic, protected by federal

71

and state antidiscrimination laws. And yet, under federal law, no individual can be employed anywhere in the United States without producing documentation authenticating identity and U.S. citizenship, or legal authorization to work as a legally-admitted noncitizen. Employers must complete a federal I-9 form, issued by the Department of Homeland Security; according to the form, "employers are subject to civil or criminal penalties if they do not comply with the Immigration Reform and Control Act of 1986," and "an individual may not begin employment unless this [I-9] form is completed."

Similarly, while the Justice Department raises objections to South Carolina's voter ID law, it ignores the fact that federal law requires states administering programs such as Medicaid to obtain proof of citizenship, nationality, and identity. South Carolinians applying for the Supplemental Nutrition Assistance Program (food stamps) must provide a "driver's license, picture ID, birth certificate, or other proof of your identity and current address." There are no claims that these federal welfare requirements are a return to Jim Crow—or that the federal requirement to prove identity in order to be employed is a Jim Crow law.

America is one of the only democracies in the world that does not uniformly require voters to present a photo ID. Across the globe, democracies administer such a requirement without problems, and without reports that their citizens are in any way burdened by it. Our southern neighbor, Mexico, which has a much larger rate of poverty than the United States, requires both a photo ID and a thumbprint to vote—and turnout has increased in Mexican elections since this requirement went into effect in the 1990s. Mexico's voter ID laws are credited with reducing the fraud that had prevailed in many Mexican elections, and with allowing the 2000 election of Vicente Fox, the first opposition-party president of Mexico in 70 years.

Asking voters to authenticate their identity is a perfectly reasonable and easily met requirement. As the U.S. Supreme Court has noted, voter ID laws protect the integrity and reliability of the electoral process. States have a valid and legitimate interest not only in deterring and detecting voter fraud, but in maintaining the confidence of their citizens in the security of all elections.

CHAPTER FOUR

Shooting the Messenger: Truth-Tellers Artur Davis and Harold Metts

Former Alabama congressman Artur Davis knew he would raise hackles on his fellow Democrats by writing the op-ed piece his hometown newspaper, the *Montgomery Advertiser*, published in October 2011.[1] He just didn't know how much anger his new support for voter ID laws would stir up.

In his essay, Davis would break many of the taboos surrounding the debate over voter fraud. Especially the one about Democrats—and especially African American Democrats—being expected to claim that voter fraud wasn't a serious concern. After all, the two-thirds-black district Davis had represented from 2003 to 2011 included Selma, home of the National Voting Rights Museum, and other landmarks of the 1960s struggle for racial equality and voting rights. He had been an active member of the Congressional Black Caucus, and his career had begun with an internship at the Southern Poverty Research Center, an iconic civil rights group. In 2007, he became the first Democratic congressman who did not live in Illinois to endorse Barack Obama for president, and the next year he seconded Obama's nomination at the Democratic presidential convention in Denver.

So it was startling to read Davis's mea culpa. "I've changed my mind on voter ID laws—I think Alabama did the right thing in passing one—and I wish I had gotten it right when I was in political office. When I was a congressman, I took the path of least resistance on this subject for an African American politician. Without any evidence to back it up, I lapsed into the rhetoric of various partisans and activists who contend that requiring photo identification to vote is a suppression tactic aimed at thwarting black voter participation."

Today Davis recognizes that the "most aggressive" voter suppression in the African American community "is the wholesale manufacture of ballots, at the polls and absentee, in parts of the Black Belt." A region in Alabama known for its dark, rich soil, the Black Belt comprises some of the poorest, predominantly black counties in the state—and some of the most prone to voter fraud.

"Voting [in] the names of the dead, and the nonexistent, and the too-mentally-impaired to function cancels out the votes of citizens who are exercising their rights—that's suppression by any light. If you doubt it exists, I don't; I've heard the peddlers of these ballots brag about it, I've been asked to provide the funds for it, and I am confident it has changed at least a few close local election results."

To rub salt in the wounds of vote-fraud deniers, Davis went on to say: "I was disappointed to see Bill Clinton, a very good president and an even greater ex-president, compare voter ID to Jim Crow, and it is chilling to see the intimidation tactics brought to bear on African American, Democratic legislators in Rhode Island who had the nerve to support a voter ID law in that very liberal state."

He concluded his remarkably candid commentary by noting that voter ID is "unlikely to impede a single good faith voter—and that only gives voting the same elements of security as writing a check at the store, or maintaining a library card." As he says, the case for voter ID "is a good one, and it ought to make politics a little cleaner and the process of conducting elections much fairer. I wish I'd gotten it right the first time."

The reaction to Davis's column intrigued him. Some people were angry. "I saw it and was frustrated by it," said Representative Emanuel Cleaver, the chair of the Congressional Black Caucus. "I don't know what that's all about. There are some people who believe he's getting ready to switch parties. I have no idea. Needless to say, he doesn't confide in the CBC."[2] Davis expressed disappointment that some critics claimed he was speaking out over bitterness that he had lost the Democratic primary for governor in 2010 to a candidate supported by local Democratic machines and the teachers union. "I gave it my best shot, but they should be concerned that in defeating a moderate like me, they handed Republicans every single statewide elected office," he told me. "But rather than look in the mirror, they prefer to cast stones."

Other critics ignored the major points Davis made in his article, and demanded he produce his evidence, as if the multiple convictions for voter fraud in counties in his district over the years weren't proof enough. Talking Points Memo asked him to provide specific examples of when he witnessed such fraud, and why he didn't report it to authorities.

"I know that those are the talking points that some groups opposed to my article have disseminated, and I choose not to play that game with you or them," Davis responded to TPM in an e-mail. "It strikes me as the 'shoot the messenger' politics both the left and the right deploy." He then noted that as recently as 2009, a former circuit court clerk in Hale County, in his district, had been convicted of voter fraud. He rattled off the names of convictions in Greene, Lowndes, Perry, and Jefferson Counties—all within his district. He pointed out that news organizations ranging from NPR to *The New York Times* had written in 2008 about the state attorney general's office seizing voting records in his district, and quoting local residents that they'd been approached by people offering them inducements to commit fraud. But those same sources said that although fraud was widespread, most people weren't willing to talk openly about it, making prosecutions difficult.

Davis also made the point that a great deal of voter fraud goes undetected because "common sense suggests that the use of the name of dead or fictitious people does not leave a victim to swear out a complaint."

He acknowledges that most of the voter fraud that's been uncovered in his old district is absentee-ballot fraud. "That means we should clean that up too, but I don't see many of my critics rushing to support those reforms," he told me. "As for voter ID, the fact that it won't stop all fraud doesn't mean we don't have laws against bribery, or that we don't have securities laws because insider trading will sometimes go on."

In April 2012 Davis expanded on his *Montgomery Advertiser* opinion piece. Then a fellow at Harvard's Institute of Politics, Davis flew to Houston to speak at the annual convention of True the Vote, a citizen's group dedicated to ballot integrity. "I congratulate you for being active on this issue in the face of the demonization you have all been subjected to," he said. He noted that many of the victims of voter fraud were minority voters who were robbed of their voice. "The most aggressive practitioners of voter fraud are local machines who are tied, lock, stock, and barrel, to the special interests in their community, the landfills, the casino operators, and they are cooking the boxes on Election Day. We need to speak out for them."

Davis concluded his speech by chiding many of his former colleagues in Congress. "We've reached a sad point where so many on the Left are now so happy to exaggerate fears about the bad old days coming back that they no longer represent a meaningful moral tenor in our national conversation. The fact is that reasonable precautions against voter fraud are nothing like the billy club, the cattle prod, and the charging state trooper of the past. We need to recognize that, and confront those critics who go over the top on this issue."[3]

WHEN DEMOCRATS VOTE IN FAVOR OF VOTER ID

As Davis indicated in his op-ed, one of those errant critics was Bill Clinton, who in the summer of 2011 portrayed the nationwide movement to pass voter ID laws as the return of Jim Crow. "There has never been in my lifetime, since we got rid of the poll tax, and all the other Jim Crow burdens on voting, the determined effort to limit the franchise that we see today," he warned in July 2011.[4]

But in an unfortunate bit of timing, Clinton gave his firebreathing criticism just days after a Democratic legislature in Rhode Island had passed a voter ID law and seen it signed into law. As Lou Jacobsen of *Governing* magazine reported, "Rhode Island is a state where both legislative chambers are dominated by Democrats and where the governor is a moderate-to-liberal independent. On paper, Rhode Island is the last place one would expect to find a voter ID law being enacted."[5]

The answer lies in the person of Harold Metts, a 69-year-old businessman who is the only African American member of the state senate. After receiving numerous complaints for almost 20 years from black and Latino residents concerned about voter fraud in his hometown of Providence, Metts decided he had to act: "I had personally reached a point where I could no longer duck the issue."

He says the issue hit him personally when he learned that his own state representative, Anastasia Williams, and her daughter had their votes stolen in 2006 by people voting in their name. "I really had to look at myself and say, 'If fraud is really happening, how long are you going to bury your head in the sand as to what is actually happening, as opposed to [worrying about] the disenfranchisement that could happen?"[6]

He quickly assembled an impressive coalition: Democratic Secretary of State Ralph Mollis; Senator Juan Pichardo, the first Dominican American elected to a state senate; and Rhode Island House Speaker Gordon Fox, the first African American to ever head that body.

They carefully crafted a bill that won support across both parties. Its provisions will be phased in, with the photo-ID requirement not fully implemented until 2014. Even then, polling places will accept a broad range of IDs, including those issued by universities and medical groups. Free IDs will be made available to those who lack them, and anyone lacking ID can vote by provisional ballot at the polls, as long as they prove their eligibility later.

Pichardo says he initially had qualms about the voter ID issue, but his time on a voter rights commission assembled by Rhode Island's secretary of state convinced him that a responsible bill could be crafted. "I think when we see a problem and we try to address it, we have to try to improve the system," he told *The Providence Journal*.

Secretary of State Mollis says proof of the law's workability came in the state's April 2012 primary. Fewer than 25 voters lacked the necessary identification, and those 25 voted by provisional ballot. "The rollout of voter went as smoothly as we could have hoped," Mollis spokesman Chris Barnett said. The secretary of state's office had prepared for primary day by handing out free state IDs at senior centers, homeless shelters, and community centers around the state. Maria Bell, a poll worker in Pawtucket, told *The Providence Journal* that voters told her they like the new law. "We had one guy show up who showed us 10 IDs," she said. "People don't mind at all. This should have been done years ago."[7]

Nonetheless, there were naysayers. The ACLU and the NAACP both claimed the successful primary rollout was invalid because too few people had voted. State senator Paul Jabour of Providence maintained that the law was a solution in search of a problem. "We haven't had those problems here," he said. "Until somebody can present me evidence that fraud has occurred, people should be allowed to vote in as free a manner as possible. This is the land of the free, not the land of restriction."

Some opponents do scoff at the idea that there is no fraudulent voting in Rhode Island. "I've seen [some voter fraud] with my own eyes," said Tony Affigne, a Providence College professor of political science. "But it's certainly not the kind of problem that [necessitates] a statewide, draconian law." Even the liberal magazine *The New Republic* found widespread concern in many Rhode Island neighborhoods. Simon van Zuylen-Wood, a recent graduate of Brown University, reported that African American councilman Wilbur Jennings told him that his 2006 opponent, Leon Tejada, illegally registered people. Former councilwoman Joan DiRuzzo, a Democrat, blamed her defeat in 2010 on text-message-coordinated voter impersonations. Representative Anastasia Williams, who has both African American and Hispanic ancestry, said that in 2010, four years after her own vote had been stolen by an illegal alien, she personally witnessed a Hispanic man voting twice at the same polling place, wearing a different outfit each time. "What caught my eye was [he] was a hottie,"[8] she told *The New Republic*.

Williams described the pattern of fraud: A candidate interested in securing an unnatural advantage hires a "recruiter," who compiles a list of likely nonvoters. The recruiter then hires people to vote in those names. African American George Lindsey, a prominent figure in Providence, told one of the authors that one recruiter he knows of routinely gets paid five to six thousand dollars by each candidate per election: "What he'll tell you is he's basically a hired gun."

It was outrages such as this that convinced Lincoln Chafee, the state's liberal governor, to sign state senator Metts's bill. According to *The Providence Journal*, Doris De Los Santos, Rhode Island's director of municipal and external affairs, told the governor the bill was needed to "eliminate or minimize any potential for voter fraud." She said that people in her Latino community were quite comfortable with showing a photo ID to vote, because it is common practice in almost every Latin American country.[9]

Chafee spokesman Steve Hourihan said that the governor's decision to sign the bill into law wasn't made lightly: "He felt there was compelling reason for him to go ahead and sign this legislation." Hourihan added that Chafee "really put a lot of energy into both sides," meeting with critics of the proposed law, and with Senator Metts, Representative Williams, and Representative Jon Brien of Woonsocket. Brien says it disappointed him that so many national Democrats attacked the legislation without knowing the details or the context. "I think that party leaders have tried to make this a Republican-versus-Democrat issue," he told Stateline, an online news service on local government from the Pew Center on the States. "It's not. It's simply a good government issue."

Secretary of State Mollis concurs. He thinks his fellow Democrats in other states should support voter ID legislation. "I believe a lot in the Democratic [Party] principles. But when the day is done, my job is to maintain the integrity of elections," he told Stateline. "I would love to see the Democratic base nationally embrace something like this."

As for complaints that there haven't been enough actual convictions for voter fraud in Rhode Island in recent years to warrant a voter ID law, Mollis points to the difficulty of collecting evidence. But even if it proves to be true that there is no current epidemic of voter fraud, he says, "I think solutions without problems are the best laws. We should be providing solutions before problems happen, not after."[10]

CHAPTER FIVE

The Problem of Noncitizen Voting

On October 13, 2010, an immigration judge in Orlando, Florida issued an order in a removal case involving Anailin Reyes,[1] a Cuban citizen who entered the United States in Miami on April 26, 2004. Four months after she arrived she registered to vote, and did vote in the November 2004 election. Reyes's aunt, Jobitza Soto, a U.S. citizen, told the court that she, Reyes, and Reyes's mother (who was also a Cuban citizen) were approached outside the Duval County Courthouse by a woman from a third-party organization holding a registration drive. Soto said she told the woman that her two companions were not U.S. citizens, but that the woman told her that "noncitizens could legally vote." So Soto filled out voter registration forms for all three of them.

That Reyes and her mother were noncitizens, and therefore not entitled to vote, was not detected by local Duval County election officials. The fraud only came to light because Reyes applied for a change in her immigration status. During that process, she at first lied to the Department of Homeland Security about registering and voting, but admitted it after "seeing evidence to the contrary" uncovered by DHS through a check of local voter registration records. If Reyes had not tried to change her immigration status, she easily could have continued to vote, illegally and without detection—as too many noncitizens (both legal and illegal) do in elections all over the country.

Unfortunately for the interests of election integrity, the immigration judge in the proceeding, Rafael B. Ortiz-Segura, refused to punish Reyes's violation of federal and state law, blaming election officials for mistakenly approving her registration, and the check-in form Reyes signed at the polling place to get a ballot, because it "made no mention of any citizenship requirement."[2] Also unfortunately, Soto was unable to identify which third-party organization had recruited her, and presumably other noncitizens, to register and vote.

This is not an isolated case. Noncitizens are on voter registration lists all over the country. In 2005, the U.S. Government Accountability Office found that up to three percent of the 30,000 individuals called for jury duty from voter registration rolls over a two-year period in just one U.S. district court were not citizens.[3] While that may not seem like many, just three percent of registered voters would have been more than enough to provide the winning presidential vote margin in Florida in 2000.

It is estimated that there are more than one million illegal aliens in Florida. In a three-year period, from October 2002 to September 2005, the Department of Justice prosecuted a dozen noncitizens for registering or voting in Florida elections since 1998, including in Broward, Miami-Dade, St. Lucie, Martin, and Palm Beach Counties.[4] One noncitizen, Rafael Velasquez, not only voted illegally, but had been a candidate for the Florida legislature![5] In 2012, a local NBC station found at least 100 individuals in one county who had been excused from jury duty because they were not citizens, but who were registered to vote.[6] A Coral Gables resident, Hinako Dennett, who is not a citizen, told the NBC reporter that she votes "every year." A Naples resident, Yvonne Wigglesworth, also a noncitizen, claimed she did not know how she had gotten registered, but records showed she had voted in six elections over the previous 11 years.

Florida is not unique. Thousands of noncitizens are registered to vote in some states, and tens (if not hundreds) of thousands in total may be on voter rolls nationwide. These numbers are significant: Local elections often are decided by a handful of votes, and even national election results have been within the likely margin of the number of noncitizens illegally registered to vote.

There is no reliable method of determining the number of noncitizens registered, or actually voting, because most laws meant to ensure that only citizens vote are ignored, are inadequate, or are systematically undermined by government officials. Those who ignore the implications of noncitizen voting are willfully blind to the problem, or may actually approve of illegal voting. Perhaps that is the objective of organizations such as the ACLU, the Mexican American Legal Defense Fund, and the League of United Latin American Citizens, which have opposed all efforts to allow states to verify the citizenship status of registered voters.

While Americans may disagree on some areas of immigration policy, the overwhelming majority agree on the basic principle that only citizens should be able to vote in elections. The law reflects that consensus, since it is a legal requirement to be a citizen to vote in federal and state elections.[7] Surprisingly, a very small number of jurisdictions, like Maryland's Chevy Chase and Takoma Park, allow noncitizens (including illegals) to vote in local elections.[8] A December 2011 proposal by the mayor of New Haven, Connecticut to allow that city's estimated 11,000 illegal aliens to vote in municipal elections came under great criticism. This is the same mayor whom the U.S. Supreme Court found in 2009 had engaged in blatant racial discrimination against white and Hispanic firefighters when he denied them promotion.[9] His proposal seemed a cynical attempt to win the votes of another voting bloc, even if it meant supporting illegal behavior.

Some Americans argue that alien voting is a nonexistent problem, or dismiss reports of fraud as unimportant because, they claim, there are no cases in which noncitizens "intentionally" registered to vote, or voted "while knowing that they were ineligible."[10] Even if this latter claim were true—which it is not—every vote cast by a noncitizen, whether an illegal alien or a resident alien legally in the country, dilutes or cancels the vote of a citizen, effectively disenfranchising that citizen. To dismiss the importance of this disenfranchisement because the noncitizens supposedly did not know they were acting illegally debases one of the most important rights of U.S. citizens.

Unless and until immigrants become citizens, they must respect the laws that bar noncitizen voting. To keep noncitizen votes from diluting election results, immigration and election officials must cooperate far more effectively than they have to date, and state and federal officials must increase efforts to enforce the laws, already on the books, against noncitizen voting.

The evidence is indisputable that aliens, both legal and illegal, are registering and voting in federal, state, and local elections. Following a mayor's race in Compton, California, aliens testified under oath in court that they voted in the election.[11] In that case, a candidate who was elected to the city council was permanently disqualified from holding public office in California for soliciting noncitizens to register and vote.[12] The election fraud would never have been discovered except that the incumbent mayor, who lost by fewer than 300 votes, contested the outcome.

Similarly, a 1996 congressional race in California may have been stolen by noncitizen voting. Republican incumbent Bob Dornan faced a spirited challenger, Democrat Loretta Sanchez. Sanchez won the election by just 979 votes, and Dornan contested the election in the U.S. House of Representatives. His challenge was dismissed when an investigation by the House Committee on Oversight and Government Reform turned up only 624 invalid votes, by noncitizens on the records of the Immigration and Naturalization Service, and another 124 improper absentee ballots[13]—fewer than Sanchez's victory margin. But the committee found "circumstantial" evidence of another 196 noncitizen votes that it did not include in its tally.

Sanchez's victory margin was just 35 votes, if one includes the 196 noncitizen voters identified by the Committee as "circumstantial." Since the California secretary of state complained that the INS refused his request to check its records against the entire Orange County voter registration file, and no complete check was made of every voter in the congressional race, that margin could be less.[14] And the investigation could not detect *illegal* aliens, who would not be in INS records. The Oversight Committee pointed out the elephant in the room: "[I]f there is a significant number of 'documented aliens,' aliens in INS records, on the Orange County voter registration rolls, how many illegal or undocumented aliens may be registered to vote in Orange County?" With about 200 votes determining the winner, the possibility is strong that undetected illegal votes changed the outcome of the election.

Many liberals assert that illegal aliens do not register to vote so as "to stay below the radar." Liberal law professor Richard Hasen, an opponent of voter ID laws, doubts that illegal aliens register to vote because "committing a felony for no personal gain is not a wise choice."[15] But he overlooks the fact that many aliens apparently believe that the potential benefits of registering far outweigh the chances of being caught and prosecuted. (That is unfortunately true, since most states have no measures in place to verify citizenship, and many district attorneys will not prosecute what they see as a "victimless and nonviolent" crime.[16])

Why would an illegal alien register to vote? Under current practice, a voter registration card is an easily obtainable document, routinely issued without any identification check, that an illegal alien can use for many purposes: obtaining a driver's license, qualifying for a job, and even voting.[17] The Immigration Reform and Control Act of 1986 requires employers to verify that all newly hired employees present documentation confirming their identity and legal authorization to work in the United States.[18] In essence, new employees must prove either that they are U.S. citizens, or legal aliens with a work permit. The federal I-9 form that employers must complete for new employees provides a list of documentation that can be used to establish identity—including a voter registration card.

The importance of this "benefit" was illustrated by a federal grand jury report in 1984 that uncovered large numbers of aliens registered to vote in Chicago. As the grand jury reported, many aliens "register to vote so that they can obtain documents identifying them as U.S. citizens" and have "used their voters' cards to obtain a myriad of benefits, from social security to jobs with the Defense Department."[19] The U.S. Attorney at the time estimated that there were at least 80,000 illegal aliens registered to vote in Chicago; dozens were indicted and convicted for registering and voting.[20]

The grand jury's probe resulted in a limited cleanup of voter registration rolls in Chicago. Just one year later, INS district director A. D. Moyer testified before a state legislative task force that 25,000 illegal and 40,000 legal aliens remained on voting rolls in Chicago. Moyer told the Illinois Senate that noncitizens registered so they could get a voter registration card to use as identification, adding that the card was "a quick ticket into the unemployment compensation system."[21] An alien from Belize, for example, testified that he and his two sisters were able to register easily because they were not asked for any identification or proof of citizenship, and lied about where they were born. After registering, he voted in Chicago.

Once aliens are registered, they receive the same encouragement to vote from campaign and party get-out-the-vote programs and advertisements directed at all registered voters—there is no way to distinguish between properly registered potential voters and illegally registered noncitizens.

An accurate assessment of the magnitude of the problem is difficult. There is no systematic review of voter registration rolls by states to find noncitizens, and the relevant federal agencies—in direct violation of federal law—refuse to cooperate with those few state election officials who attempt to verify the citizenship status of registered voters. Federal immigration law requires these agencies to "respond to an inquiry by a Federal, State, or local government agency, seeking to verify or ascertain the citizenship or Immigration status of any individual within the jurisdiction of the agency for any purpose authorized by law, by providing the requested verification or status information," regardless of any other provision of federal law, such as the Privacy Act.[22] But examples of refusal to cooperate are legion:

- In declining to cooperate with a request by Maryland to check the citizenship status of individuals registered to vote there, a spokesman for the U.S. Citizenship and Immigration Service (CIS) mistakenly declared that the agency could not release that information because "it is important to safeguard the confidentiality of each legal immigrant, especially in light of the federal Privacy Act and the Immigration and Nationality Act."[23] One result of this policy: In 2004, a guilty verdict in a murder trial in Maryland was jeopardized because a noncitizen was discovered on the jury, which had been chosen from the voter rolls.

- In 2005, Washington State's secretary of state, Sam Reed, asked the CIS to check the immigration status of registered voters in Washington; the agency refused to cooperate.[24]

- A 1998 request to the INS by the Fulton County, Georgia Board of Registration and Elections to check the immigration status of 775 registered voters was likewise refused, for want of a notarized consent from each voter to allay "federal privacy act" concerns.

- In 1997, the FBI and the U.S. Attorney's office in Dallas began an investigation into voting by noncitizens when a random check by local INS agents found 10 noncitizens who had voted in just one 400-person precinct. The criminal investigation was turned over to local prosecutors, who sent a computerized tape of the names of individuals who had voted to the INS, requesting a check against INS records. The INS refused to cooperate with the criminal investigation.[25] An INS official was quoted as saying that the INS bureaucracy did not "want to open a Pandora's box. . . . If word got out that this is a substantial problem, it could tie up all sorts of manpower. There might be a few thousand [illegal voters] in Dallas, for example, but there could be tens of thousands in places like New York, Chicago, or Miami."[26]

These incidents show that the CIS and U.S. Immigration and Customs Enforcement (ICE)—the successor agencies to the INS within the Department of Homeland Security—are either ignorant of federal legal requirements, or deliberately ignoring them. Any inquiry by a state or local election official regarding voter eligibility based on citizenship falls squarely within their statutory authority.

To be sure, CIS and ICE databases are not comprehensive; they contain information only about legal immigrants who have applied for the documentation necessary to be in the United States, and illegal immigrants who have been detained. But even access to that information would be a big step forward for election officials in their attempts to clean up registration lists and oust aliens who are voting illegally.

The refusal of federal agencies to obey the law compels local officials to rely almost entirely on the "honor system" to keep noncitizens from the polls. As Maryland's state election administrator has complained, "There is no way of checking. . . . We have no access to any information about who is in the United States, legally or otherwise."[27] Most discoveries of noncitizens on the registration rolls are therefore accidental.

But it continues to happen. The Colorado secretary of state testified before Congress in 2011 that a check of voter registration rolls against state DMV records indicated that more than 11,000 Colorado registered voters may not be U.S. citizens—and more than 5,000 of them voted.[28] New Mexico secretary of state Dianna Duran reported that a preliminary check of voter registration rolls had found 37 noncitizens who had voted in New Mexico elections.[29] In 1994, Mario Aburto Martínez, a Mexican national and the assassin of Mexican presidential candidate Luis Donaldo Colosio, was found to have twice registered to vote in California. A random examination of just 10 percent of the 3,000 Hispanics registered to vote in California's 39th Assembly District by an independent group "revealed phony addresses and large numbers of registrants who admitted they were not U.S. citizens."[30]

The large numbers of illegally registered voters may be partially explained by the testimony of a Hispanic member of the Los Angeles Police Department, who had been a volunteer for the California-based Southwest Voter Registration Education Project. When she reported to her supervisor that her fellow volunteers were not asking potential registrants whether they were citizens, she was reprimanded "and told that she was not to ask that question . . . only whether the person wished to register to vote."[31] This recalls the third-party organization registering new voters at the Duval County Courthouse in Florida that claimed that even noncitizens could vote.

The Dornan–Sanchez investigation produced an affidavit from a noncitizen similarly stating that the Sanchez campaign's field director, an elected member of the Anaheim Board of Education, told him that it "didn't matter" that he was not a U.S. citizen—he should register and vote anyway.[32] In fact, hundreds of the bogus registrations by noncitizens were blamed on an immigrant rights group, Hermandad Mexicana, which protested the investigation of the Dornan-Sanchez race. In a fitting bit of irony, the head of the organization, Nativo Lopez, pleaded guilty to voter registration fraud in 2011 for voting in Los Angeles County instead of where he lived in Orange County.[33]

In 2006, Paul Bettencourt, voter registrar for Harris County, Texas, testified before the U.S. Committee on House Administration that the extent of illegal voting by foreign citizens in Harris County was impossible to determine but "that it has and will continue to occur." Twenty-two percent of county residents, he said, were born outside of the United States, and more than 500,000 were noncitizens. Bettencourt said he had canceled the registration of a Brazilian woman in 1996 when she acknowledged on a jury summons that she was not a U.S. citizen. Despite that cancellation, however, "[s]he then reapplied in 1997, again claiming to be a U.S. citizen, and was again given a voter card, which was again canceled. Records show she was able to vote at least four times in general and primary elections."[34]

In 2005, Bettencourt's office turned up at least 35 cases in which foreign nationals applied for or received voter cards; he pointed out that Harris County regularly had "elections decided by one, two, or just a handful of votes." A Norwegian citizen was discovered to have voted in a state legislative race in Harris County that was decided by only 33 votes.[35] Nor is this problem unique to Harris County. Hundreds of illegal aliens were reported to have registered to vote in Bexar County, Texas, and at least 41 of them voted, some several times, in a dozen local, state, and federal elections.[36]

Just like Anailin Reyes, these individuals are unlikely to be prosecuted by the Obama Justice Department, given its attitude towards illegal aliens and nonenforcement of immigration laws. In fact, their violation of federal law is not even likely to prevent them from becoming citizens. This was demonstrated in 2010 in Tennessee, when Putnam County election administrator Debbie Steidl exposed a form letter sent by the Department of Homeland Security to an immigrant seeking to become a citizen, telling him to submit evidence that he had "been removed from the roll of registered voters." The Obama administration seemed uninterested that the noncitizen had actually voted in the 2004 election.[37]

In 2005, Arizona passed Proposition 200, which requires anyone registering to vote to provide "satisfactory evidence of United States citizenship," such as a driver's license, a birth certificate, a passport, naturalization documents, or any other document accepted by the federal government to prove citizenship for employment purposes. Proposition 200 has prevented at least 20,000 noncitizens from registering to vote. The law was upheld as both constitutional and nondiscriminatory by a federal court in 2008. However, in April 2012 the Ninth Circuit Court of Appeals held that it violates the National Voter Registration Act, at least as applied to the voter registration form used to register for federal elections.[38] The court did uphold Arizona's voter ID requirement; the ruling on proof of citizenship does not apply to state elections.

The case doubtless will end up on appeal to the Supreme Court, and it is very likely the Ninth Circuit Court decision will be overturned. Georgia and Kansas successfully passed similar requirements; in 2011 the Justice Department conceded that Georgia's proof-of-citizenship law does not discriminate, after the state sued for preclearance under Section 5 of the Voting Rights Act.[39] Both Georgia and Kansas now have proof-of-citizenship requirements in effect.

As the story by the local NBC station in Florida demonstrated, some noncitizen registrations can be detected through the jury process. The vast majority of state and federal courts draw their jury pools from voter registration lists, and the jury questionnaires used by court clerks ask potential jurors whether they are U.S. citizens. In most states, however, and throughout the federal court system, court clerks rarely notify local election officials when potential jurors have sworn under oath that they are not U.S. citizens.

In jurisdictions that do share that information, election officials routinely discover noncitizens on the voter rolls. The former district attorney in Maricopa County, Arizona, testified that after receiving a list of potential jurors who admitted they were not citizens, he indicted 10 who had registered to vote. (All had sworn on their registration forms that they were indeed citizens.) Four had actually voted in elections.[40]

The county recorder had received inquiries from aliens seeking verification, for their citizenship applications, that they had not registered or voted. Thirty-seven of those aliens *had* registered to vote, and 15 of them had actually voted. As Maricopa

County's district attorney explained, these numbers come "from a relatively small universe of individuals—legal immigrants who seek to become citizens. . . . These numbers do not tell us how many illegal immigrants have registered and voted." Even these small numbers, though, could have been enough to sway an election. A 2004 Arizona primary election, explained the district attorney, was determined by just 13 votes. Clearly, illegally registered noncitizens could have determined the outcome of the election.

These numbers become more alarming when one considers that only a very small percentage of registered voters are called for jury duty in most jurisdictions. The California secretary of state reported in 1998 that two to three thousand of the individuals summoned for jury duty in Orange County each month claimed an exemption from jury service because they were not U.S. citizens, and 85 to 90 percent of those individuals were summoned from the voter registration list, rather than DMV records.[41] While some of those individuals may have simply committed perjury to avoid jury service, this represents a significant number of potentially illegal voters: 24,000 to 36,000 noncitizens summoned from the voter registration list over a one-year period.

Under the Constitution, an individual's eligibility to vote is left mostly to the states. All states require individuals to be U.S. citizens to vote in state elections, and 18 U.S.C. § 611 makes it a crime for "any alien to vote in any election held solely or in part for the purpose of electing a candidate for the office of President, Vice President, Presidential elector," or Congress. Other federal laws authorize the Justice Department to prosecute noncitizens for registering and voting in elections. The NVRA requires individuals registering to vote to affirm eligibility requirements, including citizenship. The Help America Vote Act of 2002 (HAVA) added a specific citizenship question to the federal voter registration form. Since citizenship is clearly material to a voter's eligibility, aliens can be prosecuted under the NVRA for providing false registration information and for voting. They can also be prosecuted under 18 U.S.C. § 1015(f), which criminalizes the making of a false statement or claim about citizenship "in order to register to vote or to vote in any Federal, State, or local election (including an initiative, recall, or referendum)," and under 18 U.S.C. § 911, which prohibits making a false claim of citizenship.

Yet the NVRA has contributed to the problem of aliens registering to vote. The largest source of voter registrations are state programs created under Section 5 of the NVRA, known as the "Motor Voter" law, which requires all states to allow individuals who apply for a driver's license to register to vote at the same time. To comply with Motor Voter, states automatically offer voter registration to all applicants for a driver's license. Most government employees do so even when they know the applicants are not citizens, because they do not want to face claims from the Justice Department that they discriminated based on ethnicity, and because they believe it is the responsibility of election officials, not state DMVs, to determine the eligibility of voter registration applicants.

Confusion still reigns in the states. In 2004, a Maryland state legislator contacted the Justice Department to express his concern that the Maryland Department of Motor Vehicles was allowing noncitizens who were applying for driver's licenses to register to vote. When he asked the DMV to stop, he was told that the DMV was required by the NVRA to offer all applicants the opportunity to register to vote. The Justice Department quickly sent the Maryland delegate a letter pointing out that the NVRA had no such requirement, and that federal law makes it a crime for a noncitizen to register. The letter went on to say that a state that issues licenses to noncitizens should not offer such an individual the right to register to vote.[42]

Utah, which issues licenses to illegal aliens (as does New Mexico and Washington State), switched to a two-tiered system, issuing a visibly different "driving privilege" card to illegal aliens, after a limited 2005 audit by the state's legislative auditor general. The audit found that hundreds of illegal aliens had registered to vote when they obtained their Utah driver's licenses—and at least 14 of them had voted.[43] The audit used a small sample; Utah state senator Mark Madsen said that an extrapolation of the audit numbers suggested that five to seven thousand aliens were registered to vote.[44]

This problem has been exacerbated by many states' interpretation of a HAVA provision requiring a citizenship question on the federal mail-in voter registration form. The provision, in 42 U.S.C. § 15483, requires the following question: "Are you a citizen of the United States of America?" If an applicant fails to answer this question, HAVA stipulates that the local election official must notify the applicant of the failure and "provide the applicant with an opportunity to complete the form in a timely manner to allow for the completion of the registration form" prior to the election. Under the threat of lawsuits by organizations like the American Civil Liberties Union, states such as Ohio, Iowa, and South Dakota will register an individual even if he fails to answer the citizenship question. The Justice Department has never sued these states to force compliance with HAVA.[45]

CONCLUSION

America has always been a nation of immigrants, and we remain today the most welcoming nation in the world. Newly minted citizens assimilate and become part of the American culture very quickly. Requiring that our laws—*all* of our laws—be complied with requires no more of an alien than it does of a citizen.

It is a violation of both state and federal law for immigrants who are not citizens to vote in state and federal elections. These violations effectively disenfranchise legitimate voters by diluting their votes, and they must be curtailed. Election officials have an obligation not only to enforce the law, but also to implement registration and election procedures that do not allow the law to be bypassed or ignored. Anything less encourages contempt for both the law and our election process. Lax enforcement of election laws permits individuals who have not entered the American social compact, or made a commitment to the U.S. Constitution, U.S. laws, and the U.S. cultural and political heritage, to participate in elections and potentially change the outcome of closely contested races that affect how all Americans are governed.

CHAPTER SIX

Absentee Ballots— The "Tool of Choice" of Vote Thieves

Although some partisans will cling to their debunked conspiracy theories that efforts to stop and to prosecute voter fraud are attempts to "suppress" votes, those who honestly seek to protect voters' rights must study the methods and means of voter fraud in order to combat it. Absentee-ballot fraud in particular is difficult to control. It is "the 'tool of choice' for those who are engaging in election fraud," as the Florida Department of Law Enforcement concluded in its investigation of the 1997 Miami mayoral election.[1] The results of that election were thrown out because of massive fraud involving more than five thousand absentee ballots, and *The Miami Herald* won a Pulitzer Prize in 1999 for its innovative investigation into the voter fraud.[2] With the increasing use of no-fault absentee voting and all-mail elections, there is the real risk that fraud will affect more election results and potentially wipe out voting rights hard won by the civil rights movement.

The Alabama voter fraud described by former Congressman Davis, which occurs in predominantly black, poor counties, is vividly illustrated by a criminal prosecution that occurred in the 1990s in Greene County, Alabama, when local citizens, reform political candidates, federal and state prosecutors, and a hometown newspaper banded together to fight absentee-ballot fraud in the county, one of the poorest in Alabama. Unfortunately, liberal groups including the NAACP and the Southern Christian Leadership Conference worked equally hard to undermine the effort, as they have worked to undermine voter ID requirements and other reforms intended to ensure the integrity of elections. Even as the investigation uncovered massive wrongdoing, so-called civil rights groups objected at every turn, alleging a plot to disenfranchise poor and minority voters. But in the end, justice prevailed, with the convictions of 11 conspirators who had fixed local elections for years. The Greene County case proves that absentee-ballot fraud is real, and not a cover story for an imagined voter-disenfranchisement conspiracy.

The most important lesson of Greene County is that absentee ballots are extremely vulnerable to voter fraud. The case documents how absentee-ballot fraud really works, and it is a reality very different from the claims of partisans and advocacy groups. More broadly, the case shows how voter fraud threatens the right to free and fair elections, and how those most often harmed are the poor and minorities. This directly rebuts the usual partisan conspiracy theories that fighting voter fraud is a disguised attempt to suppress minority voting.

According to the self-appointed, liberal guardians of the poor, practically every effort to legislate against or prosecute voter fraud is intended to keep minorities and the poor from voting at all. Concern over voter fraud, say some partisans, is simply a Republican cover to intimidate voters and raise obstacles to minority voting. Groups like the NAACP argue that racism and intimidation are the motivation for voter-fraud prosecutions, and dismiss voter fraud as virtually nonexistent. As a result, prosecutors are intimidated by fear of the political consequences from fighting vote fraud, and elections continue to be stolen.

Greene County shows that these groups have it backwards. Voter-fraud prosecutions do not intimidate voters; what does intimidate them is the knowledge that voter fraud is routine, and goes unpunished. Too often, no one is willing to take action against it, and the organizations that victims expect help from instead take the side of the vote thieves.

What happened in Greene County also demonstrates that voter fraud need not be partisan in nature. Partisan conspiracy theories about election reform just do not apply to intraparty voter fraud in primary elections in heavily Democratic or Republican jurisdictions, where primary results determine who wins in the general election. The perpetrators of voter fraud, particularly in small rural counties, are often political incumbents whose control of local government is threatened by challengers from the same political party. In Greene County almost all of the candidates, incumbents and challengers alike, were both Democrats and African Americans.

The Greene County case is important, then, because it demonstrates the ease with which fraudulent absentee ballots can be used to steal elections, the tactics used to steal those votes, the complete failure of liberal advocacy groups to protect the interests of vulnerable voters who have been disenfranchised by fraud, and the value of vigorous law enforcement in protecting legitimate voters' rights. It also points the way toward common-sense solutions to making voting more secure, and increasing public confidence in the electoral process.

THE SETTING

Greene County is located in the west-central portion of Alabama, between the Tombigbee and Black Warrior Rivers in the region known as the Black Belt because of its dark, rich soil. Eutaw is the county seat, and it was the first Alabama county in which political power shifted entirely to blacks after passage of the Voting Rights Act in 1965.[3] By all measures, Greene County is an extremely poor, rural county. In 2010 its population was just 9,045, making it the least populated county in Alabama, and its citizenry is 81.5 percent black. Slightly fewer than 10 percent of residents have a college degree, and the median household income is just $26,131, slightly above the U.S. poverty line.[4]

The county is governed by a powerful five-member board of commissioners. The commissioners are responsible for dispensing much of the $83,876,000 in federal funds—$8,606 per person—that flows to the county.[5] Indeed, the county government is the leading source of employment, contracts, and grants.

This kind of spoils system tempts politicians to misbehave. In 1996, Greene County declared bankruptcy because a bloated county payroll, extensive debt, and "improper and illegal spending" had exhausted county revenue. The commission's financial management was so bad "that state auditors said they couldn't even audit the county's finances."[6]

The promise of spoils also led to stiff competition for seats on the commission, and to voter fraud. The Birmingham office of the U.S. Attorney and the Alabama attorney general conducted an extensive joint investigation of absentee-ballot fraud allegations in the November 8, 1994 election.[7] By the end of the investigation, nine defendants had pled guilty to voter fraud, and two were found guilty by a jury. The defendants included Greene County commissioners, officials, and employees; a racing commissioner; a member of the board of education; a Eutaw city councilman; and other community leaders.

The defendants were part of a conspiracy to manipulate the outcome of elections for local offices in Greene County and the town of Eutaw, to protect incumbents and their allies from challengers. Almost all of the candidates involved, incumbents and challengers, were African American Democrats. The case is worth studying for that reason, and because the methods the conspirators used were typical of absentee-ballot fraud.

THE CONSPIRACY

It became clear early in the campaign that the 1994 general election for seats on the Greene County Commission would be a close one. An incumbent commissioner, Nathan Roberson, had lost to challenger William Johnson by just 16 votes in the primary runoff election. After losing in the primary, Roberson requalified as a member of the "Patriot Party," and opposed Johnson in the general election.[8] Absentee ballots had been the key to victory in several of the Democratic primary races.

Even before Election Day 1994, there were signs that something was awry in the absentee ballot process. The local county newspaper, the *Greene County Independent*, reported on November 3, five days before the election, that as the county was "embroiled in one of the most hotly contested political races in many years," the number of absentee ballots being sent out by the local clerk was so high that they "could very well determine who the next county commissioners" would be. Oddly, many of the absentee ballots were not going to the registered addresses of the voters. Some 60 of the ballots in one district alone were sent to the same post office box.[9] Ballots were also sent to candidates' wives,

105

the Greene County Democratic Executive Committee, and the Greene County Sewer and Water Authority.[10]

Absentee-ballot fraud was not new to the area. In 1985 Spiver Gordon, who would emerge as a key player in the 1994 fraud, was convicted by a jury of absentee-ballot fraud. Although the Eleventh Circuit Court of Appeals found "that there was sufficient evidence to support Spiver Whitney Gordon's convictions for mail fraud arising from the mailing of fraudulently marked absentee ballots," his convictions were reversed by the U.S. Supreme Court ruling that the federal mail-fraud statute under which he had been convicted could be used only to prosecute schemes involving the deprivation of money or property, not elections.[11]

In 1994, the numbers alone were enough to raise suspicions. Greene County had 7,736 registered voters. Turnout for the November 8 election was heavy, at 62 percent, or more than 4,800 votes.[12] On the night of the election, more than 1,400 absentee ballots flooded in—greater than one-third of the total ballots cast.[13] More than a thousand of the absentee ballots were mailed by just five people "who brought in suitcases of ballots to the Eutaw Post Office the day of election in 1994."[14] More than one-third of all votes were cast with absentee ballots—far above the state average, which is normally in the single digits—a red flag for possible voter fraud.

Absentee ballots tipped several races. Garria Spencer, chairman of the Greene County Commission, had won the Democratic primary with absentee votes. His opponent, Toice Goodson, was "ahead by about 50 votes until the absentee ballots were tallied and Spencer was declared the victor by two dozen votes."[15] Absentee ballots cast in the general election helped Frank "Pinto" Smith win a seat as a county commissioner,[16] while William Johnson, who had challenged incumbent Nathan Roberson, lost due to absentee ballot votes. Johnson received

409 votes at the polls, to Roberson's 376, but just 65 absentee ballots to Rober son's 182.[17]

Tax Assessor John Kennard was the first to sound the alarm that the elections had been stolen. He called for state and federal officials and civil rights leaders to come to Greene County and ensure a fair election.[18] State and federal prosecutors answered that call, and quickly arranged interviews with absentee voters.

The backlash—that federal and state investigators were trying to intimidate African American voters—was immediate. County commission chairman Spencer, who later pled guilty to voter fraud, told the press he was receiving complaints that the agents were trying to frighten voters, who were "tired of being questioned."[19] The chorus of criticism would only rise as the investigation began to uncover evidence of fraud. But those charges rang false within the county. Neither the local probate judge, who was African American, nor the circuit court clerk received any complaints. Local voters interviewed by the newspaper called the agents "very nice" and "polite" and made clear that they did not feel "intimidated, threatened, or targeted."[20]

Most of the complaints that sparked the investigation had come from African American citizens in Greene County (not surprising in a county that was 80 percent black), and from a local, multiracial good-government group called Citizens for a Better Greene County, whose founding mission was to elect fiscally responsible officials.[21] On Election Day, the group challenged the validity of hundreds of absentee ballots, which turned out to have been fraudulently cast.[22] With absentee ballots being stolen from people's mailboxes and voters being threatened with the loss of public assistance, Pam Montgomery, one of the group's leaders, said that "[t]hey ought to send [envoys] here" rather than to Haiti.[23]

Investigators went about their task diligently. They created a computer database and sorted all absentee ballots by the names of the individuals who had witnessed the signatures. They quickly found that many of the absentee ballots "contained the same few witnesses' signatures over and over again," and that some had been cast in the names of voters who were actually dead, or no longer lived in the county.[24] Investigators decided to limit the investigation "to only those ballots on which appeared any witness who had witnessed more than 15 absentee ballots."[25] The result was a list of 800 voters to be interviewed. The investigators employed a standard interview format to determine the circumstances under which the absentee ballot had been applied for and cast. That information was reviewed, as was handwriting analysis of the absentee ballot materials. The investigative procedures did not involve the race or political affiliations of voters or the candidates in any way.

Still, the race-baiting continued. A group called the Alabama Blackbelt Defense Committee was organized to raise money for legal services for all defendants charged with voter fraud. Its leaders, including commission chairman Spencer, claimed that the investigation was intended to "discourage black voters in Greene County and other blackbelt counties"[26]—the prosecutions were simply an attempt by federal and state officials to "frame" local black leaders.

The NAACP and the Southern Christian Leadership Conference (SCLC)—liberal civil rights groups that had not responded to initial concerns about the voter fraud—joined these efforts, helping the individuals who stood accused of stealing the election and leaning on the Justice Department to drop its investigation altogether. The NAACP Legal Defense Fund actually defended the vote thieves, as did Pamela Karlan,[27] a law professor at Stanford who later criticized the Bush administration for prosecuting voter-fraud cases, and who has claimed there is little or no voter fraud. According to Spiver Gordon, a Eutaw city councilman and SCLC vice president, the Greene County prosecutions were "an extension of the harassment and intimidation carried out by the

108

FBI and state authorities. . . . It's an attempt to keep black people from exercising their constitutional rights and voting rights."[28] Gordon later pled guilty to voter fraud.[29]

Despite all the racially charged rhetoric, it was clear from the start that the defense effort, like the vote fraud, had a political genesis. According to Tax Assessor Kennard, Spencer was part of a local political machine, as was Greene County director of planning and development Booker Cooke Jr., who also eventually pled guilty to voter fraud. In fact, in 1996, as chairman of one of the local Democratic Party's committees, Cooke tried to remove Kennard from the ballot (for being "disloyal" to the Democratic Party), in addition to three other candidates who were not part of the machine.[30] One local resident said the members of the machine were arrogant, and believed they could get away with anything.[31]

Indictments issued in January 1997 charged Commissioner Smith and Connie Tyree, a county employee and Smith supporter, with 13 counts of ballot fraud. The indictments outlined how absentee ballots were stolen and used to cast fraudulent votes in the 1994 election.[32] In the two months before the election, Smith and Tyree used registered voters' names to apply for absentee ballots, used false addresses so that the ballots would be sent directly to them, convinced some voters to sign absentee ballot affidavits without actually filling out the ballots, and forged voters' signatures on other affidavits.[33] The investigation revealed that Smith and others involved in the voter-fraud conspiracy actually set up an "assembly-line process" at the Eutaw Activity Center the night before the election to fill out the fraudulent absentee ballots for mailing the next day.[34]

In 1998, six more individuals were indicted on 31 counts of voter fraud for their role in the 1994 elections. Among them were Booker Cooke Jr., county employee Flephus Hardy, Commissioner Spencer, Althenia Spencer, racing commissioner Lester "Bop" Brown, and Spiver Gordon. The charges were similar to those brought against Smith and Tyree, and included furnishing false information to election officials, voting more than once, and providing false information on absentee ballot affidavits.[35] Despite their protestations of innocence and claims that the prosecutions were "politically motivated . . . to silence those who exercise their political right to elect political office holders of their choice," all six eventually pled guilty.[36] Also convicted, Smith and Tyree claimed on appeal that they were victims of "selective prosecution" because they were black and Democrats, but the Eleventh Circuit Court of Appeals, based in Atlanta, rejected that argument.[37]

By the end of the investigation another three individuals, including a member of the local board of education, were indicted and pled guilty, for a total of 11 convictions and no acquittals. After the convictions, local black leaders, including Probate Judge Earlean Isaac (the county's chief election official) and John Kennard, expressed their relief. Isaac also expressed the hope that in the future, they would only "see clean elections." Kennard proclaimed it "a victory for the people . . . because now one vote counts. The era of stolen elections is over for Greene County."[38]

MAKING RACE AN ISSUE

The Greene County case illustrates the complete dichotomy between the views of liberal civil rights organizations and those of ordinary citizens, including African Americans, on voter-fraud issues. A spokesman for the SCLC, Randel Osburn, said in 1998 that the investigation into absentee balloting and prosecutions in Greene County amounted to "Gestapo tactics," were a conspiracy to weaken the black vote, and were having a "chilling effect" on voters.[39] Osburn said that the prosecutions "must be seen in the context of a many-pronged attack on voting rights and fair representation in this state."

But Greene County citizens and candidates, most of them African American, sharply disagreed. John Kennard held a press conference at which he maintained that national and state SCLC leaders were misinformed: "There were Gestapo tactics used, but it was blacks terrorizing blacks in 1994. Let me show you one of the victims of Gestapo tactics in 1994." Kennard then introduced Bill Johnson, a candidate whose office was stolen in the election. As Kennard said, "Johnson did everything right. He won the election in 1994—but there were those people who decided Bill Johnson was not the black candidate they wanted for commissioner." Kennard also introduced Toice Goodson, another black candidate who lost in the 1994 primary election because, as Kennard said, Goodson was not the choice of the political machine running the county.

Kennard disputes the charge that the prosecutions were an attack on voting rights. "Justice was perverted here in Greene County" in 1994, he said, by the theft of hundreds of votes cast by absentee ballot. For taking this stand against voter fraud, Kennard was labeled "Chief Uncle Tom" in anonymous leaflets distributed in Eutaw.[40]

Organizations such as the NAACP and the SCLC routinely claim that voter-fraud investigations and prosecutions intimidate black voters and deter them from the polls, but Greene County citizens and officials again disagree on this. Commenting on the 1998 election, Judge Earlean Isaac could not understand the view of the SCLC: "What are we saying if we hold up corruption? We can have a fair and clean election in Greene County. [This year] voters are not intimidated, they are not afraid to vote, and they are not afraid to vote by absentee ballot."[41] She said she had not heard of a single voter in the county who was fearful of voting because of the federal and state investigation.

Nat Winn, a former member of the school board, said that the only people who were feeling threatened were "the ones that can't get out there and steal ballots." Many black voters shared that sentiment, with one telling the local paper that only "[t]he ones who committed the crimes are afraid."[42] According to sources within the investigation, one of the FBI agents was approached during the investigation by an elderly black woman who took the agent's hand in hers, prayed with him for the investigation to be successful, and thanked him for what he was doing.

Turnout for the 1998 election certainly showed that the citizens of Greene County were not deterred from voting. Turnout in the primary election was estimated at 57 percent, compared to turnout of 25 to 30 percent elsewhere in the state.[43] A total of 3,996 people voted in the 1998 primary, compared to 3,861 in the 1994 primary.

The difference was in absentee ballots: 147 in 1998 versus 1,143 in 1994.[44] In 1998, absentee ballots accounted for only four percent of the total votes cast, which was more in keeping with levels of absentee voting throughout Alabama. In the general election, turnout was more than 70 percent, considerably higher than in 1994. And this gain came despite a massive drop in absentee ballots: Only around 200 were filed in 1998, more than a thousand fewer than in 1994. Local election officials said the turnout proved that the voter-fraud prosecutions did not deter anyone from the polls.[45]

Remarkable in the Greene County case was the NAACP's defense of the defendants accused of voter fraud. John Kennard, a member of the NAACP, was outraged over its intercession on behalf of the conspirators, instead of on behalf of the black candidates whose offices had been stolen. He wrote to Julian Bond, then chairman of the NAACP, complaining that NAACP funds were going towards "defending people who knowingly and willingly participated in an organized . . . effort to steal the 1994 election from other Black candidates in Greene County." Kennard was very frank:

Personally, I feel that if the NAACP sides with these six people who stole election after election from the people of this county[,] it is tantamount to the organization defending policemen that used the fire hoses and dogs, and Eugene "Bull" Conner in Birmingham, in the early 1960s.[46]

Probate Judge Earlean Isaac, the county's chief election official, complained that Bond did not contact her before the NAACP launched its protest. She said she didn't think "they want to find out what the facts are. . . : If they did they would have looked at the records, or at least contacted the person in charge of the elections. No one has requested a meeting with me." Kennard said the indicted commissioners and county employees were hiding behind the racial issue because they "knew that they had a fail-safe way out, when all else fails . . . cry racism, intimidation, and pretend they are the victims when they were the perpetrators of this crime."[47]

Despite the investigation and outreach efforts by local black officials, the NAACP did not change its stance. In fact, Bond responded with a letter to Kennard "basically telling him to mind his own business." Bond said that "sinister forces" were behind the prosecutions and were "part and parcel of an ongoing attempt to stifle black voting strength." He dismissed Kennard's claim that the prosecutions were a legitimate effort to uncover a criminal conspiracy directed at thwarting black voters' rights to elect candidates of their own choosing. Bond said the accused were "friends and old colleagues" and that he had to "stand by them in their hour of need." Kennard wonders whether Bond and the NAACP were more interested in defending their friends than in finding out the truth of the crimes their friends had committed.[48]

The seeming tolerance of some liberal civil rights organizations for voter fraud committed against black candidates and black voters is disappointing. Spiver Gordon, who lost his seat as a Eutaw city councilman after he pled guilty to felony voter fraud, was, according to the U.S. Attorney and his own plea agreement, one of the "leaders and organizers of voter fraud" in Greene County.[49] Yet Gordon remained an officer of the SCLC even after his conviction, serving as treasurer of its national board until 2010, when he was removed after being accused of embezzling SCLC funds.[50]

Unlike the SCLC, Greene County came out ahead from the vote-fraud investigation and prosecutions. A former resident of Greene County told one of the authors that "there was so much corruption in the county government, and votes had been stolen in elections for so long, that there was general lack of confidence that anything would be done about it or that anyone would actually be prosecuted," an extremely discouraging situation to county residents.[51] This corruption had led directly to the bankruptcy of the county government, damaging the economy of the county and the welfare of its residents. Pam Montgomery of Citizens for a Better Greene County called the voter-fraud convictions absolutely essential to cleaning up the county government and setting Greene County on the road to financial recovery.[52]

LESSONS FROM GREENE COUNTY

One of the most important lessons of the Greene County prosecutions is how vulnerable absentee ballots are to voter fraud. They are cast in unmonitored settings, where there is no election official or independent observer present to ensure that the registered voter is actually the person casting the vote, and there is no illegal coercion.

"No-fault" absentee ballot laws—laws that allow any registered voter to use an absentee ballot for any or no reason—and the growing movement toward all-mail elections threaten the integrity of elections. Absentee ballots make it much easier for corrupt campaign organizations and candidates (like those in Greene County) to manipulate the vote. Their tactics include requesting absentee ballots in the names of registered voters, particularly poor residents and senior citizens, and either intimidating them into casting votes or fraudulently completing their ballots for them.

Besides Greene County, these practices have been documented elsewhere, such as in the 2003 Democratic mayoral primary election in East Chicago, Indiana, which was overturned by the Indiana Supreme Court due to "pervasive fraud, illegal conduct, and violations of elections law" that was "voluminous, widespread and insidious."[53] Ballot fraud included "the use of vacant lots or former residences of voters on applications for absentee ballots" as well as voting by persons who did not even live in East Chicago. The court called it "a 'textbook' example of the chicanery that can attend the absentee vote cast by mail."[54]

The typical absentee-ballot fraud follows this methodology:

1. The fraud begins with the conspirator filing an application requesting an absentee ballot for a voter, either by forging the voter's signature on the application or obtaining the voter's signature through coercion, trickery, or bribery. Applications are freely distributed to anyone who asks for them, so offenders have easy and ready access to the forms needed to obtain ballots.
2. Upon receipt of the application, the election official mails the absentee ballot and the voter affidavit to the address listed on the application, which is either the true voter's address or an address selected by the conspirator.
3. Since election officials usually post the names of registered voters who have been sent absentee ballots (and the date on which the ballots were sent), the conspirator knows when the mailed ballots will arrive, and can intercept them;

in some cases, the absentee ballots are sent to addresses directly accessible by the conspirator.

4. The absentee ballot is completed by the conspirator, and the voter's signature forged; or the voter signs and completes the ballot as directed; or some combination thereof. In states that require notarized signatures, voter thieves often co-opt notaries as part of the conspiracy.

5. The ballot is then mailed or hand-delivered by the conspirator to the election official.

Greene County illustrates a key indicator of absentee-ballot fraud: turnout that is dramatically in excess of other jurisdictions, especially in the rate of absentee balloting. This is particularly true if the proportion of absentee ballots cast for winning and losing candidates is significantly different than the proportion of ballots cast for the same candidates in polling places. Turnout varies by states and locality, and certainly local races of interest may spur turnout in one particular county. But an absentee ballot rate several times higher than the average rate for the state is a sign of possible fraud. Take what happened in East Chicago, Indiana, where the candidate who received the most votes in the polls on Election Day actually lost the election, because his opponent received more absentee ballots—many of which turned out to be fraudulent. Another indication of absentee-ballot fraud is multiple ballots witnessed (or notarized) by the same person (like Connie Tyree in Greene County).

The Greene County case shows how vital it is that prosecutors vigorously investigate the claims of absentee-ballot fraud, not only to ensure a secure and fair election process, but also to maintain public confidence, and root out corruption in local government. According to a former federal prosecutor with extensive experience in prosecuting election crimes, voter fraud by incumbents is a sure sign that the local government is engaging in other corrupt practices. The incumbent mayor of East Chicago, Robert Patrick, whose reelection was thrown out because of massive absentee-voter fraud, was eventually ordered to pay $108 million in damages to the city "after the Indiana attorney general won a first-of-its-kind racketeering lawsuit that alleged Patrick and his allies ran the city as a criminal enterprise."[55] Unfortunately, the mayor elected after the successful election challenge, George Pabey, also succumbed to the local tradition of corruption—in 2011 he was sentenced to five years in prison for public corruption, which included having city workers remodel his home.

Candidates who become aware that they have lost an election because of absentee-ballot fraud have a particularly difficult job gathering the evidence needed to overturn an election. As the Indiana Supreme Court concluded in the East Chicago case, candidates and their legal counsel

> faced a herculean task of locating and interviewing absentee voters, visiting multi-family dwellings and housing projects, gathering and combing through voluminous election documents, and analyzing, comparing, sifting and assembling the information necessary to present their case. . . . In short, the time constraints that govern election contests, primarily designed to serve important interests and needs of election officials and the public interest in finality, simply do not work well in those elections where misconduct is of the dimension and multifaceted variety present here.[56]

ABSENTEE-BALLOT FRAUD TODAY

The Greene County case is relevant today because absentee-ballot fraud continues in many areas of the country. Despite the convictions and guilty pleas in Greene County, neither the

NAACP nor the SCLC has ever admitted that its claims of racism and political motivation were wrong, and as should have been apparent at the time, completely specious. Both organizations continue to oppose voter-fraud prosecutions and to discourage the investigation and prosecution of schemes to disenfranchise vulnerable voters.

A member of the NAACP executive committee in Tunica County, Mississippi was convicted of voter fraud in April 2011, for voting in the names of 10 people, four of whom were dead.[57] Lessadolla Sowers was sentenced to five years in prison on each of 10 counts of absentee-ballot fraud. But when eight individuals were arrested in Madison County, Florida in November 2011 for absentee-ballot fraud in a local school board election, the reaction of the NAACP was to make the same type of scurrilous allegations as in the Greene County case. The president of the Florida State Conference NAACP, Adora Obi Nweze, organized a town hall to protest the arrests, and claimed that the actions of the FBI and the Florida Department of Law Enforcement amounted to "voter suppression leading into the 2012 election." He seemed unconcerned by the actions of the local African American candidate and her husband, which included submitting false affidavits to obtain absentee ballots without the knowledge of the intended voters, and fraudulently submitting the ballots to election officials.[58]

Unfortunately, this type of chicanery has continued in Alabama. Eight men and women were convicted of absentee-ballot fraud and vote-buying in Winston County in the 2000 Republican primary election. They included a county commission candidate and two candidates for the county board of education, as well as the local sheriff, David Sutherland, and the circuit clerk, W.F. Bailey, both of whom were removed from office.[59] In 2002, a former Russell County commissioner, Nathaniel Gosha, and a local school board employee were convicted of absentee-ballot fraud. A former circuit court clerk in Hale County, Gay Tinker, pled guilty in 2010 to absentee-ballot fraud in the 2004 and 2005 elections to benefit her husband, Democratic state senator Bobby Singleton, and her brother, circuit court judge Marvin Wiggins. (Wiggins presided over his sister's trial until he was removed and censured for his refusal to recuse himself.)[60] After accusations of voter fraud in the 2002 primary election in Hale County, the bank where the suspected absentee ballots were being stored mysteriously burned down. Tinker's case seems to be a repeat of prior voter fraud in Hale County in the 1990s, when Alabama Assistant Attorney General Greg Biggs obtained the conviction of the local chief of police on multiple counts of voter fraud, forgery in the second degree, and possession of forged instruments (absentee ballots).[61]

And to illustrate the Supreme Court's admonition in the Indiana voter ID case that voter fraud can affect a close election, in 2010 a former county commissioner in Pike County, Alabama, Karen Tipton Berry, pled guilty to absentee-ballot fraud and perjury. Berry was running for reelection, and was initially declared the winner by six votes. But the results were thrown out over illegal absentee ballots, including a vote by someone who did not live in the district.[62]

Such fraud is not limited to Alabama. The Justice Department has prosecuted absentee-ballot fraud cases in many states, including Arkansas,[63] Missouri,[64] North Carolina,[65] Oklahoma,[66] Pennsylvania,[67] South Carolina,[68] and Texas,[69] among others. Twelve former Democratic county officials in Brooks County, Georgia were indicted for absentee-ballot fraud in November 2011 after a bitter 2010 school board election in which "the final tally was changed by an unusually large wave of absentee ballots."[70] The number of absentee ballots cast in the election was 10 times larger than in nearby Thomas County. An ongoing investigation into absentee-ballot fraud in the 2009 Working Family Party primary (the political party associated with ACORN) in Troy, New York has already resulted in guilty pleas from a city councilman, the city clerk, and two political operatives, all Democrats, in 2011. They forged numerous signatures on absentee ballots, casting votes in the names of registered individuals without their knowledge. One of the operatives, Anthony DeFiglio, told investigators that this type of voter fraud was a commonplace and accepted practice in political circles: "This is an ongoing scheme, and it occurs on both sides of the aisle. . . . The people who are targeted live in low-income housing, and there is a sense that they are a lot less likely to ask any questions."[71]

The fraud committed by county officials running for reelection in many of these cases illustrates the truth of Artur Davis's revelations:

> What I have seen in my state, in my region, is the most aggressive practitioners of voter fraud are local machines who are tied lock, stock and barrel to the special interests in their communities . . . and they're cooking the [ballot] boxes on election day, they're manufacturing absentee ballots, they're voting [in the names of] people named Donald Duck because they want to control politics and thwart progress.[72]

There is a special historical resonance to some of the convictions in Alabama. Many of the Black Belt counties in the state were the flash points of the voting rights movement. During the civil rights era struggle to register black voters, a protester in Perry County was fatally shot, inspiring the "Bloody Sunday" march over Selma's Edmund Pettus Bridge. Today, not only do African Americans vote there; they run for office—and win. Elected African American officials have controlled local government in Greene, Hale, and neighboring counties of the Black Belt for decades. But the region's black voters face another obstacle to self-determination: the threat of disenfranchisement by vote fraud. "A generation ago, civil rights leaders in West Alabama overcame entrenched power structures," observed the *Tuscaloosa News*. "What a sad irony it would be if that system were simply replaced by another undemocratic process."[73]

CONCLUSION

In the final analysis, the importance to Americans and to our civil fabric of vigorous investigation and prosecution of absentee-ballot fraud cannot be overstated. Though the distracting noise of partisan wrangling and race-baiting may have drowned out that point on the national stage, it remains clear how important such a prosecution was to the citizens of Greene County, Alabama. The local paper explained it well:

> Bankruptcy and the hopelessness of the people, because of the corruption at high levels, can be reversed now that stealing elections is no longer an accepted way of life and justice has prevailed. . . .
>
> This beautiful county, whose promise was overshadowed by corruption and greed at the hands of those who gained public office and power by theft and deception, can finally set some healthy goals and move toward economic growth and a period of prosperity. The next chapter in Greene County's history will be what honestly elected men and women make it. It will be what the people of this county make it, without the fear that the ballot brokers will be ringing people's door bells . . . when another election rolls around.[74]

☆ ☆ ☆ ☆ ☆ ☆ ☆ ☆

CHAPTER SEVEN

Holder's Justice Department

Two of the biggest barriers to the prosecution of voter fraud are the misapplication of resources within the Justice Department and the political and ideological bias of too many of its lawyers. The Justice Department divides responsibility for voting issues between its Criminal and Civil Rights Divisions. The Criminal Division is responsible for prosecuting federal election crimes, including voter fraud. Within that division, the responsibility is lodged with the Public Integrity Section, the same section whose prosecutors got into enormous trouble for their misconduct in the campaign-finance prosecution of former U.S. senator Ted Stevens. Within the Public Integrity Section is the Election Crimes Unit, which for thirty years was run by a career lawyer named

Craig Donsanto, who retired at the beginning of the Obama administration. Donsanto was well known in the election community, and was a recognized expert on election crimes—but the entire Election Crimes Unit that he headed had only two lawyers in it (including Donsanto himself) to cover the entire country.

The 93 offices of U.S. Attorneys located throughout the country share responsibility for prosecutions with the Election Crimes Unit. But given their many other responsibilities, vote fraud is not high on their priorities, particularly because they are well aware of the enormous criticism prosecutors receive from the civil rights community when they pursue election cases, as happened during the Bush administration. There is a Designated Election Officer in each office, an Assistant U.S. Attorney, who is supposed to deal with election crimes. But the vast majority have never investigated or prosecuted a voter-fraud case, and have no experience or interest in doing so.

During the Bush administration, the Justice Department increased its emphasis on prosecuting election crimes, and the number of prosecutions went up substantially compared to the Clinton administration. But there were never any additional resources or attorneys given to the Public Integrity Section. A veteran Justice Department prosecutor told one of the authors that while there was never an official memorandum delineating the Clinton administration's policy on this issue, the unofficial word had come down from the Clinton political leadership to the career prosecutors that there was "no interest" in pursuing voter-fraud cases.

In the Civil Rights Division, the Voting Section is responsible for the enforcement of the Voting Rights Act of 1965 (or VRA), the National Voter Registration Act of 1993 (the NVRA), the Uniformed and Overseas Civilians Absentee Voting Act (which protects the rights of military personnel to vote in federal elections), and several other voting rights laws. The division has enormous power over the conduct of federal, state, and local elections all over the country. Section 2 of the VRA applies nationwide, and prohibits racial discrimination in voting. Section 5 is a special "emergency" provision that covers certain states, requiring federal approval of voting-law changes. It was originally intended to last only five years, but has been successively renewed by Congress, most recently in 2006, for 25 years, despite the complete lack of evidence of any of the systematic, widespread discrimination that justified its passage in 1965.

Under Section 5, the states of Alabama, Alaska, Arizona, Georgia, Louisiana, Mississippi, South Carolina, Texas, and Virginia (as well parts of seven other states) cannot make any changes in their voting laws without the preapproval of either the Civil Rights Division or a federal court in the District of Columbia. Unlike every other federal law, which places the burden of proof on the government to prove a violation of the law, Section 5 puts the burden of proof on the states, requiring them to prove that they are not discriminating, or that the change in the law will not have a discriminatory "effect." It is Section 5 that the Obama administration has used to object to voter ID laws, even though the facts and the applicable legal standards do not support the objections. But it is expensive and time-consuming to fight the Justice Department, which has almost unlimited resources.

Unlike the tiny Public Integrity Section in the Criminal Division, which prosecutes criminal violations of election law, the Voting Section has almost 100 lawyers and support staff. The Department of Justice devotes exponentially more resources to enforcing voting rights laws than prosecuting election crimes. Unfortunately, fair and impartial enforcement of the law is hampered by the radical ideological makeup of almost all of the employees in the Civil Rights Division, especially the Voting Section. The division, one of the largest within the Justice Department with almost one thousand employees, attracts (and recruits) the most liberal applicants for career positions.

For years the division has hired almost exclusively from left-wing advocacy groups like the NAACP Legal Defense Fund, La Raza, the Mexican American Legal Defense Fund, NARAL, the Lawyers' Committee for Civil Rights, and many others. The Voting Section is a revolving door for lawyers from those organizations. Because all of the managers or chiefs of the different sections within the division are liberals, they practice political and ideological discrimination in their hiring. Conservatives need not apply—if there is anything on a résumé that indicates the applicant is a Republican or a political conservative, they will not be hired, no matter how qualified they are.

This is particularly evident in the Voting Section. When one of the authors, von Spakovsky, joined the Voting Section as a career trial lawyer in 2001, he quickly learned what a miracle it was that he had been hired. He was one of only two openly conservative lawyers in the entire section of 80-plus. There were a few other lawyers who were secretly conservative, but they hid that fact to avoid harassment, reprisals, and bad job evaluations. The only reason the author and the other lawyer, Joe Beard, avoided the normal fate of conservative applicants was because a Bush political appointee in the Office of the Assistant Attorney General for Civil Rights was monitoring the hiring by the career chiefs, and prevented the Voting Section chief, Joe Rich, from rejecting out of hand qualified applicants who happened to be politically conservative.

A personal friend of von Spakovsky, an experienced Hispanic lawyer, had applied for a career position in the Voting Section in 1999 after having worked at one of the most prominent law firms in Washington. The Voting Section would have been lucky to get him. Unbeknownst to him, one of the senior partners at his law firm—whom he barely knew, and for whom he did not work at all—happened to be a preeminent conservative litigator who had served as a political appointee in the Justice Department during the Reagan administration, and who had successfully beaten the Civil Rights Division in the Supreme Court on a number of occasions.

Following two initial rounds of interviews with section attorneys, the applicant met with section chief Joe Rich, who confronted him almost immediately in a nasty tone about his work for that conservative litigator. According to the lawyer, Rich said, "It's obvious you're a conservative, too. Why would I hire a right-winger to work in the Voting Section? This must be some sort of joke. You must be coming in as a mole to undermine me." Then in a mocking and accusatory manner, Rich demanded to know whether the lawyer had worked for or was a member of any so-called "traditional" civil rights organizations.

Stunned at the unprofessionalism of the interview, the lawyer pointed out that he had worked for various civil rights organizations in college, and that as a Hispanic himself, he considered civil rights to be extremely important. Rich angrily told the lawyer he did not believe him, because no attorney who worked for the conservative litigator at the lawyer's firm could be committed to civil rights: "I think you're nothing but a conservative. I will not let you in this Civil Rights Division. I will not have you."

This attitude was pervasive in the section. In no other workplace has this author ever encountered the fury and unrelenting hostility that he found in the Voting Section. The other lawyers made it quite clear that anyone who was not politically liberal, or a Democrat, was unqualified to work in career civil service in the division. They expressed fury that a conservative lawyer had made it through their usual screening procedures, and they shunned this author, treating him like a dissident member of a cult. And they assumed that all white Southerners (von Spakovsky was born and raised in Alabama) are racists.

This attitude is what fed the controversy during the Bush administration over supposed "political" hiring by the Civil

Rights Division. The Clinton-appointed Inspector General, Glen Fine, issued a report (prepared with the help of the Office of Professional Responsibility) that was full of bias, inaccuracies, gross exaggerations, and deliberate misrepresentations. And no wonder, since the investigators assigned to the case included a liberal former Civil Rights Division lawyer, Tamara Kessler, who had worked with the leading critics identified in the report; and Mark Massling, another former Civil Rights Division lawyer and self-proclaimed "proud Democrat." And so, left-wing lawyers who had been hired by radical managers in the division through its biased hiring process were then used to investigate the supposedly conservatively-biased hiring of the Bush administration.

What was really going on was that activist special interests had exercised exclusive control of the division for decades. When Bush political appointees threatened that control by attempting to stem the routine ideological hiring in the division, the entrenched regime responded by launching a public relations campaign counterattacking the supposedly "biased" hiring of the Bush administration.

The Bush administration was in fact trying to impose a more balanced hiring process. A very small number of experienced litigators and other lawyers were successfully hired from across the political spectrum who did not owe their allegiance to the ACLU, the NAACP, and other left-wing advocacy groups. The biggest gripe that the liberal career lawyers and civil rights organizations had against these new hires was that their first loyalty was *not* to the special interest groups who had controlled the division for decades—and the fact that they were willing to enforce the law in a race-neutral manner.

The Inspector General's report ignored the fact that not a single individual who was known to be politically conservative was hired in the Civil Rights Division during the Clinton administration. In fact, the Clinton administration engaged in raw political hiring, filling open career civil service jobs in the division even in Clinton's last month in office—something that was never investigated by the Office of the Inspector General.

On December 12, 2000, when the Supreme Court issued its decision in *Bush v. Gore*, the Clinton political appointees realized that Democrats would lose control of the Justice Department. At that time, there were more than two dozen open career lawyer positions in the Civil Rights Division. Though the federal government usually had taken six months to a year to fill such positions, the Clinton appointees (spearheaded by acting assistant attorney general Bill Yeomans, who later became chief counsel to Senator Ted Kennedy and a huge critic of the Bush administration) filled every one of those positions before George W. Bush's Inauguration Day. Each of the hires was a liberal or a Democratic activist, and, based on internal e-mails, was considered to be "loyal." This included the girlfriend of one of the counsels to the outgoing assistant attorney general, who later was assigned to the review of Georgia's voter ID law and who insisted that the division should reject it, contrary to the law and evidence. But then, that was the way hiring had always been done in the division.

The Obama administration was intent on restoring that kind of ideological hiring, and restoring left-wing control of liberals' crown jewel, the Civil Rights Division. To that aim, the president appointed Thomas Perez to be the new Assistant Attorney General for Civil Rights. Perez is a longtime Democratic activist and a former staffer to Senator Ted Kennedy. When Perez was running for a seat on the Montgomery County Council in Maryland, he was asked what was the most important thing voters should know about him. His response: "I am a progressive Democrat, and always was and always will be." Once elected, the hyper-partisan Perez made no effort to hide his contempt for Republicans. He once gave a speech claiming that conservative Republicans do not care about the poor. An article in *The Washington Post* in 2005 characterized Perez as "about as liberal as Democrats get."

Perez also served as president of Casa de Maryland, an extreme advocacy organization that opposes the enforcement of immigration laws. This group has encouraged illegal aliens not to speak with police officers or immigration agents; it has fought restrictions on illegal aliens receiving driver's licenses; it has urged the Montgomery County police department not to enforce federal fugitive warrants; it has advocated giving illegal aliens in-state tuition; and it has actively promulgated "day labor" sites, where illegal aliens and disreputable employers openly skirt federal prohibitions on hiring undocumented individuals.

It is stunning that someone affiliated with an organization that displays such contempt for federal law would even be nominated, let alone confirmed, as the nation's top civil rights law enforcement officer. But Perez has gone farther.

As a councilman in Maryland in 2003, Perez sought to force local governments to accept *matricula consular* ID cards, which are issued by the Mexican and Guatemalan governments, as a valid form of identification. He insisted that individuals with such cards should not have to show a U.S.-issued document to prove their identity, a ludicrous proposal. The *matricula consular* IDs are rife with fraud, a fact well known to Perez. No major bank in Mexico accepts them as identification for opening an account and, by last count, 22 of Mexico's 32 states and districts reject the cards as identification. But Perez was happy to have an excuse to thumb his nose at federal immigration laws. He is one of the main reasons that the division has launched unprecedented attacks on Arizona, Alabama, and Utah for their attempts to help the federal government enforce immigration laws.

Perez issued a memorandum on December 3, 2009 making it clear that he would make the final decision on *all* proposed career hires in the Civil Rights Division. He surrounded himself with equally radical subordinates to run the ever-growing division. He set up a new hiring committee to supposedly ensure that only "merit" was considered in the career-hiring process, and made a career lawyer, Karen Stevens, the co-chair of that committee. Stevens's testimony was cited in the Inspector General's report, complaining about supposedly improper "politicization" during the Bush administration. The report not only failed to identify her by name, it also neglected to mention that she had been a political appointee to the division during the Clinton administration; she burrowed into the career ranks just before the Clintonistas left office. She was one of the most partisan career lawyers in the Division when von Spakovsky worked there. She was so trusted by the Democratic leadership in the Obama administration that she was moved to the Front Office of the division on the *first day* Obama came into office—to occupy what is normally a political slot.

The Obama administration's return to the same ideologically-biased hiring practices used by the Clinton administration got almost no attention in the press. The news and opinion website PJ Media was forced to file suit over a Freedom of Information Act request for the résumés of all 113 lawyers the administration had hired into the career ranks of the division. In a series of articles in PJ Media, later nominated for a Pulitzer Prize, von Spakovsky and former Voting Section lawyer J. Christian Adams revealed that radical ideology, similar political leanings, and association with liberal civil rights organizations were prerequisites for all new hires.

For example, two new deputy chiefs were hired in the Voting Section from the ACLU's Voting Rights Project. One was Bryan Sells, who has characterized state laws that don't allow felons to vote—a power expressly authorized in the Fourteenth Amendment of the Constitution—as a "slap in the face to democracy." The other was Meredith Bell-Platts, a founding member of a Georgetown University law journal intended to complement "a long tradition of feminist scholarship and advocacy" at the law school. Sells and Bell-Platts have worked for years to stop common-sense election reforms like voter identification requirements. Bell-Platts has falsely claimed that voter ID laws are motivated by people who do not want to see blacks vote.

Another hire, Jenigh Garret, came from the NAACP Legal Defense and Education Fund, where she co-drafted the NAACP's losing amicus brief in *Crawford v. Marion County Board of Elections*, the Supreme Court case that upheld Indiana's voter ID law. Elise Shore, another outspoken critic of Georgia's voter ID law and the state's new requirement that individuals provide proof of citizenship when registering, was hired into a career position from the Southern Coalition for Social Justice, and before that worked at the Mexican American Legal Defense Fund.

The ideological bias within the Voting Section leads it to ignore or act contrary to the law as it is written and as it was intended when it was passed by Congress. The radicals who inhabit the Voting Section do not believe in the race-neutral enforcement of the Voting Rights Act. They do not believe that defendants who are racial minorities should be prosecuted—as will be explained in depth, they in essence mutinied when they were told to investigate voting discrimination and ballot theft by local black officials in Noxubee, Mississippi. They do not believe in enforcing the requirement in the National Voter Registration Act that states maintain their voter registration rolls by periodically removing the names of individuals who have died, or moved away, or otherwise become ineligible, an essential element in election integrity. They refused to file any such lawsuit during the Clinton administration, and protested the filing of the first such suits during the Bush administration.

In fact, the Obama administration dismissed without explanation a pending NVRA lawsuit against Missouri, initiated during the Bush administration, even though there were numerous counties in the state that had more registered voters than the

Census showed they had population. The case was dismissed one month after the defendant, Democratic secretary of state Robin Carnahan, announced she was running for the U.S. Senate, raising suspicions that it was dismissed to aid her campaign.

The radical career lawyers were extremely upset when the Bush administration filed briefs on behalf of states that were fighting lawsuits brought by civil rights groups claiming that prohibiting felons from voting is a violation of the Voting Rights Act. Certain of the lawyers in the Appellate Section of the division, such as Karen Stevens, could not be trusted to write briefs in those cases; the Front Office feared those lawyers would write deliberately bad briefs in the hope that they would lose. All of the federal courts of appeals issuing decisions on these cases held that felon disenfranchisement is a constitutional right delegated to the states, and not a violation of the VRA. The legal opinions of the Bush political appointees were found far superior to those of the career lawyers, whose opinions were constantly proved wrong in court.

Staffers in the Civil Rights Division are also not above violating their professional ethics by attempting to deliberately sabotage a case they do not agree with, and their supervisors allow it to happen unpunished. When he was in the Front Office, von Spakovsky quickly learned that he could trust neither the factual summaries of investigations contained in legal memoranda sent to the Assistant Attorney General for review, nor the legal analysis of applicable statutory and case law. Career lawyers in the Voting Section were willing, for ideological reasons, to twist the facts or miscite the law in order to con the Front Office into taking or not taking action that had nothing to do with an objective review of the facts—or the law.

The career staff were also willing to leak confidential and privileged internal legal opinions, a direct violation of the professional code of conduct that applies to all attorneys. In 2012 a longtime Voting Section employee, Stephanie Celandine Gyamfi, admitted to investigators from the inspector general's office that she perjured herself when she initially denied leaking confidential internal legal documents. The Obama administration did not fire, or even discipline, her. In fact, she continued to be assigned to sensitive matters, like the review of the 2011 Texas congressional redistricting plan.

The genesis of Gyamfi's perjury apparently was rooted in political attacks on the Bush Justice Department. Throughout 2005, 2006, and 2007, numerous attorney-client privileged documents, confidential personnel information, and other sensitive legal materials were leaked from inside the Voting Section to *The Washington Post* and various left-wing blogs.

One of the most prominent leaks involved the Voting Section's privileged internal analysis of the 2003 Texas congressional redistricting plan, submitted to the Civil Rights Division in October 2003 for review under Section 5 of the Voting Rights Act. The contents of the internal memorandum appeared on the front page of *The Washington Post* on December 2, 2005, to great fanfare from Democrats on Capitol Hill and their surrogates in the liberal blogosphere.

Back in 2003, Bush's political appointees had overruled the recommendation by the Voting Section career staff to object to the Texas plan. This had led to fierce and wildly unfair criticism by Democrats and the liberal media. However, as voting rights expert Abigail Thernstrom pointed out in her book *Voting Rights—And Wrongs: The Elusive Quest for Racially Fair Elections*, the career staff's leaked memorandum was a "rambling, barely coherent memo." A second confidential legal memo, prepared by von Spakovsky and two other division lawyers (and which was not leaked), found the leaked document full of "factual and legal inaccuracies, mistakes, and misrepresentations."

Not surprisingly, when the Texas congressional redistricting plan ended up before the Supreme Court in *LULAC v. Perry*, the court embraced the arguments of the Civil Rights Division's political leadership, and repudiated the claims advanced in the career staff's leaked memorandum. Specifically, the court agreed that there were only eight minority districts that needed to be preserved under the Voting Rights Act, and not 11, as erroneously argued by the career staff.

And who was the civil rights analyst whose name was on the "rambling, barely coherent memo" leaked to *The Washington Post*? It was Stephanie Celandine Gyamfi, one of the most extreme partisans von Spakovsky encountered in his four years in the Civil Rights Division—no small distinction, considering the competition among her division colleagues. As former Voting Section lawyer Christian Adams has documented, the walls of Gyamfi's office were filled with campaign signage supporting the election of Barack Obama, despite the internal Justice Department ban on displaying partisan materials.

Ms. Gyamfi made no secret of her hatred of conservatives and Republicans alike when von Spakovsky worked in the Voting Section, and later, the Front Office of the Civil Rights Division. She could not hide her contempt any time she was forced to meet with the Bush political leadership, a characteristic she shared with other career staff. She apparently went beyond hatred, and resorted to flagrantly violating Justice Department confidentiality requirements and ethical obligations.

But not only was Gyamfi not disciplined by the Obama administration, she was treated as a hero by her colleagues in the Voting Section. Many of them were gratified at her efforts—illegitimate or not—to make the Bush administration look bad in its preclearance of Texas's earlier redistricting submission. That is what passes for professional conduct within the Civil Rights Division of the Department of Justice.

Ideological decision making and ethical lapses lead to faulty lawyering. This was aptly illustrated during the Clinton administration, when the Civil Rights Division was responsible for filing 11 frivolous and unwarranted lawsuits, costing the American taxpayer more than $4.1 million in attorneys' fees and costs awarded to defendants who were falsely accused of racial discrimination.[1] One case the Voting Section filed on behalf of black voters against Dallas County, Alabama was thrown out by a federal court, which ruled that a "properly conducted investigation would have quickly revealed that there was no basis for the claim that the Defendants were guilty of purposeful discrimination against black voters." The court stated that "charging a person with depriving a fellow citizen of a fundamental constitutional right without conducting a proper investigation" of its truth is "unconscionable," and stated its hope that the court would "not again be faced with reviewing a case as carelessly instigated as this one."[2] The Voting Section lawyer responsible for that case was Gerald Hebert, one of the most virulent critics of the division during the Bush administration. That case alone cost taxpayers almost $90,000, awarded to Dallas County to compensate it for the "carelessly instigated" lawsuit filed by Hebert.

In a similar showing of how Voting Section lawyers consider themselves representatives of liberal advocacy groups rather than the American public, another "carelessly instigated" lawsuit cost taxpayers almost $600,000. In *Johnson v. Miller*, a case about Georgia's 1992 legislative redistricting plan, the federal court severely criticized the Voting Section for its unprofessional relationship with the ACLU and its "implicit commands" to the legislature over how to conduct its redistricting.

Most seriously, the court essentially accused Voting Section lawyers of committing perjury. During the redistricting process, ACLU attorneys were in constant contact with the government lawyers: "The Court was presented with a sampling of these communiqués, and we find them disturbing. It is obvious from a review of the materials that [the ACLU attorney's] relationship with the

136

DOJ Voting Section was informal and familiar; the dynamics were that of peers working together, not of an advocate submitting proposals to higher authorities."[3] The court found that the "considerable influence of ACLU advocacy on the voting rights decisions of the United States Attorney General is an embarrassment." And the court found it surprising that the Justice Department "was so blind to this impropriety, especially in a role as sensitive as that of preserving the fundamental right to vote."[4]

The Justice lawyers in the case "professed amnesia" about their relationships and communications with the ACLU over the redistricting and the lawsuit. The court found their claims "less than credible," an implicit statement that the court believed the lawyers' testimony was a lie. None of the lawyers were disciplined or terminated for their misbehavior; in fact, one of the lawyers listed on the court decision as representing the Justice Department, Loretta King, was promoted by the Clinton administration, and eventually became the highest ranking career official in the Civil Rights Division—a position she used to interfere with the New Black Panther Party voter intimidation case. In another showing of how liberals reward their loyal foot soldiers inside the division, the other lawyer representing the Department of Justice in the *Miller* suit, Donna Murphy, was nominated by President Obama to be a superior court judge in the District of Columbia.

The government's position in *Miller*, that Georgia was required to maximize black political representation to supposedly comply with the Voting Rights Act, was severely criticized by the court. It shows how politics, rather than the fight against discrimination, too often drives division lawyers. As the Supreme Court said, "Instead of grounding its objections on evidence of a discriminatory purpose, it would appear the Government was driven by its policy of maximizing majority-black districts."[5] In related cases filed in the early 1990s, the courts similarly criticized the Voting Section, finding that it was trying to use its power under the Voting Rights Act "as a sword to implement forcibly its own redistricting policies."[6] The courts found that the Louisiana legislature "succumbed to the illegitimate pre-clearance demands of the Justice Department" that "impermissi-bly encouraged—nay, mandated—racial gerrymandering."[7] Those cases cost the American public $1.1 million in attorneys' fees and costs awarded to Louisiana.

Loretta King, by the way, was appointed by the Obama admin-istration as the acting Assistant Attorney General of Civil Rights as soon as Barack Obama was inaugurated. She had been so frustrated during the Bush administration that she once told von Spakovsky she was considering resigning to run for office as a Democrat in Maryland. According to Christian Adams, the former Voting Sec-tion lawyer and author of *Injustice: Exposing the Racial Agenda of the Obama Justice Department*, King told staffers in the Voting Sec-tion how excited she was at seeing the photos of Eric Holder and Barack Obama in her office, because "we now have two black men running the country." If a white supervisor had made such a com-ment inside the Justice Department about two white men running the country during the Bush administration, he would have been charged with racial discrimination and insensitivity, disciplined, and probably terminated, and there would have been screaming headlines about a racist government employee on the front pages of *The Washington Post* and *The New York Times*.

After King was put in charge by the Obama administration, she hauled the chief of the Voting Section, Christopher Coates, into her office to reprimand him for his hiring practices. Because of problems he had with hostile career staff in the prosecution of black defendants for discrimination against white voters and candidates in Noxubee County, Mississippi, he had begun asking job applicants whether they believed in the race-neutral enforce-ment of voting rights laws. Numerous career staff had refused to work on the Noxubee case because they opposed prosecuting black defendants; Coates wanted to be sure he was hiring lawyers who were not racially biased. King had heard of his practice, and angrily denounced him for it. He was ordered to cease and desist immediately, and to not ask that question—the Civil Rights Division was not interested in hiring anyone who believed in the race-neutral enforcement of the law.

This ideological bias of lawyers in the Civil Rights Division, including Loretta King and the political appointees of the Obama administration, can also be seen in their mishandling of the New Black Panther Party voter intimidation case, and the objection made to a change in town elections in Kinston, North Carolina.

The New Black Panther Party is a notorious black Muslim separatist hate group whose openly virulent anti-Semitism and hatred of whites has been catalogued by everyone from the Anti-Defamation League to the Southern Poverty Law Center. Its leadership has included Khalid Abdul Muhammad, a former member of Louis Farrakhan's Nation of Islam who was kicked out for being too radical—something that is a little hard to imagine, given the ravings of Farrakhan and his racial vitriol. Despite its violent racist views, Obama had "appeared and marched with members of the New Black Panther Party as he campaigned for president in Selma, Alabama in March 2007."[8]

In 2008 the head of the NBPP, Malik Zulu Shabazz, stationed two of its members, King Samir Shabazz and Jerry Jackson (a registered Democratic Party poll watcher), at a polling place in Philadelphia located in a retirement community. They stood smack in front of the entrance, dressed in black Fascist-style paramilitary uniforms, Shabazz carrying a billy club, as part of a supposedly nationwide NBPP "security" program. The New Black Panthers were threatening, hurling racial epithets at poll watchers and scaring off voters. Shabazz had once been interviewed for a *National Geographic* documentary about the NBPP in which he talked about how much he hates and wants to kill white people, including white babies. The documentary includes a truly ugly scene (one among many) in which he confronts an interracial couple in a Philadelphia neighborhood.

Two roving poll watchers, Chris Hill and Bartle Bull, each responded that Election Day to a desperate call for help from another poll watcher, a black man.[9] The poll watcher told Hill, a former infantry soldier who lived nearby, that the Panthers had called him a "race traitor" and had threatened him, saying "there would be hell to pay if he came out." The poll watcher was visibly scared, and had clearly been intimidated. Hill testified that the poll watcher was afraid to appear before the U.S. Commission on Civil Rights, which conducted a hearing on the case, or to testify in the lawsuit filed by the Justice Department, because "he lives in that neighborhood," and was scared that the NBPP would come after him—a problem the Justice Department encountered many times in the South in the 1960s, when it was trying to root out discrimination, intimidation, and threats by local white officials.

In the incident, the New Black Panthers called Hill a "white devil" and a "cracker," and said he would be ruled by the black man the next day—Hill would have to get used to "living under his boot." The pair tried to prevent Hill from entering the polling place. Hill saw several voters, including two elderly women, stop abruptly when they saw the two Panther thugs standing in front of the door to the polling place; these voters all left without casting a ballot, Hill testified. There is no telling how many voters were scared off by the New Black Panthers. But in a sign of how biased the mainstream media's coverage of this was, a *Washington Post* reporter who attended the commission hearing wrote that "there was no evidence that voters had been prevented from casting ballots in Philadelphia."

Bartle Bull—a well-known Democratic lawyer (and a former publisher of *The Village Voice*), who worked in the South during the height of the civil rights campaign—gave similar testimony. He had also responded to the call about intimidation, and recounted that one of the New Black Panthers had pointed a billy club at Bull and said, "Now you are going to find out what it is to be ruled by the black man, cracker"—this to a man who had been a volunteer for Adlai Stevenson, who had headed Robert Kennedy's presidential campaign in New York in 1968, and who, in 1971, worked to get civil rights stalwart Charles Evers elected governor of Mississippi.

Bull testified he saw the New Black Panthers "confront voters, and attempt to intimidate voters;" voters would walk up the long driveway to the polling place, stop, and leave when they saw the duo in their paramilitary garb and combat boots, one of them slapping a truncheon in his hand. In an affidavit filed in the Department of Justice lawsuit in Pennsylvania, Bull said that:

> the men created an intimidating presence at the entrance to a poll. In all of my experience in politics, in civil rights litigation, and in my efforts in the 1960s to secure the right to vote in Mississippi through participation with civil rights leaders and the Lawyers Committee for Civil Rights Under Law, I have never encountered or heard of another instance in the United States where armed and uniformed men blocked the entrance to a polling location. Their clear purpose and intent was to intimidate voters with whom they did not agree. . . . To me, the presence and behavior of the two uniformed men was an outrageous affront to American democracy and the rights of voters to participate in an election without fear. It would qualify as the most blatant form of voter intimidation I have encountered in my life in political campaigns in many states, even going back to the work I did in Mississippi in the 1960s.[10]

Fox News aired video of the incident; the video was posted by DrudgeReport.com and viewed by Americans nationwide. The chief of the Voting Section, Christopher Coates, immediately dispatched lawyers, including Christian Adams, to investigate the incident. As Adams later said, it was a "slam dunk" case of voter intimidation, a violation of Section 11b of the Voting Rights Act, which prohibits anyone from intimidating, threatening, or coercing (or attempting to intimidate, threaten, or coerce) any person from voting, or a person who is "urging or aiding any person to vote," which would include poll watchers. The New Black Panthers' threats against and intimidation of both voters and poll watchers was a *per se* violation of the law.

Yet liberals, Democratic Party officials, and members of the mainstream media would spend the next two years doing everything they could to excuse what happened and to belittle any attention being paid to it, as if it was nothing out of the ordinary. This included Democratic members of the U.S. Commission on Civil Rights, who made every effort to stop the commission's investigation of the incident. Imagine what the reaction would have been if members of the Ku Klux Klan had been standing in front of the polling place in full robed regalia, acting in exactly the same manner. The reaction all over the country, especially in the editorial pages of *The New York Times*, would have been absolute outrage. If the Bush administration had failed to prosecute such a case, the attorney general might have been impeached.

The reaction inside the Voting Section was similar—liberal lawyers and staff resented the attention being paid to this incident, and did not think it should be investigated or prosecuted, because they did not believe in enforcing the Voting Rights Act against black defendants. But Christopher Coates, the chief of the Voting Section, persisted; as he wrote in an internal Justice Department e-mail: "If standing in front of a polling place with a stick in Black Panther clothing and talking about how you are going to keep whites from voting . . . does not violate the intimidation prohibition in 11(b), I don't know what does."

In the waning days of the Bush administration, the Voting Section filed a lawsuit against the NBPP; its head, Malik Zulu Shabazz; and the two New Black Panthers who had threatened voters and poll watchers at the polling place in early January, just two weeks before Barack Obama was inaugurated and his political appointees took over the Justice Department. None of the defendants answered the lawsuit, which accused them of intimidation and attempted intimidation. On April 1, 2009 the Justice Department filed a motion asking for a default judgment. But through the political interference of Loretta King, the political leadership of the Justice Department, and the Obama White House, justice was thwarted.

Just before the deadline to file pleadings with the federal court in Philadelphia in order to obtain a final judgment against the NBPP, Loretta King and her deputy, Steven Rosenbaum, suddenly called Coates to a meeting in the Front Office of the Civil Rights Division. They berated him about the suit, claiming there was no evidence to support it and that the New Black Panthers were exercising their First Amendment rights. At one point, Rosenbaum was forced to admit he hadn't even read the Voting Section's extensive and detailed internal legal memorandum that summarized all of the facts, the evidence, and the applicable law. Coates and his trial team were ordered to dismiss the lawsuit, except for an injunction against club-wielding King Samir Shabazz, and to drop the nationwide injunction that the team had originally proposed against the NBPP. The injunction against Shabazz was watered down; it was the first time in the history of the Civil Rights Division it had ever dismissed a lawsuit it had already won.

The division leadership's unfamiliarity with the case became obvious when they helped draft a letter that the Justice Department's Office of Legislative Affairs sent to Congress on June 13,

2009, in response to a congressional inquiry. The letter stated that charges against Jerry Jackson were dismissed because he was a resident of the apartment building where the polling place was located, and that he was a certified poll watcher. The first claim was absolutely false. Jackson did not live at the retirement community, a fact that would have been obvious to King and Rosenbaum if they had read the internal legal memorandum. The second point is irrelevant; Jackson's status as a poll watcher did not immunize him from compliance with the anti-intimidation prohibition of the VRA, a fact that King and Rosenbaum were well aware of.

But the actual facts in this case did not matter to King, Rosenbaum, or the Obama political appointees they reported to in the top leadership of the Justice Department, like associate attorney general Thomas Perrelli, whom the Justice Department admitted had been consulted in the case.

White House visitor logs revealed that Perrelli, who as a private attorney was extensively involved in some of the Democratic Party's biggest redistricting fights, had met with White House deputy counsel Cassandra Butts on key dates in the sudden reversal of the NBPP case. Butts had worked at the NAACP Legal Defense Fund, and has described herself as being "as close to Barack as anyone" when they were classmates at Harvard Law School. While Butts was at the Center for American Progress, she complained on CAP's blog that John Ashcroft had allowed conservative views to influence decisions in the Civil Rights Division, and specifically the Voting Section. The suspiciously-timed meetings between Perrelli and Butts raise the question of just how involved the White House was in the decision to abandon the NBPP case.

The New Black Panther Party prosecutions had ignited the same fury among the civil rights establishment that the case against Ike Brown in Noxubee, Mississippi had sparked six years earlier. Liberal activist lawyers, including those in the Civil Rights

Division, were outraged that the Voting Rights Act was again being applied to black defendants. One career lawyer who had left the Voting Section for the NAACP, Kristen Clarke, admitted to the *Washington Times* that she had talked to the division's new political leadership after Obama was inaugurated, berating them for pursuing the NBPP case.

Meanwhile, the forced dismissal of the New Black Panther Party prosecution turned out to be just the beginning of the misery heaped on Coates. King and the political appointees who came in soon after Obama's inauguration (particularly Julie Fernandes, an ideological firebrand and former lawyer for the Leadership Conference for Civil Rights) put severe restrictions on Coates; they almost immediately began micromanaging his work. The new apparatchiks stripped Coates of virtually all discretionary authority, delegated responsibility for most decisions to more "results-oriented" underlings in the Voting Section, and rendered him a virtual figurehead. He was eventually relieved as the chief of the section and exiled to the Office of the U.S. Attorney in South Carolina—outside of the subpoena power of the U.S. Commission on Civil Rights, which had opened an investigation into why the case had been dismissed.

The Justice Department refused to turn over key documents to the commission and to a number of congressmen, including Republicans Frank Wolf of Virginia and Lamar Smith of Texas, who were tireless in their efforts to have the department explain its actions. And when the commission subpoenaed Coates and Christian Adams to testify before it, the division ordered the lawyers to ignore the subpoena, in violation of federal law. Since the commission must rely on the Justice Department to enforce its subpoenas, Justice knew it could get away with this outright contempt for the rule of law.

Representative Wolf called the Justice Department's obstruction of congressional oversight into the NBPP case "a shameful example of the types of partisan obstruction that undermine our nation's civil rights laws." He revealed that Justice had admitted that Attorney General Holder "was made aware—on multiple occasions—of the steps being taken to dismiss this case."

Both Adams and Coates eventually testified before the Civil Rights Commission: Adams after he resigned in disgust at the lies told by the head of the Civil Rights Division, Thomas Perez, about the handling of the NBPP case when Perez appeared before the commission; Coates after he defied his superiors at the division. Coates's testimony before the commission, in September 2010, was as riveting as it was shocking. He supported the prior testimony of Christian Adams, and knocked down the Potemkin village the Obama administration had built to obscure why Justice officials had dismissed the NBPP case: because they didn't want to enforce the Voting Rights Act against minorities accused of violating the law.

Coates described the culture of animus within the Civil Rights Division toward race-neutral enforcement of federal voting rights laws. He described an atmosphere of harassment directed at lawyers and paralegals who worked on the NBPP case, and on the earlier case filed in Noxubee, Mississippi against Ike Brown, a twice-convicted felon and political activist who runs Noxubee County. Lawyers and other staff within the Voting Section refused to work on the NBPP and Brown cases, Coates testified, because they did not believe the Justice Department should prosecute blacks or other racial minorities—*no matter what law they violated*. Coates testified that he had complained about this unwritten policy to Assistant Attorney General for Civil Rights Perez, a political appointee. Yet when Perez testified before the Civil Rights Commission, he said that no such policy or attitude existed.

Coates recounted directives received from political appointee Julie Fernandes, who had made it clear in meetings with Voting

Section staff that the Obama administration was interested only in filing "traditional types" of voting rights cases that would "provide political equality for racial- and language-minority voters." Coates testified that everyone in the room understood what that meant: "No more cases like the Ike Brown or NBPP cases."

Coates testified that in another meeting with Voting Section staff, Fernandes had said the Obama administration was not interested in enforcing the provision of Section 8 of the National Voter Registration Act, which requires states to maintain voter registration lists by regularly removing ineligible voters—for instance, the names of voters who have died or moved away. In September 2009, Coates testified, he sent a memorandum to Fernandes and the Front Office in which he recommended opening investigations of eight states that appeared to be in noncompliance with procedures for maintaining these lists as outlined in the National Voter Registration Act. He did not get approval for the project, and the Obama administration has never filed a single suit to enforce this provision of the NVRA. Prosecutorial discretion does not allow prosecutors "to decide not to do any enforcement of a law enacted by Congress because political appointees determined that they are not interested in enforcing the law," Coates testified. "That is an abuse of prosecutorial discretion."

Coates testified that King, Fernandes, and other lawyers within the Justice Department violated their oath to faithfully execute the law when they selectively enforced the Voting Rights Act based on the race of the victim and the perpetrator. Biased enforcement, he testified, will encourage violations by election officials who happen to be minorities, because they will not fear repercussions from the law. In our "increasingly multiethnic society, that is a clear recipe to undermine the public's confidence in the legitimacy of our electoral process," he told the commission.

An example of exactly what Coates was talking about was an outrageous objection by the division in 2009, under Section 5 of the Voting Rights Act, to a voting change in the small town of Kinston, North Carolina. In November 2008, when Barack Obama was on the ballot, the residents of Kinston overwhelmingly passed a referendum to change elections for city council from partisan to nonpartisan. But the Justice Department refused to give the referendum preclearance, claiming that it was discriminatory towards local black voters.

At the time of the November 2008 election, Kinston had about 15,000 registered voters, of whom 64.6 percent were black. This is a higher registration rate than one would expect, since the 2000 census showed that the black voting-age population was lower, at 58.8 percent of the total population. At the time, of the town's five-member city council (elected at large), two of the councilmen were black, and all five were Democrats. Although the mayor at the time was white, the longtime prior mayor was black. Thus, there was no evidence whatsoever that blacks faced *any* barriers to registration and voting in Kinston, which is what Section 5 was designed to prevent. And in an election in which blacks comprised the majority of registered voters, and turned out in droves to support Barack Obama's candidacy, the referendum passed with a two-to-one margin—although you would never have known that from reading the Justice Department's objection. Moreover, the actual racial voting minority in Kinston was whites, not blacks.

None of these facts could dissuade the career ideologues in the Voting Section, who showed their disturbing and paternalistic distrust of the capability of black voters to understand the impact of the referendum vote. And they used Section 5 as a political weapon in Kinston, to protect the electoral success of the Democratic Party. In the Kinston objection letter, the Justice Department stated that changing to a nonpartisan election would have a discriminatory effect on black voters because "it is the partisan makeup of the general electorate" that allows the winner of the Democratic primary to win in the general election. The Justice Department expressed concern that changing to nonpartisan elections would "likely eliminate the party's campaign support" for black candidates.[11] But the VRA is supposed to protect *voters*, not particular political parties. The fact that blacks are a controlling majority in the city, and can affect election outcomes when they turn out to vote, plus the fact that black voters themselves voted for the change, was essentially deemed irrelevant. It was no surprise that this racially-biased decision was issued by Loretta King, who was instrumental in the dismissal of the New Black Panther Party prosecutions.

The Civil Rights Division's action rests on the presumption that blacks simply cannot be trusted to make their own decisions as to which individual candidates to support, and will be presumed to vote against their own self-interest unless candidates on the ballot have the "right" party label. In short, the Justice Department "knew" for whom Kinston's black community should vote, and that certainly couldn't be Republicans. This approach to enforcement stands the Voting Rights Act on its head, and is anathema to all of our constitutional requirements for fair elections. It shows how a handful of Justice Department bureaucrats have effectively been empowered to control much of the political structure of the South in aid of Democratic Party interests.

Given the frequent partisanship demonstrated by the Civil Rights Division in Section 5 proceedings, there is little doubt that if the members of the Kinston city council had been Republicans, the division would not have objected to the switch to nonpartisan elections. In fact, it's more likely that the division would have sued the city under Section 2 of the Voting Rights Act, either to force the change, or to switch to a single-member district system rather than at-large elections, to ensure that Democratic candidates could get elected.

This cynical manipulation of federal power to benefit one political party over another—an all-too-common feature of the

Civil Rights Division's agenda during Democratic administrations—underscores that the only real source of refuge from these political machinations is the Supreme Court. Only the Supreme Court, by striking down Section 5 as unconstitutional, can cauterize the bleeding. The court passed up that opportunity in 2009, when it avoided the constitutional question in a case out of Texas that allowed a small local utility district to bail out from coverage under Section 5.[12]

Several residents of Kinston and a candidate from that election filed suit against the Justice Department in federal court in the District of Columbia, claiming that Justice's objection to the referendum was wrong, and that Section 5 is unconstitutional. They sued because Kinston's Democratic town officials, who could have contested the objection, failed to do so—as Democrats, they were happy that the citizen referendum had been voided. The residents lost at the district court level, and appealed the decision. In an interesting development, however, the Civil Rights Division suddenly notified Kinston in January 2012 that it was "reconsidering" its objection to the nonpartisan referendum, even though there had been no request by the town of Kinston for reconsideration. One week later the Department of Justice withdrew its objection, making a laughable claim that there had "been a substantial change in operative fact."[13]

One of the "changes" was that the voter registration rate for blacks in Kinston was now 65.4 percent— an increase of only 0.8 percentage points over 2008, when the registration rate was 64.6 percent, and when black voters had overwhelmingly approved the referendum. The only real "change in operative fact" was that it seemed likely the Kinston lawsuit was headed for the Supreme Court. The facts in the case were so bad, and made the political manipulation of the VRA by the Civil Rights Division so visible, that the Justice Department clearly wanted to withdraw its objection so as to convince the appeals court that the case had been mooted and should be dismissed, averting a Supreme Court review of the viability of Section 5. It apparently worked, because the appeals court dismissed the lawsuit in May 2012.

The Kinston case highlights the Civil Rights Division's refusal to recognize an electoral fact. In many localities covered under Section 5, former racial minorities are becoming the majority. Whether in Kinston, in the Mississippi Delta, or along the Rio Grande, Hispanics and blacks have become the numerical majority. Yet the division has still not enforced Section 5 in a race-neutral manner to protect white voters when they are a minority, as they are in Kinston. The division's failure to acknowledge this change, and protect the actual minority voting population in a jurisdiction, reveals the biases of the lawyers who work there.

The Voting Rights Act is designed to break down racial barriers to voting. It is intended at its core to ensure equal opportunity for all voters, regardless of race or politics. The National Voter Registration Act was intended to both improve the ability of individuals to register, and to make sure states clean up their voter registration rolls. But when enforcement of these laws is left in the hands of the left-wing partisans who dominate the ranks of the Civil Rights Division, federal laws become a political tool, and one that is all too easily abused. This is the sad reality of today's Justice Department.

Christopher Coates, when he was forced out as chief of the Voting Section by the Obama administration, captured this succinctly in a speech he gave at his going-away party. He describes the danger we face from the politicized enforcement of laws affecting elections and the voting process:

> Without question, the most controversial cases I have been involved in during my time in the Voting Section were the prosecution of the Voting Rights Act cases in Noxubee County, Mississippi, against Ike Brown, and in

Philadelphia, Pennsylvania, against the New Black Panther Party.

Many people inside and outside the Civil Rights Division have criticized me for those cases. . . . I actively participated in the prosecution of those two cases for four reasons. The first is that a plain reading of the statutory language of the Voting Rights Act indicates that it is aimed at protecting all American voters from racial discrimination and voter intimidation. . . . Before I became a DOJ attorney, I read the Voting Rights Act to protect all voters; but especially as a government lawyer, I have never assumed that I was entitled to ignore that clear language in federal law and therefore ignore incidents where evidence showed white voters were discriminated against or where the wrongdoers were themselves members of a minority group . . . I was not willing to look the other way just because the victims were white and the wrongdoers were black.

The second reason I supported the prosecution of these two cases is because the race-neutral enforcement of the Voting Rights Act is imperative to the holding of racially fair elections. . . . As anyone knows who has observed human behavior, all races have their bad apples. Sometimes members of minority groups—like Ike Brown in Noxubee—violate the antidiscrimination provisions of the Voting Rights Act. Having worked in the Voting Section and responded to many complaints filed by voters, I know that the racially discriminatory and intimidating behavior that occurs in the voting area is not committed just by whites, although whites certainly commit their share, and that some of these outrages are committed by members of minority groups.

Since many minority officials are now involved in the administration of elections in many jurisdictions, it is imperative that they believe that the antidiscrimination and anti-intimidation provisions of the Voting Rights Act will be enforced against them by the Justice Department, just as it is imperative that white election officials believe that Justice will enforce the provisions of the Voting Rights Act against them. I fear that actions that indicate that the Justice Department is not in the business of suing minority election officials, or not in the business of filing suits to protect white voters from discrimination or intimidation, will only encourage election officials, who are so inclined, to violate the Voting Rights Act. . . .

The third reason for race-neutral enforcement of the Voting Rights Act so that all persons are protected from discrimination or intimidation regardless of their race is that fair enforcement of the VRA is important for its very survival. America is increasingly a multiracial, multiethnic, and multicultural society. For such a diverse group of people to be able to live and function together in a democratic society, there have to be certain common standards that we are bound by and that protect us all. In fact, as we become more diverse, it is even more important that our national standards of nondiscrimination are enforced by the federal government.

One of these most basic standards is equal protection under the law. When that is violated, America does not live up to the true meaning of its creed. When it is followed, the country functions the way it was intended to. For the Department of Justice to enforce the Voting Rights Act only to protect members of certain minority groups breaches the fundamental guarantee of equal protection, and could substantially erode public support for the Voting Rights Act itself.

My fourth reason for this kind of law enforcement is very simple: Selective enforcement of the law, including the Voting Rights Act, on the basis of race is just not fair and does not achieve justice. . . .

Some who criticized the two cases about which I speak claim that they are not opposed to protecting the rights of white voters, but question using the resources of the Voting Section in that manner. I question the validity of that criticism. Given the number of cases the Voting Section has filed during the past 40 years on behalf of racial minorities, I do not understand why a mere two cases on behalf of white voters would have raised the ire of most of the critics of the Ike Brown and New Black Panther Party cases to the level that has been observed. Those critics are not motivated primarily by resource concerns, but rather, in my opinion, by a strongly held but erroneous view that the work of the Civil Rights Division in its enforcement of the VRA should be limited to protecting racial-, ethnic-, and language-minority voters. The resource issue is a red herring raised by those who want to continue to enforce the Voting Rights Act in a racially biased fashion and to turn a blind eye whenever incidents arise that indicate that minority persons have acted improperly in voting matters.

A lot has been said about the politicization of the Civil Rights Division. I believe that one of the most detrimental ways to politicize the enforcement process in the Voting Section is to enforce the provisions of the Voting Rights Act only for the protection of certain racial or ethnic minorities; or to take the position that the Voting

Section is not going to enforce certain provision of any of the voting statutes the Voting Section has the responsibility to enforce. Such decisions carry with them obvious, enormous implications for partisan political struggles.

CHAPTER EIGHT

Tennessee Two-Step Fraud

Opponents of all forms of election reform constantly claim that vote fraud is a myth. Yet the Supreme Court's admonition, in the Indiana voter ID case, that voter fraud can make the difference in a close election was proven in a state senate race in Tennessee. The details illustrate that people convicted of felony voter fraud for stealing elections all too often receive minimal punishment and no jail time, which merely encourages more fraud.

In May 2005, Democratic state senator John Ford was arrested by the FBI, and resigned from office. He is the brother of former congressman Harold Ford Sr. (Tennessee's first black congressman) and the uncle of former congressman Harold Ford Jr. (who succeeded his father in his congressional seat and later ran unsuccessfully for the U.S. Senate). Ford was indicted, along with four other legislators and several local government officials, in a bribery sting operation called Operation Tennessee Waltz. Ford was eventually convicted of accepting $55,000 in bribes; the trial evidence included videos showing Ford stuffing his pockets with hundred-dollar bills "counted one by one by an undercover FBI agent."[1]

Ford had represented the 29th Senate District, centered in Shelby County and the home of the blues—Memphis, Tennessee. A special election was held on September 15, 2005 to fill Ford's seat. Ophelia Ford, the accused senator's sister, ostensibly beat her opponent, Republican candidate Terry Roland, by only 13 votes. Ford received 4,333 voters, while Roland received 4,320 votes, in a district in which three-quarters of the voters were black.[2]

Roland contested the close election, filing a petition with the state senate on September 23, 2005 in accordance with Article II, Section 11 of the Tennessee Constitution, and filing a lawsuit in the Chancery Court in Shelby County. The Chancery Court lawsuit was dismissed for lack of jurisdiction; under the state's constitution and § 2-17-102 of state law, the state senate has exclusive jurisdiction over such election contests.

Lieutenant Governor John Wilder, as Speaker of the senate, impaneled a special senate ad hoc committee to investigate the election. The committee consisted of five senators and was chaired by a nominal Republican, Michael Williams, the Speaker Pro Tem, who often voted with Democrats on legislation. Of the other committee members, two were Republicans and two Democrats. The Tennessee Bureau of Investigation also conducted an investigation, following on the heels of an exposé by the local newspaper, *The Commercial Appeal*, which found, among other irregularities, "that someone forged the names of two deceased elderly voters" and that votes were cast in the names of voters whose registered addresses were vacant lots.[3]

Roland hired an investigator, John Harvey, a lieutenant in the local sheriff's office, to check the validity of the voter registration list and the individuals who were recorded as having voted in the election. Harvey not only compared the voter registration list to county tax and court records, he used commercial databases, such as utility connection records, tax liens, business and marriage licenses, and real estate data. He also did online checks, and made personal visits to the registered addresses of voters.

In an affidavit filed with the Tennessee Senate on December 11, 2005, Harvey reported he had found at least 43 voters who did not live in Senate District 29, yet had cast votes in the election. One of these illegal voters was Ophelia Ford's nephew, Sir Isaac Ford, who had registered at his business address, a local funeral home owned by the Ford family in the district. Harvey also reported that he had visited the registered addresses of several voters; two of them were vacant lots, another was a business address for a development corporation, one was an apartment that was uninhabitable due to rehabilitation efforts, and four were federal housing projects where none of the registered voters were residents. Another voter had died six weeks before the special election in which he had supposedly cast a ballot in person.[4]

Harvey submitted a second affidavit, including photographs, dated February 6, 2006 and showing the registered addresses of two more voters. Both locations were vacant lots that had been public housing developments before they were razed, well before the election.

Harvey told *The Commercial Appeal* that he had "logged countless hours" investigating the voter registration list.[5] His work demonstrates how time-consuming these types of voter-fraud investigations are—a difficult prospect, given the short deadlines that usually exist under state law for contesting an election.

The deceased voter who supposedly cast a ballot in person was Joe L. Light, a renowned folk artist whose works are in the

Smithsonian and "in private collections of celebrities Susan Sarandon and Tommy Lee Jones."[6] Light had lost his home to foreclosure five years before the election, and ended up in a nursing home. But "his" signature was on the poll book in his former precinct near his old home. The senate committee reported it found a second deceased person in whose name "an unknown person or persons fraudulently cast a ballot."[7] The Shelby County Election Commission acknowledged that in addition, at least three felons had illegally voted in the race, while the senate committee noted that at least seven felons had voted, even though their voting rights had not been restored.

Either intentionally or due to their own negligence, poll officials apparently did not check the identification of many voters, require them to fill out the "application for ballot," or sign the computerized signature list, as mandated by state law. The ballot application that voters must complete contains an affidavit that the voter is who he says he is, and lives where he is registered. That is the point at which a voter's ID is checked by election officials. Oddly, the number of votes cast in the precinct exceeded the number of ballot applications that had been completed—which means that election officials had to be allowing individuals to vote without checking their identification, their signatures, or their addresses.[8] Observant poll watchers in the precinct could have reported and corrected this unlawful behavior.

In addition to Joe Light, Harvey found a local radio talk-show host who had voted in District 29 even though he admitted in an interview with *The Commercial Appeal* that he had not lived in the district for years. He cavalierly justified his violation of the law by saying that his vote hadn't affected the outcome "because he voted for eccentric businessman Robert 'Prince Mong' Hodges, who says he's from the planet Zambodia" (Hodges received 89 votes in the election). In total, Harvey found at least 69 ineligible individuals voting in an election that was decided by only a 13-vote margin. If photo IDs with current addresses that matched registered addresses were properly checked, and impersonators or other ineligible individuals were promptly prosecuted, the overall incidence of all kinds of election fraud could be greatly reduced.

But in a key demonstration of how local election officials often ignore voter fraud to protect candidates who belong to the same political party, the three Democratic members of the county election commission voted to certify Ophelia Ford's 13-vote victory, overriding objections from two Republican commissioners. Ford was sworn in minutes later. The Democratic chairman of the commission, Greg Duckett, was "impatient" with candidate Roland's attempt to contest the election, despite the initial evidence of irregularities and bogus votes.

Ophelia Ford was provisionally seated pending the outcome of the election contest. The state senate eventually voted to overturn the election, based on the faked votes and other irregularities. The senate, acting as a Committee of the Whole, on January 17, 2006 voted to send to the floor a proposed resolution finding the special election so tainted with irregularities that the results were untrustworthy, and should be voided. The vote was 17 in favor to 14 against, with Democratic senators voting to seat Ford.

Ford immediately sued in federal court, making claims under the Voting Rights Act and the Equal Protection doctrine.[9] Although the federal court acknowledged that the "Tennessee Senate is the final arbiter of the election contest," it issued an injunction ordering the senate to resolve the contest "in accordance with Equal Protection and Due Process requirements" that applied a standard "uniform with past elections," and to provide due process to any voters whose residency was being challenged.[10] The court found no discriminatory actions that violated the Voting Rights Act, and refused Ford's request for an order preventing the senate from investigating the election or throwing out the results.

The senate ad hoc committee adopted a standard that provides a model for other states to follow in election contests. It decided it would void the election if it found either that "the number of illegal ballots cast equals or exceeds the difference between the two candidates" or "a sufficient quantum of proof that fraud or illegality so permeated the conduct of the election as to render it incurably uncertain, even though it cannot be shown to a mathematical certainty that the result might have been different."[11] After eight hearings, the senate committee issued a final report recommending that the election be overturned. It found at least 12 votes that were invalid because the "voters were either dead, felons, or residents of other districts."[12]

The many other questionable votes were not considered by the committee, despite the compelling evidence submitted by Harvey and by Roland's attorneys, one of whom was a Democrat. According to one of the attorneys involved in the case, the committee was incorrectly advised in testimony by Brook Thompson, the state coordinator of elections, that votes could not be declared illegal if their invalidity was the result of mistakes made by election officials, not the voter—a proposition that is manifestly wrong under applicable law. The committee also ignored the fact that there were more votes than voters' applications for ballots, which means that there was no verification of these additional voters and their identities, addresses, or signatures. Those potentially invalid votes alone (cast in violation of state law) should have been enough to render the election results "incurably uncertain."

The senate voted 27 to 6 to adopt the committee's recommendation on April 19, 2006, and Ford was removed from office.[13] Senator (now lieutenant governor) Ron Ramsey, a Republican who led the opposition to Ford, said that the senators "did what we had to do to restore the integrity of the ballot box."[14] Democratic senator Roy Herron, who had originally voted against removing Ford, changed his vote in favor of removal, saying that the evidence uncovered by the investigation proved that a true election result was "incurably uncertain."

Ford went back to federal court, unsuccessfully seeking an order overturning the senate's decision. But in the general election of November 7, 2006 Ford ran against Roland again, and this time won in a landslide.

Three local poll officials were indicted and eventually pled guilty to voter fraud, including illegal voting and altering official election documents. They never said why they had engaged in such fraud, although at one point one of the officials, who was a Democratic Party activist who had served as the "poll boss" of heavily Democratic Precinct 27-1, suggested in a media interview that an election commission inspector "played a role in the scandals." That inspector, Eddie Hayes, who was previously convicted of forgery and therefore was ineligible to work as a poll official, was a funeral director at the Ford Funeral Home,[15] which is owned by relatives of Ophelia Ford. (She lists on her senate website that she is a "certified funeral service practitioner," and includes in her "community involvement" that she is "an Ambassador for the Academy of Professional Funeral Service Practice.") But local prosecutors claimed there was no evidence that Ford or others were involved in the fraud.[16] No one else was ever charged—even the voters who had registered at vacant lots or who did not live in the district.

One poll official was not even at her assigned polling place on Election Day. She was a member of a local authority, and was attending a convention out of state. A relative, who was on probation for her part in a drug-dealing conspiracy, impersonated the election official at the polls, forging the official's initials on election documents and voting under the official's name. Although

named in the indictment, the impersonator was never charged—
and her drug charge was dropped in accordance with a diver-
sion deal with prosecutors.[17] And the senate committee did not
investigate the potentially invalid ballots of individuals who were
unlawfully approved to vote by the imposter.

The state judge in the case, John P. Colton, expressed his outrage at the fraud, saying that "[v]oting to me is . . . [the] high[est]
honor this country has. When it is desecrated, it makes me sad
and it makes me shudder." Despite his concern, and the fact that
the three former poll workers pleaded guilty to eleven felonies,
they only received probation, community service, and minimal
fines. The fraud they admitted to committing did not include the
dozens of invalid votes made by nonresidents and uncovered by
John Harvey.

Senator Ford, like her older brother John, had quite a col-
orful history after the initial scandal over her election. She was
accused in 2007 of assaulting a taxi driver in Nashville, the state
capital. The police incident report, dated May 22, 2007, says
that the taxi was called to pick up Ford at the Wildhorse Saloon.
According to the police report, she "was brought out to the cab
under a blanket to keep the media from seeing her" intoxicated.
The driver said that Ford grabbed his shirt from behind while he
was driving, tearing a button off the collar; the other passenger
restrained her. The cab driver had to help Ford to her hotel room
because she was unable to do so on her own. In a separate incident, Ford fell off a bar stool at the Sheraton Hotel that is across
from Nashville's Legislative Plaza, engaging in "a puzzling public
tirade." Ford missed most of her first legislative session because
of a supposed illness.[18]

Local poll officers were involved in some of the fraud in this
election. That type of insider fraud can be hard to deter and hard
to detect. The importance of poll-watching programs cannot
be overstated. They allow poll watchers and election observers

to verify that officials are not violating the law, or even sloppily failing to follow the law, by allowing individuals to vote whose IDs don't match their registered names or registered addresses. The Memphis case is a perfect example of how close elections are changed due to voter fraud, and why security measures should be put in place to ensure that elections are decided only by legitimate voters.

CHAPTER NINE

The Anti-Federalist National Popular Vote Scheme— The Vote Stealer's Dream Come True

Our system for electing a president has worked pretty well. There is no real case being made that it will work better if changed—only that it will look nicer if one subscribes to one particular vision of how democracies should work. . . . We are so accustomed to stable, generally good government that we sometimes forget that failure of government structures is historically much more common than success . . . [W]e tinker with our success at our peril.

—Bradley A. Smith, former chairman
of the Federal Election Commission

Since the 2000 presidential election, there have been many ill-informed calls to abolish the Electoral College. Even before that contentious election, there were more than 700 proposals introduced in Congress down the years seeking to amend the Constitution to change the Electoral College—more than on any other topic.[1] The "National Popular Vote" plan (NPV) is just the latest in a long line of schemes that are bad public policy.

The Electoral College has proven both effective in providing orderly elections for the presidency, and resilient in allowing a stable transfer of power of the leadership of the world's greatest republic. While it would be a mistake to replace the Electoral College, replacing it with the NPV would be a disaster.

The NPV devalues the minority interests that the Founding Fathers sought to protect, and could radicalize the U.S. political system. The NPV plan would:

- diminish the influence of smaller states and rural areas of the country;
- lead to more recounts and contentious conflicts over the results of presidential elections; and
- encourage voter fraud.

The NPV plan strikes at the Founders' view of federalism and a representative republic—one where popular sovereignty is balanced by structural protections for state governments and minority interests. It likely would violate the Constitution's Compact Clause. In an age of perceived political dysfunction, effective policies that already are in place—especially successful policies established by this nation's Founders, like the Electoral College—should be preserved.

The Constitution provides that "Each State shall appoint, in such Manner as the Legislature thereof may direct, a Number of Electors, equal to the whole Number of Senators and Representatives to which the State may be entitled in the Congress."[2] Although electors were initially appointed directly by state legislatures, some states like Pennsylvania and Virginia allowed popular election even in the first presidential contest.[3] However, by 1836 only South Carolina did not provide for the direct election of electors, and "since the Civil War, electors have been popularly chosen in all states."[4] The electors chosen by voters cast their votes for president and vice president in their respective states on the first Monday after the second Wednesday in December.[5] Forty-eight states have a winner-take-all system that allocates all of their electoral votes to whichever presidential candidate wins the popular vote in that state.[6]

Changing or eliminating the Electoral College can be accomplished only by an amendment to the Constitution, which requires the consent of two-thirds of Congress and three-fourths of the states.[7] From a political standpoint, there is almost no probability that such an amendment will happen in the near future.

Consequently, the NPV[8] scheme proposes an interstate compact, in which participating states agree in advance to automatically allocate their electoral votes to the winner of the national · popular vote, disregarding the popular vote results in their state, or what the relevant legislature might then desire. The NPV would "put the fate of every presidential election in the hands of the voters in as few as 11 states and thus . . . give a handful of populous states a controlling majority of the Electoral College,"[9] undermining the protections of the Electoral College.

This agreement would go into effect only after "states cumulatively possessing a majority of the electoral votes" needed to win an election—270 votes—join the purported compact. Because it is far easier politically to get a smaller number of states with the required electoral votes to join the compact than it is to get two-thirds of Congress and three-fourths of the states to pass an amendment, the scheme is an expedient way for proponents to circumvent the Electoral College without formally amending the Constitution.

So far eight states, representing a combined 132 electoral votes, have approved the proposed National Popular Vote plan: Illinois, Washington, New Jersey, Hawaii, Maryland, Vermont, California, and Massachusetts, as well as the District of Columbia. The NPV is nearly halfway to its goal of 270 votes—and to the activation of this unconstitutional, politically dubious, and dangerous cartel.

The millions of dollars being used to finance the lobbying for the NPV plan in state legislatures come from, among others, John Koza, the founder of Scientific Games and the inventor of the rub-off instant lottery ticket, who has pledged $12 million to the effort. He is a former Bill Clinton/Al Gore elector who has contributed hundreds of thousands of dollars to Democratic political organizations, including the Democratic National Committee and the Democratic Congressional Campaign Committee, as well as to Democratic candidates including Harry Reid and John Edwards.

Koza's nonprofit, National Popular Vote, Inc., based in Los Altos, California, has a board of advisors that is a microcosm of the progressive movement. It includes Democrats like Birch Bayh of Indiana and former independent presidential candidate John Anderson of Illinois. It is co-chaired by New York businessman Tom Golisano, the co-founder of the Independence Party of New York, who claims he is a Republican "even though he supported John Kerry and gave a cool $1 million to the Democratic National Convention in 2008."[10]

Koza and Golisano don't have a problem convincing liberal state legislators to back the NPV plan. So they have hired Republican lobbyists, including former Senator Fred Thompson and Republican National Committee member Saul Anuzis, to convince Republican state legislators and organizations such as the American Legislative Exchange Council to adopt the NPV. They falsely claim that the NPV would help Republicans politically—a strange claim, given the support for NPV from individuals like Jonathan Soros, George Soros's son; and left-wing organizations including Demos, the ACLU, Common Cause, and FairVote.

In creating the basic architecture of the American government, the Founders struggled to satisfy each state's demand for greater representation while attempting to balance popular sovereignty with the risk posed to the minority from majoritarian rule.[11] Smaller states in particular worried that a system that apportioned representatives on the basis of population would underrepresent their interests in the federal structure.

Out of this concern arose a compromise, proposed by the Committee of Eleven at the Constitutional Convention,[12] that helped to balance the competing interests of large states with those of smaller states. By allocating electors on the basis of a state's cumulative representation in the House and Senate, the Electoral College system avoided purely population-based representation, but still gave larger states greater electoral weight.

This arrangement prevents candidates from winning an election by focusing solely on high-population urban centers, and forces them to seek the support of a larger cross section of the American electorate. This aspect of the U.S. election system addressed the Founders' fears of a "tyranny of the majority," a topic frequently discussed in the *Federalist Papers*. In the eyes of the Founders, this tyranny was as dangerous as the risks posed by despots like King George, and had the potential to marginalize sizeable portions of the population, particularly in rural and more remote areas of the country. The Electoral College was devised as a response to these fears, as a means of "ensuring the participation of a broad regional diversity in the outcome of elections."[13]

This fear of marginalizing large portions of the population is also the reason that the Constitution calls for a representative republic, and not a direct democracy. Under the National Popular Vote plan, this electoral benefit to states would disappear, and presidential candidates could win elections by catering to high-density population centers and ignoring the rest of the country. The NPV would "encourage presidential campaigns to focus their efforts in dense media markets where costs per vote are lowest"; states that are sometimes ignored now will "continue to be ignored under NPV."[14] There is no question that smaller states do receive less attention than larger states, but any direct national election system "would magnify, not improve, this problem."[15]

Despite all this, both large and small states have joined the National Popular Vote movement. The NPV, at face value, may appeal to traditionally democratic notions of "every vote being equal." But its supporters seemingly have no concern for the many other nonmajoritarian aspects of the governmental structure established by the Constitution, including:

- every state having two senators, regardless of its size or population;
- a president's ability to veto legislation passed by a majority of the people's popularly-elected representatives;
- the lifetime appointment of federal judges whose power is inherently undemocratic;
- the unequal representation in the House of Representatives due to widely varying populations in congressional districts in states, such as Delaware (with a population of almost 900,000) and Wyoming (with a population of only 600,000); and
- the unequal apportionment among the states of House districts caused by the inclusion of large numbers of ineligible voters (including noncitizens) in the census count.

As former Federal Election Commission chairman Bradley Smith says, "If such direct checks on popular majorities can be reasonable and acceptable in a democracy, then it is difficult to argue that indirect checks on popular majority such as the Electoral College are inherently illegitimate."[16] Do not forget that one of the major purposes of the Bill of Rights is to protect us from majoritarian rule—otherwise, popular democracy could abolish freedom of religion, limit political speech, or restrict the ability to assemble and associate with unfavored minorities. The NPV movement seeks to create an unfair and unconstitutional system that diminishes the voting rights of citizens throughout the country, and raises the prospect of increased voter fraud and post-election litigation over the outcome.

Supporters of the NPV claim that because the Constitution gives state legislatures the power to determine how electors are chosen, "[c]ongressional consent is not required for the National Popular Vote compact."[17] The claim is specious: The NPV is unconstitutional, because it would give a group of states with a majority of electoral votes "the power to overturn the explicit decision of the Framers against direct election. Since that power does not conform to the constitutional means of changing the original decisions of the framers, NPV could not be a legitimate innovation."[18]

The Constitution's Compact Clause provides: "No State shall, without the Consent of Congress . . . enter into any Agreement or Compact with another State."[19] The Founders created the Compact Clause because they feared that compacting states would threaten the supremacy of the federal government in matters of foreign affairs and relations among the states.[20] If states could make agreements among themselves, they could damage the nation's federalist structure. Populist states, for example, cannot agree to have their U.S. senators only vote to seat one senator from the less populous states. Such a compact would overturn an essential part of the constitutional design. The very purpose of this clause is to guard against this; the plain text makes it clear that all such state compacts must be approved by Congress.

Undoubtedly, many liberal activist groups would like either the ability to create their own compacts or to lobby states individually to join compacts. Such compacts could then create *de facto* constitutional amendments regarding many different public policy issues—including purely federal matters. By circumventing the checks and balances of Congress, the NPV would risk setting the precedent that states can validate noncongressionally approved compacts as a substitute for a constitutional amendment.

Even though the plain text of the Constitution makes it clear that no compact shall be made by states without the consent of Congress, courts have recognized certain narrow agreements as exceptions to the limitations of the Compact Clause.[21] Interstate compacts that govern boundary disputes between states are almost always upheld as valid.[22] Although states sometimes submit their compacts to Congress for ratification, there has been an implied understanding that interstate agreements are legitimate as long as they have a limited—specifically local—impact, and do not affect national prerogatives.

No other interstate compact would have the impact on the federal government or on nonparticipating states to the extent that the NPV plan would. The NPV addresses national concerns by effectively abolishing the Electoral College and changing the method of choosing the president. But unlike other agreements that are exempt from the requirement of congressional approval, the NPV aims to control the behavior of compacting and noncompacting states alike, and it "harms those states whose citizens benefit from the current system of election."[23] Should the NPV movement reach its target of 270 electoral votes, those states not involved in the compact will have been co-opted into an electoral regime, despite having never consented to the compact. This distinction delineates this compact from all others.

In *U.S. Steel Corp. v. Multistate Tax Commission*,[24] the Supreme Court held that the Compact Clause prohibits compacts that "encroach upon the supremacy of the United States."[25] The court emphasized that the real test of constitutionality is whether the compact "enhances state power *quoad* the National Government."[26] To determine this qualification, the court questioned whether:

1. the compact authorizes the member states to exercise any powers they could not exercise in its absence;
2. the compact delegates sovereign power to the commission it created; or
3. the compacting states cannot withdraw from the agreement at any time.[27]

Unless approved by Congress, a violation of any one of these three points is sufficient to strike down a compact as unconstitutional; the NPV plan violates two. And congressional approval of a compact that attempts to change a provision of the Constitution without following the amendment requirement of Article V would also be invalid.

By eliminating the requirement that Congress approve a virtual constitutional amendment, the NPV would enhance the power of certain states at the expense of the national government—a conflict with the first prong of the *U.S. Steel Corp.* test. Without question, the NPV deprives nonparticipating states of their right, under Article V, to participate in deciding whether the Twelfth Amendment, which governs the Electoral College, should be changed.

From a constitutional standpoint, one could argue that, while states are given the power to decide how electors will be chosen, that power is not completely unrestricted. The Constitution "presupposes that the electors belong to each individual state and the state may not delegate this responsibility outside of state borders."[28] For example, in *Clinton v. New York*, the Supreme Court struck down the presidential line-item veto because it disrupted "the 'finely wrought' procedure that the Framers designed" in the Constitution for the enactment of statutes—a procedure that was "the product of the great debates and compromises that produced the Constitution itself."[29]

Similarly, in *U.S. Term Limits, Inc. v. Thornton*, the Supreme Court threw out state-imposed term limits on members of Congress.[30] A state-imposed qualification that was intended to evade the requirements of the Qualifications Clauses of the Constitution could not stand: "To argue otherwise is to suggest that the Framers spent significant time and energy in debating and crafting Clauses that could be easily evaded."[31] Such an argument would trivialize the principles behind the Qualifications Clauses, and treat them as an "empty formalism" rather that "the embodiment of a grand principle. . . . 'It is inconceivable that guaranties embedded in the Constitution of the United States may thus be manipulated out of existence.'"[32]

By disrupting the "finely wrought procedure" the Framers designed into the presidential election process, the NPV would trivialize the federalism principles behind the Electoral College, a product of the great debates and compromises that produced the Constitution. The supporters of NPV are not hiding their goal: to manipulate the Electoral College out of existence, an objective that cannot and should not be achieved by state compact, especially without congressional approval.

There is another component of the NPV that potentially violates the first prong of the *U.S. Steel Corp.* test: the plan's guarantee that "electors would no longer be accountable to the voters in the states they are from."[33] As a result, voters—such as felons—

who are eligible to vote in some states could influence the electoral votes of other states where they would be ineligible to vote.

Furthermore, "candidates could end up being elected with the electoral votes of a state in which they weren't even qualified to be on the ballot."[34] Even more disconcerting, the NPV provides that if the "number of presidential electors nominated in a member state" is less than what the winner of the national popular vote is entitled to, that winner "shall have the power to nominate the presidential electors for that state."[35] In other words, a winning candidate (say a governor from another state like Texas or Massachusetts) could appoint the electors for New York even if the candidate *never* qualified to get on the ballot in New York; he or she could even designate as electors individuals who are neither residents nor qualified voters in New York.

Under the third prong of the constitutionality test delineated in *U.S. Steel Corp.*, the compact must allow states to withdraw at any time. The NPV, however, places withdrawal limitations on compacting states. The plan states that "a withdrawal occurring six months or less before the end of a President's term shall not become effective until a President or Vice President shall have been qualified to serve the next term."[36] This provision is in direct conflict with the *U.S. Steel Corp.* test, and alone renders the compact unconstitutional without congressional approval.[37] It could also cause an unresolvable election crisis: If a state withdrew in violation of the provision, it would throw into doubt the results of a presidential election. There is no provision in the NPV for enforcing this limitation, or indeed for compliance with any of the provisions of the compact.

Moreover, this withdrawal limitation is in explicit violation of the Article II provision that gives the legislatures of each state the power to select the manner in which electors are chosen. A legislature can delegate to the people of its state the ability to choose electors, but the legislature retains the power to withdraw that delegation. The NPV scheme would temporarily suspend that legislative power, which again would violate the Constitution.

Outside of the question of constitutionality, there are a number of public-policy reasons that such a compact would be detrimental to America's unique democratic system.

SWING STATES AND POLITICAL INFLUENCE

Although the point has been argued that under the current electoral system, swing states garner the majority of candidates' attention, swing states can change from election to election; many states that are today considered to be reliably "blue" or "red" in the presidential race were recently unpredictable. For example, "California was competitive for decades, only becoming a Democratic presidential bastion in the last 15 years. Florida was considered a safe Republican seat as late as 1996."[38] With rare exceptions, however, established urban centers like Houston, Chicago, New York City, and Los Angeles will always have high populations that vote in a predictable fashion. While the Electoral College assures that minority interests in a variety of geographic regions are protected, the NPV plan would help protect only select urban interests. The Electoral College "embodies the balance [the Founders] aimed to achieve through deference to states with smaller populations and by ensuring that the interests of these states be reflected in national decision-making."[39]

Although some state legislators have embraced the NPV, their support appears to be rather shortsighted: Under the NPV, a majority of states will see their influence over the presidential election decrease. The influence of a state under the Electoral College can be measured by dividing the state's electoral votes by the total electoral votes; the measure under the NPV is the number of a state's eligible voters divided by the total eligible votes in the country.

When these measurements are compared, states that have adopted the NPV—such as California, Hawaii, and Vermont, as well as the District of Columbia—*lose* influence with the switch. While California's loss is relatively small (1 percent), Hawaii would lose 42 percent of its influence, Vermont 58 percent, and the District of Columbia a stunning 62 percent. Twenty-nine states and the District of Columbia would lose influence under the NPV.[40] Based on the 2006 elections, "59 percent of voters . . . lived in states that would either lose influence under direct election or would be indifferent about moving away from the Electoral College."[41]

RECOUNTS

Under the NPV, recounts would be both more prevalent and more problematic. The basic principles of federalism—the principles upon which this nation was founded—were used to design the U.S. electoral process. As such, federal elections are decentralized affairs; each of the 50 states and the District of Columbia run their own elections on the first Tuesday of November every four years, or for a varying period before then in early voting states. Every state has different procedural rules for the administration of elections, from the definition of what constitutes a vote to how recounts are triggered and conducted.

The presidential election of 2000 saw an unprecedented vote recount in Florida. This recount was a belabored, emotional, costly process—even though it was limited to only one state. For the most part, only one set of state laws was applicable in that recount. Under the NPV, however, any suspicions necessitating a recount in even a single district would be an incentive for a national recount. And why not? Every additional vote a losing candidate could obtain anywhere in the country could make the difference in winning or losing the national election—even if the extra vote would not change the results of the electoral vote in that particular state under the current system. The lengthy and contentious recount in the 2008 Minnesota senate race between Al Franken and Norm Coleman cost each candidate upwards of $10 million in legal fees and costs—imagine such a recount going on in every state!

The winner-take-all system for electoral votes reduces the possibility of a recount, since popular vote totals are often much closer than Electoral College totals. In fact, former FEC chairman Bradley Smith points out that "recounts may have been necessary in as many as six presidential elections since 1880, if a national popular vote system had been in place. That's nearly one out of every six elections."[42]

The prospect of a candidate challenging "every precinct, in every county, in every state of the Union" should be abhorrent to anyone who witnessed the drama, cost, delay, and undue litigation sparked by the Florida recount.[43] Worse still, there is little chance that the ballots would be recounted in a consistent manner across the nation, or that there would be a national, as opposed to piecemeal, recount.

Election laws vary by state, which means that 50 different standards (51, including the District of Columbia) would be applied to a recount.[44] And no state or group of states that wanted a national recount could force other states to participate. Ironically, the NPV, which is supposed to make each vote count equally, would likely result in varied and even conflicting decisions among the states as to the validity of each vote.[45]

While the total of the national popular vote may be close, the vote totals in particular states may not be close at all—certainly not close enough to trigger a recount under that particular state's recount laws, even if a losing candidate believed a national recount is warranted. The margin of victory in the popular vote could be enough to warrant a recount in the eyes of some, yet not large enough to trigger a recount in specific states with large vote margins.

The Florida recount madness could be replicated on a national level, with new complexities added if some states refused to participate in a recount, or even devised their own recount rules. Such a national recount could result in 51 potential lawsuits heading to the Supreme Court—or more, if lawsuits are filed in each relevant state and federal court. The votes for the presidential ticket could get recounted in some jurisdictions across the country, but not others—leading to virtually the same type of equal-protection problems the Supreme Court found in *Bush v. Gore*[46] because of the unequal treatment of ballots by election officials in separate Florida counties.

Such a national recount would result in protracted litigation and confusion, weakening public faith in the election process, delaying the final resolution of a presidential election, and exacerbating the exact "problem" that the NPV plan claims to be solving. The 2000 election crisis was a temporary one—and a testament to the strength and reliability of this nation's electoral system. The current electoral system has consistently produced presidents without producing a constitutional crisis. The burden is on the NPV's supporters to justify changing a system that has functioned well for more than two hundred years—not those defending that system.[47]

CLOSER ELECTIONS AND MORE CRISES

The NPV awards the presidential election to whichever candidate receives the "largest" national vote, not a majority of the national popular vote. In an electoral system defined by the NPV, numerous fringe parties and radical candidates appealing solely to the largest population centers would likely emerge, destabilizing America's two-party system and leading to a higher incidence of close elections. Consequently, "[p]residential campaigns would devolve into European-style, multi-candidate races. As more candidates enter the field, individual votes will necessarily be divided among an ever-increasing number of candidates. The result will be lower vote totals per candidate and an increased likelihood that two or more candidates will have close popular vote totals."[48]

The winner-take-all allocation of electoral votes within 48 states necessitates that a candidate be popular enough to appeal to a broad electorate, including moderate voters, and it provides the winner of the presidential race with both finality and a mandate, even if his popular vote total is slightly below 50 percent. With its plurality requirement, the NPV could lead to presidential candidates being elected with unprecedentedly small margins. These smaller victory margins, combined with an overall decrease in popular support for a single candidate, could trigger chaotic and contentious elections. Furthermore, a president elected by only 25 to 35 percent of the American people would not truly have a mandate to govern, and questions about his legitimacy could pose grave consequences for the nation, and for any actions he took as president.

The Electoral College system requires a presidential candidate to win simultaneous elections across 50 states and the District of Columbia; the concurrent majorities means that "the president gains a popular legitimacy that a single, narrow, national" election does not provide, and emphasizes "the breadth of popular support for the winner."[49]

PROVISIONAL BALLOTS

Under the NPV plan, provisional ballots also could lead to an extensive, widespread, and complex battle that could delay and confuse the results of a presidential election.

Federal law requires provisional ballots for all voters whose eligibility is called into question, or who are unable to cast a regular ballot at the polling place because they are not on the list of registered voters.[50] Provisional ballots are only counted if local election officials can verify that the voter was entitled to vote; the verification happens after the election, and after an investigation of the circumstances by election officials. Provisional ballots may not affect the outcome of the majority vote within a state under the current system, because the number of provisional ballots is less than the margin of victory. However, if the total number of provisional ballots issued in all of the states is greater than the margin of victory, or if it could make a difference in the outcome when combined with all of the other ballots in dispute, a national battle over provisional ballots could ensue.

Losing candidates would have the incentive to hire lawyers to litigate the ballot verification process of election officials in every corner of the nation. This could make the isolated fights over chads in punch-card ballots in Florida in 2000 look almost insubstantial by comparison. Legally contesting the legitimacy of decisions made by local election officials on provisional ballots nationwide could significantly delay the outcome of a national election.

VOTER FRAUD

Another ignored consequence of the NPV is that the plan would encourage vote fraud. Currently, a fraudulent vote is counted only in the district where it was cast, and therefore can only impact the electoral votes in that particular state. Under the NPV, however, vote fraud in any state would affect the aggregate national vote. To a would-be wrongdoer, this is a drastic increase in the potential benefit obtained from casting fraudulent ballots. Fraudsters would be encouraged to cheat to obtain further votes for their national candidate, or to deny votes for the opposition candidate. Under the Electoral College system, there are some states where such fraud would make no difference, because not enough fraudulent votes could be cast to change that state's Electoral College outcome. But with the NPV, every fraudulent vote obtained anywhere could make a difference in changing the outcome of the national race.

This prospect is even more worrisome in strongly partisan neighborhoods and one-party districts where there are no (or few) members of the opposition party to work as election officials or as poll watchers. There is little incentive now to engage in such partisan fraud where it is most possible, since the dominant party is likely to win anyway. But under the NPV scheme, there is an increased incentive to engage in fraud in states that are the most corrupt and one-sided. Under NPV, all states—especially one-party states and those with a history of tolerating fraud—become targets for fraud, with likely increases in this type of misbehavior nationwide.

It should be noted, "the popular vote winner has triumphed in 42 of 45 elections."[51] Supporters of NPV point to those elections (1876, 1888, and 2000) where the popular vote winner did not prevail. But "the Electoral College clearly played a democratizing and equalizing role" in the 1876 and 1888 elections that "almost certainly better corresponded to true popular sentiment than did reported popular vote totals." Why? Because in the 1876 election, for example, where Samuel Tilden defeated Rutherford B. Hayes in the popular vote, there was "rampant vote fraud and suppression in the southern states [that] make the actual vote totals from that election unknowable." In the 1888 election, Southern states voted overwhelmingly for Grover Cleveland, the national popular vote winner, while Republican Benjamin Harrison carried the rest of the nation, winning 20 of 25 states and the presidency. If blacks had not had their votes suppressed, there is little doubt that Harrison, as a Republican, would have received almost the entire black vote, and would have won the national popular vote, which he lost by fewer than 100,000 votes.[52]

The NPV is both unconstitutional and bad policy. If the proponents of the NPV believe that a change to the electoral system is necessary, they should convince Congress and the American people, and use the proper method for amending the Constitution.

The United States should maintain the Electoral College. It has enabled us to successfully elect presidents throughout this nation's history in a way that best represents the diverse and various interests of America:

> America's election systems have operated smoothly for more than 200 years because the Electoral College accomplishes its intended purposes. . . . [It] preserves federalism, prevents chaos, grants definitive electoral outcomes, and prevents tyrannical or unreasonable rule. The Founding Fathers created a stable, well-planned and carefully designed system—and it works.[53]

In an age of perceived political dysfunction, effective policies already in place—especially successful policies established by this nation's Founders—should be preserved.

CHAPTER TEN

How a Machine Steals
an Entire Town

In 2003, Mississippi senator Thad Cochran sent a letter to the Justice Department's Voting Section complaining about the conduct of that year's primary in Noxubee, Mississippi, joining numerous complaints from white voters and candidates there. Over the next four years, attorneys in the Civil Rights Division investigated and sued perpetrators of vote fraud, vote suppression, and discrimination in Noxubee—but the investigation faced its biggest opponents within the division itself.

The career lawyers in the section, including the chief of the Voting Section, Joe Rich, wanted to ignore the complaints. They were coming in from white voters and a white Republican senator, and the miscreants who were violating the law were black.

After internal debates and conflict, the division eventually initiated the first Voting Rights Act lawsuit it had ever filed against black defendants on behalf of white voters, which it won in 2007. Even though conditions in Noxubee were "the most extreme case of racial exclusion seen by the [department's] Voting Section in decades," the case would never have happened under the normal conditions in the division.

Noxubee County is in east-central Mississippi, adjacent to the Alabama border, and was one of 26 counties carved from the last great Indian land cession east of the Mississippi River, in 1830. General Andrew Jackson built the Jackson Military Road through the county on his way to New Orleans in the War of 1812, yet today many of its county roads remain unpaved. Noxubee County is extremely poor, over 70 percent black, and has a shrinking population of only 11,000; the average family income is a little over $22,000. More than 35 percent of the population is below the poverty level, and only 13 percent have a college degree.

Agriculture has been Noxubee's main industry throughout its history, and it still produces timber, corn, soybeans, catfish, cotton, and wheat. It is about 50 miles northeast of Philadelphia, Mississippi, where three civil rights workers were murdered during the Freedom Summer of 1964. When the Voting Rights Act was passed in 1965, 100 percent of the elected officials in the county were white.

By 2007, 93 percent of the elected officials in the county were black. Four of the five members of the county commission were black, all members of the election commission and the board of education were black, and with the exception of the county district attorney, all countywide elected officials, including the sheriff, were black.[1] As one expert said in the government lawsuit, you had "a situation in which whites are the minority and blacks are in a position to discriminate against them very much in the same way as whites discriminated against blacks in the history further back."[2] And that was apparently the attitude of many local officials and party activists—it was payback time.

Noxubee County was exactly the kind of desperately poor place that was ripe for political corruption. That corruption was represented by Ike Brown, a twice-convicted felon who was the head of the local Democratic Party executive committee. Brown had his own racist Mississippi version of Tammany Hall, a local political machine that Boss Tweed himself would have admired.

Despite widespread illegal activities by Brown over the years, the Department of Justice investigation, and prosecution of the case, almost didn't happen. One of the authors, Hans von Spakovsky, was the counsel to the assistant attorney general for civil rights overseeing voting matters when Mississippi senator Cochran sent his letter to the Voting Section about the primary, and complaints started coming in from voters. However, the career lawyers in the Section, including the chief of the Voting Section, Joe Rich, wanted to ignore the complaints, since they believe that the Voting Rights Act protects only minority voters.

The Justice Department was familiar with Noxubee, which has seen many federal officials since 1965. Federal observers were often sent to monitor elections in Noxubee under the authority of the Voting Rights Act, and all of the barriers that had kept blacks from registering, voting, or running for office had been removed. Federal observers continued to be sent to Noxubee in the 1990s, often at the behest of Brown, to protect the rights of local black voters. The observers apparently turned a blind eye to Brown's antics and discriminatory tactics towards white voters. One resident told Christian Adams, one of the Voting Section lawyers assigned to the case, that Brown had a close relationship with the observers and one of the supervising Justice Department lawyers. As Adams said, the "stinging message to opponents of

Brown's anti-white crusade—you can't count on the federal government to protect you."[3]

But Christopher Coates, the special counsel in the Voting Section who later became its chief, took an interest in opening an investigation. Coates was probably the most experienced trial attorney in the section, with more courtroom experience than all of the other lawyers combined. He had been a staff attorney for the ACLU's Voting Project in Atlanta for many years before coming to the Justice Department during the Clinton administration. He had filed numerous cases on behalf of minority voters across the South. The civil rights community—before the Noxubee case—so admired his work that he received the Thurgood Marshall Decade Award from the Georgia NAACP in 1991. In 2007, the Civil Rights Division gave him its second highest award, the Walter Barnett Memorial Award for Excellence and Advocacy. What civil rights organizations did not realize was that, contrary to their orthodoxy, Coates had a firm and principled belief that the Voting Rights Act protects *all* voters from discrimination, and that it should be enforced in a race-neutral manner.

Other career attorneys were against sending observers to the primary runoff election, but the Front Office of the Civil Rights Division overrode that, and Coates led a team of observers to Noxubee. Based on their findings, Coates wrote a memorandum summarizing the evidence the section had at that point, and recommended that an investigation be opened. He argued that a civil injunction against Brown and his allies "was the most effective way of stopping the pattern of voting discrimination" in Noxubee.

Normally, the section chief forwards these types of memoranda up through the chain of command, for the assistant attorney general and his assistants in the Front Office to review and decide how to proceed. However, unbeknownst to Coates, Voting Section chief Joe Rich deleted the recommendation about opening an investigation or filing suit before forwarding the memorandum to von Spakovsky, who was responsible for reviewing all recommendations and memoranda from the Voting Section. Rich deleted the recommendation not only because he believed the law should not be applied to white voters, but because of advice from another career lawyer, Chris Herren (who later became chief of the Voting Section in the Obama administration), that proceeding with the Noxubee investigation would upset civil rights organizations.

By coincidence, von Spakovsky ran into Coates at a special presentation in the Great Hall, a grand room at the Main Justice Building used for presentations and ceremonies. Von Spakovsky knew Coates from his time as a trial attorney in the Voting Section, which was located in a separate office building across town. Unlike the majority of the Voting Section staff, Coates did not treat von Spakovsky with hostility because he was a political conservative. Coates asked von Spakovsky if a decision had yet been made about sending observers to Noxubee and opening an investigation. Von Spakovsky had just read the Noxubee memorandum, and was taken aback by Coates's question, since there had been no mention of filing litigation.

Von Spakovsky told his boss, Deputy Assistant Attorney General Brad Schlozman, about the altered memorandum. They were both astonished and angry at Rich's unprofessional conduct and his efforts not only to stop an investigation of blatant racial discrimination against voters, but also to deceive the Front Office of the division. Everyone in the Front Office had long recognized what a political animal Rich was, but almost no one—up to that point anyway—thought that Rich would go so far as to sanction outright racial disenfranchisement as part of his ideological agenda.

The Front Office decided to approve Coates's recommendation, and von Spakovsky placed a call to Rich telling him that the Voting Section was sending a team, headed by Coates, to Noxubee to open an investigation. When von Spakovsky added a reprimand about Rich's unprofessional behavior in his end-of-the-year job evaluation, Rich objected, and appealed the review; he lost. The Front Office never trusted Rich's judgment again.

But even though the Front Office had approved opening an investigation, Coates ran into further problems within the section. Opposition was widespread among other career lawyers within the Voting Section to investigating the Noxubee matter. They refused to work on the investigation, did not want to be part of any observer teams, and began harassing Coates for having persisted in getting the investigation opened. They did not believe that the Voting Rights Act should be used against black defendants, or to protect white voters, no matter how egregious the behavior.

As Coates related to von Spakovsky, one career attorney told him "[i]n no uncertain terms that he had not come to the Voting Section to sue African American defendants." Another told Coates that he was opposed to bringing voting rights suits against black defendants "until we reached the day when the socioeconomic status of blacks in Mississippi was the same as the socioeconomic status of whites living there."[4] The section leadership was no different. Coates told von Spakovsky that the then deputy of the Voting Section, Robert Kengle, expressed his disgust to Coates, saying, "can you believe that we are going to Mississippi to protect white voters?"[5]

After multiple visits to Noxubee and an extensive investigation conducted with a few volunteers who were willing to risk ostracism by their colleagues, Coates prepared and eventually sent what is called a "j-memo" ("justification memorandum") through Joe Rich, to the assistant attorney general, in August 2004. It recommended that a Voting Rights Act lawsuit be filed against Brown, the local election commission, and the Noxubee

Democratic Party executive committee. This time, Rich did not delete the recommendation to file suit.

Coates and his observers had themselves seen much of the illegal and discriminatory behavior of the Brown political machine—Brown had apparently gotten away with it for so long, he saw the Justice Department as an ally, and it did not occur to him that he should curtail his activity in front of federal observers. In fact, Coates said it "was some of the most outrageous and blatant racially discriminatory behavior at the polls" that Coates had "seen or had reported to me in my thirty-three-plus years as a voting rights litigator."[6]

But others within the Voting Section continued to refuse to work on the case, including the section's historian, Peyton McCrary, whose job it was to research the history of discrimination. Coates complained to von Spakovsky about this, but because of the protections of civil service rules, there was almost nothing that could be done about McCrary's unprofessional attitude. (McCrary was given an award by the Obama administration for his behavior.) This was a common problem that applied to all of the insubordinate and recalcitrant staff within the Voting Section. Fortunately, newly hired career attorneys Christian Adams and Joshua Rogers believed in the race-neutral enforcement of the Voting Rights Act, and both of them agreed to work with Coates on the case.

Their investigation revealed that Ike Brown had created a widespread and pervasive system to disenfranchise white voters and elect black candidates. Brown made no secret of his hatred of whites. The Voting Section's internal memorandum summarizing the results of the Section's investigation, dated August 13, 2004, concluded that Brown was "profoundly racist toward white citizens and is willing to act in blatantly unlawful ways to defeat white candidates in their bid for local office."

Brown had been involved in Noxubee politics since moving there in the 1970s to help state representative Reecy Dixon become the first black superintendent of education in the county. Brown ran unsuccessfully for the chancery clerk position in 1983, and never ran for office again. But he became, according to the internal 2004 Justice Department memorandum, "the most powerful political organizer in the county" who "exerted enormous influence on the local political process." As head of the Democratic Party, he was in a position to control the process of selecting Democratic candidates, who then were practically guaranteed election in the overwhelmingly Democratic-voting county.

In 2000 he was elected chairman of the local Democratic Party's executive committee, and became an officer in the Mississippi NAACP and the state Democratic Party, as well as chairman of the East Mississippi Voters League. Brown believed that there should not be a single white elected official in Noxubee, and that any black officials who cooperated with whites should be replaced. He once called a black county supervisor who had voted to fire two black justice court clerks who had stolen money "a white man's nigger" who had sold "out to the white folks."[7] He constantly used racial appeals in soliciting votes "to get the job done," often making false accusations of racial discrimination (and drug dealing) against the few remaining white elected officials in the county.

On his route to political power in Noxubee, Brown was convicted in 1994 of nine counts of income tax fraud, for which he initially served 14 months of a two-year sentence. But in a display of his contempt for the law and his unapologetic nature, he was returned to prison for seven months in 1996 and 1997 for violating the terms of his release. He had a previous conviction on state charges of insurance fraud and forgery, but had been pardoned by Mississippi Governor Ray Mabus—another reason why Brown seemed to think he was immune to the law. His voting rights were also restored by the Mississippi governor after his release from federal prison.

An interview conducted by Department of Justice lawyers revealed that "even during the time Brown was in prison, he instructed members of the Board of Supervisors how they were to vote on issues before the Board," reminiscent of Al Capone or many a Hollywood Mafia movie. He even sent a letter from prison to the county's "BLACK VOTERS" telling them he would "be back soon" and urging them to vote only for an all-black slate of candidates. He had made many other similar statements. In 1994, he entered a polling place and announced loudly to all of the voters in the room, "You've got to put blacks in office, our candidates, because we don't want white people over us anymore."

In an article in the local newspaper, *The Macon Beacon*, Brown reminded county elected officials that they would "suffer consequences at the ballot box" if they did not do what he wanted. On July 29, 1999, Brown ran an advertisement in *The Beacon* telling voters that he would "be at the polls" all day, a not-so-veiled threat that he would be checking how they would be voting.

The Department of Justice filed a lawsuit in 2005, and two years later obtained a judgment in federal court that found that Brown and the local Democratic Party had "engaged in racially motivated manipulation of the electoral process." In fact, the court did not have "to look far to find amply direct and circumstantial evidence of an intent to discriminate against white voters."[8] Brown and his cohorts "engaged in improper, and in some instances fraudulent conduct, and committed blatant violations of state election laws" to stuff ballot boxes with invalid votes.[9]

Among the abuses catalogued by Judge Tom Lee was the wholesale harvesting of absentee ballots, which are required to be notarized under Mississippi law. A front company owned by Brown, RMB Enterprises, paid the registration fees of more than 50 notary publics. These notaries, all part of Brown's political machine, fanned out across the county contacting blacks, making sure they voted the way Ike Brown wanted them to, often fraudulently completing absentee ballots without the knowledge or consent of the voter. The absentee ballot rate in the county was routinely more than 20 percent, compared to the average rate in Mississippi of three to six percent. That kind of high absentee voting rate is almost always a clear sign that there is unlawful conduct going on. As the government's expert testified:

> . . . even taking into account that there could have been an exceptionally efficient 'get out the vote' campaign at work here, this level of absentee voting cannot happen except when you're generating absentee ballots on a fraudulent basis.[10]

The importance of this absentee ballot scheme to Brown's ballot-box-stuffing operation was pointed out by the testimony of a notary public who was not part of Brown's crew. After she helped some voters notarize their absentee ballots, she received an angry call from Brown warning that she "shouldn't be picking up his ballots."

Brown then put in place a nearly all-black force of loyal poll workers and managers over whom he "had effective influence and control." Under the direction of Brown, they acted in "blatant disregard of applicable law" in counting all absentee ballots coming in from black voters "by preventing, ignoring or rejecting challenges," while systematically throwing out the absentee ballots of white voters. At one point a poll manager called Brown on her cell phone when a poll watcher for a white candidate for sheriff started to challenge a ballot. The poll manager reported that Brown had told her to count all of the ballots, and then, in direct violation of Mississippi law, told the poll watcher that she could not issue any other challenges, saying "No. Ain't no ballots being challenged. I was instructed by Ike not to—can't no ballots be challenged."

The candidate challenging the incumbent sheriff was present during the counting of absentee ballots in another precinct, where poll workers were tearing open the absentee ballot envelopes and stacking the ballots together on a table. They refused to "call out the names of the voters, check the register to see if the person had voted at the polls, or take the time to check the envelope and application to ensure the statutory requirements were met," and worked so fast that the poll watchers "didn't even have time" to take any action. When the candidate tried to get the poll officials to comply with legal requirements, Deputy Sheriff John Clanton told the poll officials to ignore the protests:

> "Don't listen to him. He can't tell you how to do your job. You know what you're supposed to do. You know what you've been told to do. You open those envelopes now and get those ballots down to the end."[11]

Brown himself engaged in similar behavior. A controversy had developed over the absentee ballot of a person who had already voted at the polling place, and whose absentee ballot had been separated from its envelope and mixed in with all of the other ballots. Brown came charging in to the polling place, yelling at the poll workers to count "every vote, count them right now." Thus, that particular voter cast two ballots; who knows how many other illegal ballots Brown forced to be counted?

Brown even took absentee ballots home with him the night before an election and "put Post-it notes on a number of the ballot[s] identifying reasons for rejecting the ballots." He ordered the poll managers to reject all of the marked ballots, and to count all the rest. The evidence in the lawsuit showed that "ballots of black voters with defects similar to those of white voters with yellow stickies were not marked by Brown for rejection and were counted." For example, ballots of white voters whose signatures were not directly on the signature line were rejected, while the ballots of black voters whose signatures were not directly on the signature line were accepted.

Brown and his political allies also interfered with black voters who voted for white candidates. According to the Justice investigation, the county clerk failed to place the absentee ballot of Aldine Farmer Cotton into the ballot box in the 2003 Democratic primary because Cotton hadn't voted for the black clerk, but had "voted for the white folks." The husband of a local black woman who was helping Samuel Heard, a white candidate running for sheriff, was told by state representative Reecy Dixon, a Brown ally, that his wife should not be supporting a white man. The woman was told the same thing by a clerk at the county justice court; she was derisively referred to as "a white man lover" to her face.

There is also a strong probability of impersonation fraud in Noxubee's elections. A former Noxubee County deputy sheriff testified that during the 2005 election, he saw Brown outside a polling place talking to a young black woman. He heard Brown "tell her to go in there and vote, to use any name, and that no one was going to say anything."[12] Mississippi had no voter ID requirement at the time.

In order to cover up his absentee-ballot fraud, Brown was not above soliciting perjury or threatening the government's witnesses. A black voter testified in court that one of Brown's notaries recruited her and her mother to vote absentee, even though they had no reason to do so. That same notary picked up their absentee ballots, but neither the signature on the absentee ballot application or the ballot envelope was the voter's. As the witness left the federal courtroom, Brown was overheard telling the notary and another one of his "people", as the court referred to them, to pay the witness a "visit." His "people" confronted the witness at her home, telling her that "we black people need to stick together" and suggesting that she tell the court that "she probably didn't understand" what she was being asked, and that she change her testimony.[13]

Only three days after appearing on the government's witness list, the deputy sheriff who testified to observing impersonation fraud was arrested by Noxubee Deputy Sheriff Terry Grassaree, a member of Brown's Democratic Party executive committee. Grassaree stopped the witness on a city street and told him that the sheriff, Albert Walker, wanted to talk to him. The witness told the deputy that he was busy, and would speak to the sheriff later. Grassaree yelled, "Motherfucker, I'll put you [out] of this damned truck and kill you." According to an affidavit filed by the witness, he drove off, and Grassaree then drove his patrol car into the back of the witness's car. The witness then headed for the courthouse, where he thought he might be safer, but Grassaree arrested him for disorderly conduct, resisting arrest, failure to yield to a blue light, and dangerous driving. Grassaree "expressly warned [the witness] that he should not speak to attorneys or investigators" from the government. At the time of his "arrest," the witness was a police officer in Aberdeen, Mississippi.

In a most unusual move, the Justice Department filed a motion with the federal judge presiding over the lawsuit, asking for an order prohibiting Brown and his allies from threatening, harassing, and intimidating the government's witnesses. Instead, the federal judge issued an injunction staying the county's criminal prosecution from going forward, saying that there did not "seem to be any basis for a criminal prosecution."[14] It was clear that the government witness had been targeted by Brown and his Brownshirts in the sheriff's department for helping the Justice Department in the Voting Rights Act case.

Sheriff's departments in rural states like Mississippi have tremendous power, and under Sheriff Albert Walker, the Noxubee

County sheriff's department operated as the "strong arm" of Brown and his vote-stealing machine. Brown regularly threatened "to call 'the law' on people and to have them arrested" if they tried to interfere with his lawlessness.[15] He used the sheriff's office as his headquarters on Election Day, and the sheriff's department chauffeured Brown "around to polling places on Election Day."

Sheriffs also hauled voters to the polls. According to the Justice Department's internal memorandum, one deputy sheriff, John Clanton, actually worked as a poll manager in the 2003 primary in uniform, with a weapon strapped to his waist, while another deputy, Darryl Mitchell, was seen tearing down campaign signs for white candidates.

In fact, Sheriff Walker owed his job to Brown. Walker lost the 1999 Democratic primary runoff by 22 votes to black challenger Earnest Eichelberger. In a recount, Walker was declared the winner when invalid ballots that had been discounted were suddenly considered valid. Eichelberger went to court and obtained an order setting aside Walker's victory because of the discovery of 52 invalid absentee ballots. But the judge failed to specify when a new election should be held, and Brown refused to allow one to be scheduled; Walker served out his full four-year term, even though there was a judicial finding that Walker had not won the election.

Brown thought he was the ultimate authority in elections, and used the sheriff to enforce it. For example, he refused to allow the candidate challenging the sheriff to have more that one poll watcher in a precinct where there was ballot counting going on at multiple tables. The challenger's daughter telephoned Brown to explain that state law allowed one poll watcher for each table. Brown refused to listen, finally telling her, "I said you can only have one. This isn't Mississippi state law you're dealing with. This is Ike Brown's law."[16] When she insisted that she would send four poll watchers, Brown threatened her: "Fine, fine, have as many as you want. I'll send the police on around to arrest you."

The sheriff and his henchmen would enforce the state law prohibiting campaign activity within 150 feet of the polls against white candidates, but assisted, and engaged in, that same prohibited campaigning on behalf of Brown's candidates. When a challenger for the sheriff's office protested this treatment, the chief deputy threatened him, saying, "I'll put your ass in jail." Brown and the chief deputy even cited the state campaign ban in trying to prevent another candidate from voting in his own precinct.

Brown and his machine repeatedly offered improper and unsolicited "assistance" to black voters throughout the county. Under federal law, any voter who is disabled, illiterate, or who otherwise needs assistance is entitled to ask for help with voting. In Noxubee, Brown's enforcers approached black voters and offered them "unsolicited assistance, which 'assistance' consisted of the poll workers taking the ballots and marking them without consulting the voters." An elderly white voter who had difficulty marking her ballot was refused assistance by these same poll workers, who "instead ran the voter's blank ballot through the machine and thereby denied her the opportunity to cast a ballot."

Joe Prince, a black resident of Noxubee who had moved back from Detroit in 2001, told the Department of Justice investigators that two black incumbents, supervisor George Robinson and county clerk Carl Mickens, insisted that he vote by absentee ballot at the courthouse before the election, even though he told Robinson he planned to be at his polling place. When he went to the courthouse to vote, Robinson and Mickens told Prince which candidates to vote for, including themselves, and looked on as he marked the ballot, to make sure Prince followed their directions.

The court concluded that the actions of Brown and the local Democratic Party executive committee were "designed, from start to finish, to minimize white voter participation."[17] At one point Brown sent a press release to the local paper with a list of 174 voters, all of them white, and mostly from the sole remaining district with a white supervisor. The paper published the press release, which said Brown would challenge these voters if they attempted to vote in the Democratic primary, because they were not "loyal Democrats." The court said that Brown had published the names "to discourage white voters from voting in the 2003 Democratic primary," concluding that race was a factor, since Brown was otherwise unable to identify more than a few persons "for whom he had any concrete basis for suspecting they were not true Democrats." And Brown was effective—the court heard testimony that "one voter was so intimidated that she did not vote; another was intimidated to the point that she did not feel she could approach the polls alone."[18]

Brown's attitude was shared by other county officials. The investigation included an interview with one witness who said that Sheriff Walker had made statements to the effect that blacks had suffered in the past, and now it was time for blacks to do whatever they wanted in Noxubee County. Similarly, Essie Brooks, who defeated a white member of the local election commission, told a witness, "It's payback time."

Brown's exclusionary practices extended to candidates as well. He did everything he could to exclude white candidates from the Democratic Party. He would keep the location of precinct caucuses secret from all but his most loyal supporters, all black, making it nearly impossible for white Democrats to attend, so that, as the probe found, he could "retain his position and power . . . by whatever means were necessary, namely, connivance, manipulation and prevarication." This is almost a mirror image of tactics used in the 1950s and 1960s, when voter registration offices would change their office hours or even close when blacks were attempting to register to vote.

Brown also recruited blacks who were not residents of the county to run as candidates. He recruited a black lawyer to run against the local prosecutor, the only white to hold an elected countywide office. To qualify, the challenger, who practiced law in Ridgeland, Mississippi, rented an apartment in Noxubee that had no utilities, appliances, or furniture; the apartment was arranged by Brown, who also paid the first month's rent. The incumbent attempted to challenge the black lawyer's nonresidency at a Democratic Party meeting held at Brown's house, but Brown forced the prosecutor into the kitchen, refusing to allow him into the meeting to present his petition or the evidence of nonresidency. Brown also banned two white members of the Democratic Party executive committee from attending the meeting, telling them falsely that they had been put off the committee. The prosecutor ultimately went to chancery court to get the spurious candidate disqualified. Brown fumed about having a white official still in office, telling *USA Today* in an April 2, 2006 article that if Brown "could find a black lawyer who lives in the county, we'd get him [the prosecutor], too."

Once the Noxubee case was filed in 2005, critics lost no time in condemning it. *The New York Times* said the action was "a sharp shift and it has raised eyebrows outside the state."[19] The president of the Mississippi NAACP criticized the Justice Department, expressing his deep concern over the Noxubee lawsuit "because of the historic pattern of voting rights abuses— including voter intimidation and registration challenges—against blacks in Mississippi." He claimed those abuses had continued, and were not being "sufficiently investigated," and that voters in Noxubee were just choosing their candidates, not engaging in racial discrimination.[20]

Demonstrating this pattern by the NAACP in supporting voting abuse and ballot theft, its Noxubee County branch actually placed an ad in the local paper after the trial, but before the verdict, inviting "citizens of Noxubee" to a "pre-victory celebration and reception in honor of . . . the outstanding performance" of the attorney representing Ike Brown. The liberal political appointees who were put into the Civil Rights Division at the start of the Obama administration, many of whom came from the NAACP and other civil rights organizations, made it clear that there would be no more Noxubee-type cases filed.

Robert Kengle, the deputy chief of the Voting Section who had told Coates, "Can you believe that we are going to Mississippi to protect white voters?" left the Voting Section in 2007 to join the liberal Lawyers' Committee for Civil Rights. He has since claimed, in an affidavit filed with the U.S. Commission on Civil Rights during its investigation of the New Black Panther Party voter intimidation case, that he made that statement because he felt that the Front Office was "rejecting" recommendations to monitor elections "based upon concerns of discrimination against minority voters" and that there was a "double standard" in place for complaints from minority voters.

But the history of extensive election monitoring conducted by the Bush Civil Rights Division, which broke all prior records for the number of observers sent to monitor elections, belies that claim. In 2004 alone, when observers were being sent to Noxubee, the division monitored 162 elections in 29 states, with 1,463 federal observers and 533 division personnel. With the exception of the Noxubee mission, *all* of those observers were monitoring elections on behalf of racial, ethnic, and language minorities. The only double standard that existed was the double standard of lawyers like Rich and Kengle, who wanted to ignore voting discrimination and illegal behavior by blacks like Ike Brown.

Critics of the Bush administration bitterly complained about the Noxubee case, asserting that the division's priorities had shifted from so-called "traditional" voting rights enforcement, and that it should not be filing "reverse" discrimination cases. After Joe Rich left the division for the liberal Lawyers' Committee for Civil Rights, he asserted that it was "really a question of priority" for a department with limited resources. Rich said that the division's "core mission is to fight racial discrimination," and he claimed that did not "seem to be happening in this administration."

That claim was false; numerous other cases had been filed by the Bush administration's Voting Section, all on behalf of racial and ethnic minorities that included blacks, Hispanics, Asians, and American Indians. In fact, the Bush administration filed almost the same number of lawsuits under Section 2 of the Voting Rights Act as the Clinton administration. Taking into account all lawsuits the Bush administration filed in enforcing provisions of the Voting Rights Act, the National Voter Registration Act, and two other federal voting rights laws, the Bush administration actually filed twice as many enforcement actions as the prior Clinton administration.

The problem Rich and others had with the Noxubee prosecution was not that it was a matter of limited resources or misplaced priorities. What Rich was mad about, as was the rest of the civil rights community, was that the Voting Rights Act had been enforced against black defendants and black officials on behalf of white voters. They did not believe that the resources of the Justice Department should have been used to stop Ike Brown's outrageous behavior, or to protect the white voters and white candidates whose rights were violated in Noxubee County.

Doubtlessly, many critics of the Justice Department's suit agreed with the defense that Brown raised: that it was "preposterous" for the department to bring such a case in a county where blacks had been "oppressed by the white establishment for 135 years and finally gained the reins of power a mere 12 years ago."[21] This was government persecution of "the victim for fighting back when a crime has been committed against him." In other words, past misdeeds justify current misdeeds, and we should look the other way when black officials discriminate and violate the rights of white voters, no matter how egregious their conduct.

In an atypical verdict, the court ruled that Section 2 of the Voting Rights Act "provides no less protection to white voters than any other class of voters." The VRA was "viewed essentially as a restatement of the Fifteenth Amendment" and the Fifteenth Amendment *"grants protection to all persons, not just members of a particular race."* [22] The "heretics" of the trial team and division leadership were vindicated—the Voting Rights Act applies to all citizens, regardless of race.

Even after the Justice Department won a judgment against Brown, the monumental arrogance and hubris he had displayed throughout his trial continued.

The judgment against Brown was awarded at the end of June 2007. The court held an evidentiary hearing on possible remedies at the end of July, just before the August primary. Although the government wanted a third party appointed to administer the Democratic primary, Brown remained in charge, promising that he would not participate in the absentee ballot process, that challenges would be permitted, that there would be no unsolicited "assistance," and that poll managers would be told to follow Mississippi law.

But according to federal observers who were stationed in Noxubee County during the 2007 primary, most of the same illegal and unlawful practices continued.

Contrary to his promises, Brown had access to the absentee ballots the night before election, chose the poll managers, and once again "interjected himself" into the ballot-counting process. Brown even told one of the federal observers: "I don't care what the court says. I am still primarily responsible for running this election." The federal observers "recorded numerous instances of improper voter assistance," including one where 15 black individuals, who refused to identify themselves, stationed themselves outside a polling place and escorted black voters into the polls, "where they told the voter for whom to vote." Federal observers "tallied as many as 180 instances of such" illegal behavior.[23]

As a result, the court held a second hearing after the primary, in which it appointed former Mississippi Supreme Court Justice Ruben Anderson to carry out the "electoral duties" of administering Democratic Party primaries until 2011. Ironically, it was this kind of defiance by local white officials in the late 1950s and early 1960s that led directly to the passage of the Voting Rights Act in 1965.

Over the years, the state Democratic Party in Mississippi did nothing to stem Brown's illegal and unethical behavior and theft of votes. The district court concluded that "the State Democratic Party was remiss in failing to take action to rectify his abuses."[24] The Justice Department would also have done *nothing* about Brown's blatant discrimination and vote fraud, as it had done nothing for years, if not for a few lawyers, including the Bush political appointees in charge of the division, who were willing to fight the entrenched power of the liberal ideologues who occupy most of the career civil service legal positions within the Civil Rights Division and the Voting Section. It is no wonder that Brown knew he could get away with his illegal behavior in Noxubee—he had been doing so for a long time with the knowledge of the Justice Department, which took no interest whatsoever in curbing his crimes.

Brown appealed the judgment against him to the Fifth Circuit Court of Appeals, but the judgment was upheld. Yet Brown seemingly remained undeterred. An Associated Press article in 2009 described Brown, after his appeal was rejected, as "[s]till defiant. Still cocky. Still unbowed." [25] No criminal case was ever filed against him by the Public Integrity Section of the Criminal Division of the Justice Department, as it should have been. The Obama administration was apparently so embarrassed by the Court of Appeals ruling, made after Obama entered office, that contrary to its regular practice, it did not issue a press release highlighting the victory.

Fifty years ago, during the height of the civil rights movement, the issues involved were literally black and white. Now they are subtler, more nuanced. As both the Noxubee and New Black Panther Party incidents show, not all villains in voting rights cases are white. Vote fraud and discrimination in the election process is an equal-opportunity crime. Voters in Noxubee, both black and white, who supported candidates other than those chosen by Ike Brown's corrupt political machine, had their votes stolen and their voting rights violated.

Reading the decision in the Noxubee case, in which the judge describes the extensive and pervasive wrongdoing by Ike Brown, it is shocking that government lawyers—who are charged with enforcing the law, pursuing justice, and protecting the rights of all Americans—wanted to ignore Brown's perversion of the election process. We need a Justice Department that enforces our voting rights laws, and prosecutes election crimes no matter what the race is of criminal or victim. That is something we don't have today.

☆ ☆ ☆ ☆ ☆ ☆ ☆ ☆ ☆ ☆

CHAPTER ELEVEN

Voter Fraud Cinema Verité

It was the day of Washington, D.C.'s presidential primary, April 3, 2012. A 22-year-old white man with a beard entered a polling place in the District, carrying a hidden camera.

He walked up to the check-in desk and asked a poll worker if an Eric Holder was registered there. He gave U.S. Attorney General Holder's address, which he had gleaned from public records. The worker began to hand him a ballot, at which point the young man said that he wanted to show his identification. "You don't need it," the poll worker replied. "It's all right. As long as you're in here, you're on our list, and that's who you say you are, you're okay." The young man replied, "I would feel more comfortable if I just had my ID. Is it all right if I go get it?" The poll worker agreed. "I'll be back faster than you can say furious," the man joked as he left, a sly reference to the Fast and Furious gunrunning scandal that has bedeviled Attorney General Holder.

The young man was an accomplice of James O'Keefe, the conservative filmmaker whose hidden-camera stings helped bring down ACORN and top NPR management. The young man and his companions twice more pulled off the same stunt, stopping just short of obtaining ballots in the names of NAACP head Benjamin Jealous and David Brock, founder of the liberal group Media Matters for America. Only one attempt failed; when one woman tried to obtain the ballot of Alicia Menendez, a political commentator and daughter of New Jersey Democratic senator Robert Menendez, she was erroneously told she must show an ID to vote in a District of Columbia election. This simple precaution, although not actually in place in the District, prevented voter fraud.

O'Keefe released the polling-place footage on the web, causing quite a stir. After all, Attorney General Holder is a staunch opponent of laws requiring voters to show photo ID at the polls to improve ballot security. He calls them "unnecessary," and has blocked their implementation in Texas and South Carolina under Section 5 of the Voting Rights Act, citing the fear that such requirements would discriminate against minorities. The Justice Department responded with outrage to the O'Keefe video: "It's no coincidence that these so-called examples of rampant voter fraud consistently turn out to be manufactured ones."[1]

Except, of course, that wasn't the point. O'Keefe's activists weren't voting fraudulently; they were showing the public how easy it would be for someone with sinister motives to vote fraudulently. And the Justice Department knew that—it would take a full-on fool not to understand. But the Justice Department has no interest in that point. It is far more interested in ignoring the potential for voter fraud, and blaming the messengers like O'Keefe who point out the absurdity of the department's positions. The ease with which a nonresident can vote illegally in the District of Columbia had already been demonstrated in 2011, when Andi Pringle, the deputy chief of staff to Mayor Vincent Gray, was forced to resign for voting in the District, despite the fact that she was a resident of Maryland.

O'Keefe has struck several times in other states. In New Hampshire, three of his assistants visited precincts during the state's January 2012 presidential primary. They asked poll workers whether their books bore the names of several voters, all deceased individuals still listed on voter registration rolls. Poll workers handed out 10 ballots, never once asking for a photo ID. The ballots were immediately given back, unmarked, to precinct workers.

Debbie Lane, a ballot inspector at one of the Manchester polling sites, later said she had had suspicions about the O'Keefe activist who approached her table, but she handed him a ballot anyway. "I wasn't sure what I was allowed to do. . . . I can't tell someone not to vote, I suppose."[2] The only precinct in which O'Keefe or his crew did not obtain a ballot was one in which the local precinct officer knew the dead voter.

New Hampshire Governor John Lynch, who had vetoed a state photo ID bill, sputtered when asked about O'Keefe's videos, focusing on the messenger, rather than his message—that polls are dangerously vulnerable to fraud. "They should be prosecuted to the fullest extent of the law, if in fact they're found guilty of some criminal act," he roared. But cooler heads in his government quietly issued new guidelines to local election workers on how to better maintain voter records, and the New Hampshire state senate promptly passed another version of the photo-ID law that Lynch had vetoed earlier. No charges have been filed in New Hampshire against any of O'Keefe's accomplices.

In February 2012, O'Keefe sent a crew to Minnesota's presidential caucus, where they asked for voter registration applications in the names of NFL quarterbacks Thomas Bray and Tim Tebow. They were offered applications that could be mailed in with no proof of identification, notarization, or other means of verification. When one investigator asked an election worker, "There would be no way of knowing if someone was misrepresenting themselves on the form, is this correct?" the worker replied: "We're not the police." But election officials should be concerned with the security of the election process—they have an obligation to verify the accuracy of voter registration information.

In neighboring Vermont, O'Keefe struck again in March, during that state's presidential primary. His assistants were freely offered ballots at several locations without being asked to produce identification. In his videos, O'Keefe then documented the same people ordering drinks in bars or trying to rent a hotel room. In each case, they were asked for an ID.

O'Keefe's conclusion was pointed: "Given that a comedian from Minnesota was elected to the United States Senate in 2008 with a margin of 312 votes, and that a much larger number than that consisted of votes from convicted felons who obtained ballots and voted illegally, this is an issue that demands urgent attention."[3] Governor Mark Dayton, a Democrat, has twice vetoed photo-ID bills presented by the Republican legislature. The issue will now go to voters in November 2012 in the form of a state constitutional amendment.

O'Keefe, a 2006 graduate of Rutgers University, first became interested in exploring voter fraud in his native New Jersey, when one of his videos reaped a bizarre self-confession from a top official of the New Jersey Education Association (NJEA), the state's teachers' union. "I helped take down ACORN, but many people already knew they were corrupt. I caused NPR to fire two senior executives, but it was generally known they were liberal and arrogant before my videos," he says. "But no one knew the teachers' union was tied up with voter fraud."

O'Keefe was referring to his infamous *Teachers Unions Gone Wild* videos, filmed at the East Brunswick Hilton during an October 2010 NJEA leadership conference. The tapes, which document union members cursing, discussing involvement in voter fraud, and laughing about how hard it is to fire tenured teachers, were dismissed by an NJEA spokesman as a "complete fabrication."

But New Jersey Governor Chris Christie praised O'Keefe's filmmaking, and said that "nothing on it surprises me." He told a town hall meeting, "If you need an example of what I've been talking about . . . about how the teacher's union leadership is out of touch with the people and out of control—go watch this video."[4]

Employing "citizen journalists" who wore hidden audio and video recording devices, O'Keefe's Project Veritas group captured union members threatening to kick Christie "in his toolbox!" Passaic special education teacher Alissa Ploshnick was caught laughing about how hard it is to get a tenured teacher fired: "Once you get that third year [and get tenure], it's like 'Schwing!'"[5]

But the most disturbing video featured the voice of NJEA associate director Wayne Dibofsky, boasting off-camera about how he cooperated in an attempt to steal a 1997 mayor's race in Jersey City, the state's second biggest municipality.

Jersey City is home of the legendary Democratic political machine founded by Frank ("I am the law") Hague early in the twentieth century. The jailing of Democratic Mayor Gerald McCann on fraud charges in 1992 weakened the local machine, and allowed Bret Schundler, a former finance executive, to win a crowded, 19-candidate special election as a Republican on a reform platform. In 1993, he won a full four-year term, with 69 percent of the vote.

As mayor, Schundler infuriated public employee unions by forcing police officers out from behind their desks and making them walk neighborhood beats. He cut the number of city workers, and pressed for school choice to help turn around Jersey City's dismal schools. For all that and more, the political machine and their public-employee-union allies were out for revenge when he ran for a third term in 1997.

A last-minute mailing by opponents featured Schundler standing near a Confederate flag at a Lincoln Day dinner, and implied he favored racism. Schundler failed to punch back, and won re-election by just five votes over the 50 percent required to avoid a runoff.

But the machine didn't concede. Jerramiah Healy, the Democratic candidate, filed suit, charging election irregularities. Superior Court Judge Arthur D'Italia ruled that there was a seven-vote discrepancy between the votes cast and the number of people who actually showed up to vote. He subtracted all seven from Schundler's total, leaving him two votes shy of a majority, and forcing a runoff. Schundler complained that the judge was a former lawyer for the county executive who runs the local political machine, but did not contest the ruling, and decided instead to take his case to the people.

With a higher turnout than in May, Schundler won a solid 59 percent of the runoff vote, including a near majority in minority neighborhoods. But even though he won, Schundler wondered about reports of massive voting fraud in the initial election. They seemed credible, but no hard evidence had turned up. Until Wayne Dibofsky opened his mouth.

O'Keefe's video from the NJEA event records Dibofsky recounting that he was at the offices of the Jersey City Education Association, coordinating get-out-the-vote efforts for the

1997 mayor's race, when a man arrived and announced that he had two voting machines to deliver. Dibofsky told him the JCEA office was not a voting precinct. The unidentified man winked at him and said, "I don't care; I was told to deliver these machines." When Dibofsky asked more questions, he was told, "It doesn't matter."

The two voting machines, Dibofsky recounted, "were already locked, loaded, and voted," which he said meant they had "vote tallies that were already added," ready to be printed out at the end of the day. "Nobody came through; we weren't a voting location. They came back later on, they took the machines, I called the [city] clerk's office," Dibofsky recounted. "They said, 'Just leave well enough alone.' And I knew that meant, 'Keep quiet.' That was a tough district for a Democrat to win in, and they carried the district with those voting machines. And nobody came in and voted. That's Hudson County."

The machines involved were the century-old Print-O-Matic machines that are now relegated to scrap heaps. But for decades they were popular in Jersey City; votes could easily be "created" by simply loading the machines with bogus vote totals, and then reporting them as actual votes. Robert Byrne, the city clerk in Jersey City at the time, denied that Dibofsky's story could be true, and offered to retire if it could be proven (a safe offer, given the number of intervening years and lapsed statutes of limitations). Dibofsky refused to respond to the media about the video, not even to claim he had been joking or making up stories. The NJEA had no comment on the incident.

Schundler found the facts in Dibofsky's statement "entirely credible." He was disappointed that, even with the passage of time, there was zero media interest in following up on the story. "Everybody knows there is still voter fraud in Jersey City, and it seems to be accepted. When I ran for state senate in the 1990s, we found slam-dunk evidence that voters in the geriatric ward of the

Pollack Hospital had their ballots filled out by people who visited them,"[6] he said. The Schundler campaign passed the matter to the office of New Jersey's attorney general, but no action was ever taken, despite the videotaped confession of voter fraud.

That is in keeping with Jersey City's reputation as the jurisdiction that takes first prize for electoral corruption over the last century. Mayor Frank ("I am the law") Hague's political machine controlled gritty Jersey City from 1917 to 1947. His desk famously had a special drawer that opened from the front, allowing visitors to deposit bribes. On a yearly salary of $8,000, he amassed a fortune of at least $10 million. The Hague machine turned vote fraud into a science, and there is evidence its practitioners still use Jersey City as their laboratory.

In 2007, former Mayor McCann, whom Schundler replaced after McCann was convicted of fraud, ran for the Jersey City school board with the support of public employee unions. He won by a whisker, by only 21 votes. Jenny Garcia, one of the losing candidates, sued him, claiming he hoodwinked "incompetent or otherwise elderly and ill" residents of multiple nursing homes into casting absentee ballots for him.

McCann admitted signing up nursing home residents for ballots, but said he never actually filled any out. But Garcia obtained a sworn statement from a man who witnessed chicanery inside one nursing home—Carl S. Czaplicki Jr. It contended that McCann attempted to get Czaplicki's father to fill out an absentee ballot. When he refused, the statement says, a person McCann later acknowledged was a campaign supporter came to help fill out the ballot. Czaplicki refused again, according to the statement.

McCann said he was furious at being accused of fraud.

"I plan to shoot bullets," he told *The New York Times*.[7] "She shoots at me, I'll shoot right back at her. Except my bullets will be bigger." He went on to say, "Remember, you throw a rock, I'm throwing a boulder. You throw mud, I'll throw a mountain."

During a hearing on the Garcia lawsuit, Judge Maurice J. Gallipoli said that one didn't "need to be a rocket scientist" to conclude something fishy might be afoot, and wondered why McCann was spending so much time looking for votes in nursing homes. "Do you think these people in the nursing homes were fully interested in a school board election?" Judge Gallipoli asked McCann's lawyer, Mark C. Curtis, saying that under normal circumstances, "You have to drag them out to get them to vote." The suit was eventually dropped, but not until credible evidence was submitted that as many as 216 suspect votes had been cast.

In 2010, McCann ran for re-election to the Jersey City school board. His opponents banded together to form "oversight" committees of volunteers to police the election. He was overwhelmingly defeated, and in a not-too-surprising turn of events, the number of ballots cast in nursing homes declined dramatically.

James O'Keefe's innovative work vividly exposes flaws in the security of voter registration and voting processes in many states. The confessions of fraud from union members in Jersey City, captured on film, demonstrate the absolute brazenness of some in their willingness to steal elections. It also shows the unwillingness of prosecutors to pursue vote fraudsters, and the anger displayed by election officials and law enforcement when flaws are exposed. Rather than correct those security breaches, they instead talk about prosecuting the messengers who have alerted them to the flaws.

☆ ☆ ☆ ☆ ☆ ☆ ☆ ☆

CHAPTER TWELVE

America's Military Heroes— the Real Disenfranchised

Misinformed liberals constantly make unsubstantiated claims that certain groups of voters are disenfranchised, and that their votes are "suppressed" by reasonable and common-sense measures such as voter ID requirements or state laws that prohibit felons from voting. But they seemingly have no concern about the one group of voters who really are disenfranchised—members of America's military. Election after election, service members have shockingly low turnout rates, as severe as any minority demographic in our nation's history, including those that resulted in the passage of the Voting Rights Act in 1965 that struck down barriers to voting by black Americans.

While the 2008 presidential election saw record levels of turn-out nationwide, and high levels of voting by many demographics which have not traditionally participated in the election process, the turnout by members of the military and their dependents was dismal. The overall turnout rate of the voting-eligible population was almost 62 percent in 2008, the highest since the 1964 presidential election. In contrast, the estimated military voter turnout rate was approximately 30 percent.[1]

Unfortunately, the 2008 election was not an anomaly. In 2006, only 22 percent of nearly 2.6 million military voters cast ballots, compared to 41 percent of the general voting-age population.[2] The U.S. Election Assistance Commission found that only 16.5 percent of an estimated six million eligible military and overseas civilian voters requested an absentee ballot, and only 5.5 percent of these ballots were returned and counted.[3] Data from 24 states on the 2010 election shows that only 4.6 percent of eligible military voters cast an absentee ballot that was actually counted.

The major reasons for this disenfranchisement are the transitory life of a member of the military, and the delays associated with delivering absentee ballots to remote locations across the world, especially in war zones such as Iraq and Afghanistan. A survey by the Overseas Vote Foundation found that nearly 22 percent of respondents never received their requested absentee ballot for the 2008 presidential election, and 10 percent received them less than seven days before the election.[4]

But another reason for the high disenfranchisement rate is the Pentagon's failure to provide military voters with timely registration and voting assistance, and the Justice Department's failure to properly enforce the 1986 federal law guaranteeing the right of overseas civilians and members of the military to vote by absentee ballot. That law, the Uniformed and Overseas Citizens Absentee Voting Act (UOCAVA), requires the Federal Voting Assistance Program (a Department of Defense program) to administer UOCAVA, and requires the Justice Department to enforce it.

One of the most significant problems with UOCAVA is that it does not specify when states are required to mail absentee ballots to overseas military voters. Every federal agency and nonprofit group examining the issue, including the Election Assistance Commission, had concluded that, to provide enough time for absentee ballots to be returned from overseas, they would need to be sent out at least 45 days before a state's deadline for receiving absentee ballots. Yet nearly one-third of states refused to follow the 45-day standard, and at least 10 states gave military voters less than 35 days to receive, cast, and return their ballots.

In 2009, Congress attempted to solve this problem by amending UOCAVA, as part of the Military and Overseas Voter Empowerment Act, or MOVE Act. The MOVE Act not only requires states to send absentee ballots to military voters at least 45 days before an election, it requires states to provide at least one form of electronic delivery for providing blank absentee ballots and other election materials, such as e-mail, facsimile, or a web-based method. The Pentagon is required to use expedited mail service to ensure that overseas military ballots are returned by Election Day. In a sign of how politics infects almost everything done in Washington, due to pressure from its unions, the U.S. Postal Service was made the exclusive carrier for this expedited mail service, rather than allowing competitive bids from private carriers such as Federal Express or DHL. But because the USPS could not meet the three-day international service guaranteed by most private carriers, the statute gives USPS seven days to return completed ballots to election officials in the United States.

The MOVE Act also requires the Pentagon to create installation voting assistance offices on every military base that, upon approval by the secretary of defense, would become designated voter registration agencies, covered by the National Voter Registration Act. These new offices, much like a state DMV branch or public assistance office, would provide a "one-stop shop" for military voting assistance, and enable higher participation rates among military voters.

But in the 2010 election, a report by the Military Voter Protection Project (MVPP) found that local election officials in at least 14 states and the District of Columbia failed to comply with the 45-day mailing requirement for absentee ballots, affecting more than 65,000 voters. Based on a combined count of military members who voted in person and by absentee ballot, MVPP estimated that the overall military participation rate was 11.6 percent. Since the turnout rate of all voters was 41.6 percent in the 2010 election, this means that military personnel were 3.5 times less likely to vote than other voting-age citizens.

One troubling provision of the MOVE Act allows states to apply for a one-time waiver from the 45-day deadline. Ten states and the District of Columbia applied for a waiver, most of them submitting their applications a little more than three months before the election, and approximately 50 days before the deadline for mailing absentee ballots. The problems created by these late applications were exacerbated when the Defense and Justice Departments delayed decisions on these applications for waivers until the eve of the deadline for sending absentee ballots. Military voters had no idea when they might receive ballots.

New York was one of the states that received a waiver from the 45-day deadline. It then violated the terms of that waiver, sending out ballots even later than the date agreed to by the Department of Defense. Many of New York City's military and overseas ballots, more than 40,000 of them, were sent 25 or fewer days before the election, even though it can take 30 or more days for mail to be delivered to a war zone in Iraq or Afghanistan.

New York was not the only state or local jurisdiction that delayed sending absentee ballots. St. Clair County in Illinois, home to Scott Air Force Base, mailed more than a thousand absentee ballots less than 30 days before the election. When asked about his failure to comply with the MOVE Act, the local election official in St. Claire County openly challenged the law by telling one reporter, "This is not just like sending out your grocery list. . . . I really don't care what the Department of Justice thinks."[5] If it had been directed toward nonmilitary populations, this kind of attitude would raise howls of outrage and cries of "Jim Crow" from leading civil rights organizations.

The MVPP report on the 2010 election details errors by localities and egregious mistakes made by the Justice Department. States were advised they could avoid the need for a waiver by sending a ballot that contained only federal races at least 45 days before the election, even though that meant depriving military voters of their right to vote in state elections. Fortunately, a federal court disagreed with that advice, in a lawsuit filed against the State of Maryland by the MVPP and a Maryland National Guard service member serving in Iraq.

Many of the problems in 2010 could have been avoided, or minimized, if the Justice Department had been willing to enforce the MOVE Act aggressively. From late decisions on states' waiver applications to inexplicable delays in pursuing clear violations of the law, the Justice Department's dilatory actions caused delays that disenfranchised military voters in the 2010 election. As Eric Eversole, the executive director and founder of MVPP, emphasized, "Justice delayed is justice denied. To bring a case a couple of weeks before the election, what is the remedy to getting ballots to troops on the front lines? You can't move the election."

To make matters worse, many of the settlement agreements did not ensure that absentee ballots—especially those being sent to war zones—would arrive before the election, rendering them pointless. These failures were most evident in New York, when more than 40,000 ballots were mailed 25 or fewer days before the election. Rather than requiring the state to send tardy ballots via express mail, the Justice Department agreed to allow New York to use standard mail to deliver absentee ballots to troops. Not surprisingly, nearly one-third of all absentee ballots that were returned by military personnel to New York were rejected by state or local election officials, many because they were either cast after the election or returned after the deadline negotiated by the Justice Department.

The Pentagon also had problems implementing the MOVE Act. In particular, it failed to create the installation voting assistance offices that would be covered by the NVRA. These offices were supposed to provide, on military installations, the same type of voting assistance received by civilians at their local driver's license bureau or public assistance office. Not only would these offices provide voter registration assistance to military voters when they moved to a new duty location (which helps provide up-to-date address information to the states), but they would ensure that any completed registration or absentee-ballot request form was transmitted to the appropriate state or local election official in a timely manner. The creation of these offices was the "capstone" of the MOVE Act; it addresses the problem of chronically low participation rates among military voters.

The Pentagon failed to create most of these offices prior to the election, or to designate them under the NVRA. In fact, the Pentagon waited until two weeks after the November 2010 election to designate these offices as voter registration agencies under the NVRA. Nor is it yet clear whether all offices are fully operational. A March 2011 letter to Congress, from the Under Secretary of Defense for Personnel and Readiness, indicated that several military branches were still in the process of creating such offices.[6] In any event, the continuing low enfranchisement rate leaves no doubt that military voters did not benefit from these voter registration offices in 2010.

Worse yet, the Pentagon appears to be "cooking the books" on military voter participation as a basis for not complying with the MOVE Act. In 2011, it released a survey in which it claimed a remarkable 21 percent increase in military voter participation— notwithstanding the fact that it had failed to create installation voting assistance offices.[7] The survey was in sharp contrast to data and reports from nonpartisan groups and the U.S. Election Assistance Commission. Unlike the EAC, which relies on data from actual absentee ballots sent and received by state officials, the Pentagon reached its conclusions based on survey responses from 15,037 military members and their spouses, out of more than 123,376 surveys sent.

The low response rate is a red flag about the credibility of the report—a fact that the Government Accountability Office has repeatedly emphasized to the Pentagon. In 2010, the GAO criticized the Pentagon's reporting methodology because it "does not conduct a nonresponse bias analysis" that the Office of Management and Budget has said is "a necessary step in determining whether survey findings are biased. Not conducting such an analysis limits data reliability." The report was aptly named "DOD Can Strengthen Evaluation of Its Absentee Voting Assistance Program."

Nor did the survey respondents accurately reflect the overall military population. Twenty-five percent of the surveys were completed by senior officers and their spouses, even though they represent only 12 percent of the actual military population, thus giving a biased and skewed view of the voting experiences of the military. There were very low response rates from combat troops, who have the greatest difficulties in voting. Tellingly, the response rates from members of the United States Navy, Air Force, and Coast Guard were nearly 70 percent higher than the response rates from those serving in the Army and Marine Corps. Yet army and marine corps personnel make up more than half of the armed forces.

Whether a member of the military is in the field, on the front lines in Afghanistan, or sitting at a desk in the Pentagon can have a significant effect on his ability to receive, vote, and return an absentee ballot. Yet the Pentagon report didn't appear to account for this critical difference, or many others. It painted a far rosier picture than actual reality.

The difficulties members of the armed forces have with voting, especially during periods of prolonged conflict, have always existed. From the Civil War to World War II to America's conflicts in Iraq and Afghanistan, the logistical challenges associated with delivering absentee ballots to a war zone have been significant and undeniable. But they are not insurmountable. Both the federal and state governments have an absolute obligation to do everything they can to address the shortcomings in the current system, and ensure a complete commitment to promoting and protecting the voting rights of service members.

☆ ☆ ☆ ☆ ☆ ☆ ☆ ☆

CHAPTER THIRTEEN

What Is to Be Done?

Catherine Englebrecht was a mother and small-business owner in Houston, Texas until what she saw in the summer of 2010 turned her into a "mama grizzly" crusader against voter fraud, and the leader of a growing nationwide movement to improve the integrity of American elections.

That summer, a group called Houston Votes and its parent organization, Texans Together Education Fund, a teacher union subsidiary, made headlines by declaring their intention to register 100,000 new voters in Harris County (which includes Houston) before the November election.

"The folks I talked to who worked the polling places as volunteers became concerned," she recalled. "If they could register that many citizens legally and accurately, great; but if not, then our registry was at great risk of being overwhelmed with fraudulent registrations." Nor was this the first time her contacts at the polling places would have seen suspicious behavior. "Flooding the rolls with suspect registrations had already been tried in 2008 in Houston. Those suspect registrations had bad results on Election Day. No one had checked IDs, election judges voted for people who asked for help, and oversight was pathetic."[1]

Englebrecht and a few allies in a Tea Party group called the King Street Patriots began submitting open-records requests to Harris County, asking for publicly available information for all 1.9 million registered voters, including copies of applications that had been completed inaccurately or incompletely. Their review didn't single out any particular group at first, but then it became clear that Houston Votes had far and away the worst record of any in submitting unacceptable applications. "We started to look at houses with more than six voters in them," Englebrecht said. "We came across one voting district with more than 24,000 such homes, and that's where we found things like an eight-bed halfway house with 40 people registered."

Using hundreds of volunteers and resources like Google Earth, King Street Patriots spinoff group True the Vote cross-referenced voter registration information with other public records to determine whether registered addresses were truly residences, and matched driver's license information. They even paid visits to some addresses, vetting 3,800 voter registrations. But they also found hundreds of problems, including multiple active registrations for a single voter, voters whose registered addresses were vacant lots, voters registered at business addresses, and active registrations of deceased voters.

The King Street Patriots presented its findings to Harris County officials, and asked that they undertake a comprehensive audit of applications collected by Houston Votes. The county chose to review a sampling of 25,640 registrations. What it found was stunning. Only 7,193 were deemed legal, and able to be added to the voting rolls. The rest were put aside, listed as "problematic." These included registration forms from 1,597 people who applied to vote at least twice, 235 who were underage, 25 from people who said they were noncitizens, and 1,014 from people who were already voters.[2] Many of the rest were set aside because the information in their applications did not match their driver's license or Social Security numbers.

Harris County tax assessor–collector Leo Vasquez, who oversaw the county clerk's election office, accused Houston Votes of submitting thousands of bogus voter registration applications, in what he said appeared to be a campaign to taint the voter rolls.

"The integrity of the voter roll of Harris County, the second largest county in the country with 1.9 million people, appears to be under an organized and systematic attack by the group operating under the name Houston Votes," Vasquez told a news conference in August 2010.[3] He announced he was disqualifying 200 deputy voter registrars his office had appointed, almost all of them linked to Houston Votes. "There is no excuse for this," he told a news conference, noting that other groups, such as the League of Women Voters, had a 99 percent success rate with their applications.

Texans Together president Fred Lewis accused Vasquez of attempting to suppress voter registration. He said that when the irregularities in registration applications had been brought to his attention, he had fired employees, and put in more controls. Lewis rationalized that duplicates easily occur, because people sometimes are not sure whether they are registered, or cannot remember if they have registered since they last moved. "He is a disgraceful liar," Lewis said of Vasquez. "We need to have the Justice Department come in and see what Mickey Mouse stuff he and his office are doing to suppress people."[4]

But problems continued to mount for Houston Votes. Sean Caddie, its project director and a former official of the Service Employee International Union, soon had to admit to serious problems in its management structure. He acknowledged that several of its canvassers had submitted fraudulent applications, including some with addresses that corresponded to vacant lots, some from fictitious people, and some from people who had been signed up without their permission.

The number of voter registrations submitted by Houston Votes dropped from a thousand a day to approximately fifty a day after Vasquez's news conference. Mysteriously, only three days after the news conference, a warehouse containing the county's election equipment burned to the ground, at a loss of $40 million. No direct evidence of arson has been uncovered.[5]

As Election Day neared, the controversy escalated. A week after early voting began in October, volunteer poll watchers were being verbally and physically harassed by loiterers at polling places.

Houston representative Sheila Jackson Lee was seen inside a polling place engaged in illegal electioneering; upon being challenged, she threatened to turn a poll watcher's name over to the Department of Justice for voter intimidation. Other poll watchers filed written descriptions of election judges and clerks attempting to influence citizens' votes, telling them to vote a straight Democratic ballot, shadowing voters as they cast ballots, pushing "assistance" on voters and casting their ballots for them regardless of the voter's intent, and even casting votes for people who did not know for whom they wanted to vote.[6]

Once it became clear that the King Street Patriots wasn't backing down, its opponents switched tactics. The state's Democratic Party sued it for defamation. In a clear attempt to intimidate, a group called Texans for Public Justice filed an ethics complaint against the group with the Texas Ethics Commission.

"As a matter of law, corporations cannot sue individuals for defamation; this attack is baseless," said Kelly Shackelford, the president of the public-interest law firm Liberty Institute, which represents Catherine Engelbrecht and King Street Patriots. "All these attacks are clearly an attempt to bully and silence a group of volunteer citizens who are just trying to keep the election process honest."[7] Shackelford noted that in pretrial discovery, it was revealed that both Texans for Public Justice and Texans Together have received more than $100,000 in contributions from the Open Society Institute, of which liberal supporter George Soros is founder and chairman.

Almost two years after the King Street Patriots uncovered the scandal, the lawsuits and ethics complaints were still grinding through the courts, but Catherine Englebrecht said her group was unbowed and undeterred, and she was confident of victory. The King Street Patriots had spun off a separate group called True the Vote, which is organizing volunteers in 30 states to help police the 2012 election and verify the accuracy of voter registration lists—an obvious need, given the findings of a Pew Report on the millions of ineligible individuals registered across the country.

"There is enormous money behind people who seem not to care if our election laws are enforced—especially from public employee union groups such as Texans Together," Englebrecht said. "It's one thing for them to take taxpayer money and contribute it to politicians they want to have elected, but for them to then take yet more of our money, combine that with George Soros money, and try to fraudulently register people to vote just adds insult to injury."[8]

Englebrecht's True the Vote group held its annual summit meeting in Houston in April 2012, where she hosted more than 300 leaders of True the Vote chapters. Their priorities: to watch the polls, monitor absentee ballots, and clean up existing voter registration lists, a model for all citizens who want to help improve the integrity of our election process.

But longer-term reforms still must be enacted to address the chaos, incompetence, and outright fraud that menace our election system. The leaders in any society are unlikely to change their habits, or the rules they lay down for others, unless pressured to do so by the governed. If corruption exists, it is in part because we the people permit it, either by silence, by inattention, or by misunderstanding. If persistent vote fraud and outdated election procedures are to be remedied, the public and the media will have to demand it. Ignoring, or refusing to recognize, the enduring problems of election fraud and mismanagement that plague many parts of our country will ensure that they spread, mutate, and grow more toxic.

The United States has one of the most decentralized systems of administration for its national elections of any country. We don't have a central government agency charged with overseeing the process. This is in accordance with the Constitution, which reserves for the states the exclusive authority for most election decisions, including voter qualifications; Congress may alter only "the Times, Place and Manner of holding Elections" for Congress.

State legislators and local officials can take several steps to safeguard America's elections and improve the integrity of the process. While there are some steps that only Congress and the federal government can take, here are some improvements to voter registration and voting procedures that states can—and should—implement.

A QUESTION OF IDENTITY—REQUIRING VOTER ID

The most often discussed proposal to limit fraud and irregularities at the polls is a requirement that all voters show a photo ID before voting, much as they now do when they take an airline flight, donate blood, fill a prescription, buy an Amtrak ticket, cash a check, rent a video, or check into a hotel.

The vast majority of eligible voters already have such identification. During litigation objecting to Indiana's and Georgia's voter ID laws, plaintiffs were unable to produce a single individual who would be unable to vote because of the identification requirements. A survey by Robert Pastor of American University found that across three states—Mississippi, Maryland, and Indiana—less than one percent of all voters did not have the required ID, and the number was even smaller (0.3 percent) in Indiana, the state with the strictest ID rules.[9] Indiana's law has been upheld by six justices of the U.S. Supreme Court. In Georgia, in an election with exceptionally high turnout, only 0.23 percent of more than five million registered voters obtained a free voter ID from the state for the 2008 presidential election after Georgia's voter ID law became effective in 2007. In most years, Georgia has issued fewer than three thousand IDs to registered voters. It is clear that upwards of 99 percent of the state's registered voters already have a government-issued photo ID.

Poll after poll shows that the concept of voter identification is popular, and easily understood by the American people. Yet it is one of the most bitterly fought reforms. Opposition has often reached comical levels—but voter identification is a basic requirement for secure elections, and should be implemented in all states.

CITIZEN CHECK—MAKING SURE
ALL VOTERS ARE AMERICANS

Individuals who are not U.S. citizens can easily register and vote without detection.

Federal law and all fifty states provide that only U.S. citizens may vote in federal and state elections; a few local jurisdictions may allow noncitizens to vote in local elections. States have an interest in preventing dilution of the votes of their citizens at the state level, and must maintain citizen-only voting rolls for federal elections. All states should require that anyone who registers to vote provide proof of U.S. citizenship. Only three states have so far mandated this: Arizona, in 2004, through the initiative process; and Georgia and Kansas, in 2009 and 2011, via legislation.

Congress and state legislatures should require all federal and state courts to notify local election officials when individuals summoned for jury duty from voter registration rolls are excused because they are not United States citizens. U.S. Attorneys are already under a similar obligation: Under the NVRA, they must notify local election officials of felony convictions so that the felons can be removed from voter registration rolls.[10]

The Department of Homeland Security should comply with federal law, and confirm the citizenship status of registered voters when it receives requests for such information from state and local election officials. If the federal agency declines to do so, states should demand that it be investigated by Congress and the Inspector General of the DHS for its failure to follow the law.

American employers use a government database known as E-Verify to check the citizenship status of prospective employees. It should be utilized by state election officials and administrators to verify citizenship when individuals register to vote. States should not allow an individual to register when he or she has not answered the citizenship question, required by HAVA, on the voter registration form. Citizens should demand that local district attorneys treat registration and voting by a noncitizen as a serious offense against the basic principles of our democratic system.

State DMVs must train their employees to prevent noncitizens who apply for driver's licenses from registering to vote. All states should implement legislation requiring that a license clearly indicate when it is issued to a noncitizen—this will prevent it from being used as a photo ID for voting or other purposes.

A voter registration card should not be accepted as a valid identifying document for obtaining a driver's license, unless states have implemented proof-of-citizenship requirements for voter registration.

PREVENTING ABSENTEE-BALLOT FRAUD

To reverse the trends of "no-fault" absentee voting and all-mail elections, absentee ballots should be reserved for individuals who cannot vote in person at their assigned polling place on Election Day, or at early-voting sites prior to the election. Absentee ballots are appropriate for individuals who are too ill or disabled to vote in person, as well as those who have legitimate reasons why they cannot vote in person (such as soldiers stationed overseas); they should not be available just for convenience's sake, because the risk of fraud is too high.

Many states have early-voting statutes that allow in-person voting at government-run polling places for a certain amount of time prior to Election Day. From a standpoint of election integrity, early voting is a much safer alternative to expanded absentee balloting, although it does make campaigns more expensive, and makes it harder for candidates and political parties to observe election procedures with poll watchers.

To increase the difficulty of fraudulent voting with absentee ballots, individuals should be required to provide a copy of an identification document containing a photograph (e.g., a driver's license) when submitting an absentee ballot, or provide their driver's license number, as is now required by Kansas. While it is relatively easy to forge a voter's signature on an absentee ballot, it is more difficult for a conspirator to provide a photocopy of the voter's identification or obtain their driver's license number.

To deter the forgery of voter signatures, the signatures on absentee ballots should be either notarized, or witnessed by at least two individuals who provide their addresses and telephone numbers; any single individual should be allowed to witness only a limited number of signatures. For most jurisdictions, though, signature verification should be a last resort, because it is too difficult for untrained clerks to perform. In many jurisdictions, election officials—overwhelmed by the sheer number of absentee ballots—do not even attempt signature verification. Nonetheless, these steps would make forgery both more difficult, and easier to detect in any post-election law-enforcement investigations.

To help detect fraud, states with "no-fault" or relaxed absentee ballot rules should require voters wishing to cast mail-in ballots to provide a sample of their signature at least every five years. This would ensure that election officials have an up-to-date specimen of the voter's signature for comparison with an absentee ballot affidavit's signature.

To prevent intimidation and fraud, unrelated third parties, including campaign workers and candidates, should be prohibited from delivering or collecting absentee ballots. State laws should allow only voters, their immediate family members, or their caregivers to deliver absentee ballots, whether to the post office or directly to election officials.

MAKING SURE VOTER REGISTRATION DATABASES CONTAIN REAL DATA

State and local election officials should verify the accuracy of new voter registrations by comparing them to other available federal and state databases.

The Help America Vote Act requires states to coordinate their voter registration lists with "other agency databases," and to "verify the accuracy of the information provided on applications for voter registration." However, some election officials are not complying with the federal law, and are not verifying new voter registration information against available databases (such as DMV and Social Security Administration records), or are not investigating discrepancies when such comparisons are made. During the 2008 election, for example, the Ohio secretary of state refused to investigate the accuracy of 200,000 new voter registration applications whose information did not match information in other state databases. Although it is the duty of the Justice Department to enforce compliance with this HAVA requirement, it refused to do so in Ohio, and is unlikely to do so in the future, due to the views of both the department's current leadership and its liberal career lawyers. Only by implementing database verification as state law can legislators ensure that their state's officials will follow this common-sense electoral requirement.

States would also be well advised to use available commercial databases and web tools such as Google Earth to check the accuracy of voter registration information. There is nothing like a satellite photograph of a vacant lot to show that someone has filed a false address when registering. Property tax records should also be utilized to verify that registered addresses exist and are residential properties, not commercial establishments.

We should also prevent future ACORNs. All third-party voter registration groups should be required to put the name of the group and the person handling each new registration on each voter registration form, and return forms to election officials in a specified period of time after collection. These measures will allow election officials to identify which organization and individual handled forms that are found to be incomplete or fraudulent, and ensure that completed registration forms are provided to election officials on a timely basis so they may be properly processed before the state's pre-election registration deadline.

STATE COMPACTS—KEEPING THE LISTS CLEAN

States should enter into agreements with other states to compare voter registration lists so as to expose voters who are registered in more than one state. Numerous reports comparing voter registration lists among different states show thousands of individuals registered in multiple states, especially in Florida, Arizona, and other snowbird havens. The *New York Daily News* found that in 2004, some 46,000 New Yorkers were registered to vote in both New York City and in Florida, and that between 400 and 1,000 registered voters have voted twice in at least one election.[11] As everyone knows, Florida was won by George W. Bush in 2000 by only 537 votes out of some six million cast.

Because there is no national voter registration list, it is relatively easy to register in more than one state without detection. Regional agreements would be a good start in the detection (and deterrence) of double registration and possible double-voting.

HONORING OUR TROOPS

The long transit times for overseas mail and the difficulty of voting from combat zones has led to the disenfranchisement of many military personnel, particularly those in Afghanistan and Iraq. Most states did not mail absentee ballots to service members in time for them to be received and returned.[12]

In October 2009, Congress passed the most comprehensive military voting reform of the last twenty years. This legislation, known as the Military and Overseas Voter Empowerment Act (MOVE Act), promised to revolutionize the military voting process by increasing the use of technology, removing unnecessary obstacles to absentee voting, and providing greater opportunities to register and request an absentee ballot.

But the MOVE Act's promise was not fully realized, and in the 2010 election, many military voters were again disenfranchised.

Evidence from that election is that the current administration failed to implement and enforce the law—a failure that had an undeniable impact on military voters' ability to cast a ballot. And too many states failed to fully comply with the law, particularly the requirement that absentee ballots be sent out at least 45 days prior to an election.

We must address the shortcomings displayed in the 2010 election, and ensure a top-down commitment from the executive branch to promote and protect U.S. service members' voting rights. At a time when members of America's military are in harm's way in remote parts of the world, this nation should spare no expense or effort in making sure that the MOVE Act's promise is realized.

SAME-DAY REGISTRATION

A contentious proposal for reform of the election system—which is not reform at all, but an added opportunity for mischief—comes from those who believe it is vitally important to make sure as many people as possible vote. The "reform"? Same-day voter registration, which would allow new voters to register on Election Day, at the polls. It is now used in Wisconsin, Minnesota, and four smaller states.

In 2002, two liberal millionaires put the idea on state ballots in California and Colorado. They argued that registration deadlines of 15 days before Election Day in California and 30 days in Colorado prevented some people from voting. The proposals would have allowed anyone to show up at the polls, present a driver's license or some other document bearing a name and address, register on the spot, and vote.

State and local election officials generally were opposed. Colorado's former secretary of state, Donetta Davidson, said the program would prevent counties from checking for fraudulent registrations, and would require her to train thousands of poll workers to handle new computer equipment.[13] In California, Connie McCormack, then the voter registrar of Los Angeles County, warned that "Elections are in danger of collapsing under the weight of their own complexity."

Other registrars opposed Proposition 52, as the same-day registration idea was identified, because it would not require the use of provisional ballots (which require later verification of identity) by those who register at the polls, as current law does. If the initiative had passed, voters who registered on Election Day would have had their ballots mixed in with everyone else's. If investigators later proved there was fraud, there would be no way to know who was responsible. An aide to Bill Jones, California's secretary of state at the time, warned that under Proposition 52, busloads of people could "move into" a close, targeted district for a day, vote, then leave town, without technically breaking the law.

Mary Kiffmeyer, former Minnesota secretary of state, said she is tired of hearing her state's same-day registration extolled. She compared it to holding a party and not knowing how much food to buy because no one sent an RSVP—some precincts run out of ballots, while others are overstocked. "We have long lines because of same-day," she said. "People get frustrated and leave."[14]

The states that have tried same-day registration are mostly small, with stable populations and long traditions of good government. Even so, problems crop up. In 1986, Oregon voters overwhelmingly scrapped the idea after a cult that wanted to take over a town government tried to register hundreds of supporters on Election Day. In 2000, a New York socialite working for Al Gore scandalized Wisconsin when a television camera caught her bribing street vagrants with packs of cigarettes in return for voting (she pleaded guilty to fraud). At Marquette University in Milwaukee, 174 students boasted that they had voted more than once. They quickly changed their stories when prosecutors pointed out that voting twice is a crime. Also that year, the Postal

Service returned at least 3,500 Election Day registration confirmations as undeliverable in Wisconsin—meaning that thousands of people had registered to vote, and probably cast ballots, with an unverifiable address. For what it's worth, Al Gore won Wisconsin by 5,700 votes.

Even some supporters of same-day registration in smaller states quail when asked about its use in America's most populous state. Curtis Gans, director of the Committee for the Study of the American Electorate, says the risk of fraud in California is too great to consider it. "It's not beyond the imagination that one party or another will register aliens on the last day," he said. "And there's no protection against that except criminal penalties, which have not been effective."

Proponents of same-day voter registration spent millions in both California and Colorado promoting their initiative. But liberal newspapers shrank from the idea, with the *San Francisco Chronicle*, the *Los Angeles Times* and *The Denver Post* all editorializing against it. Even California's liberal governor, Gray Davis, opposed the idea. "His view is that voters who go to the polls ought to have a minimum amount of information about what they are voting on," explained Davis aide Garry South.[15] Same-day registration failed to pass in California, at 59 to 41 percent against, trailing in 45 out of 53 congressional districts. In Colorado, it garnered less than 40 percent, losing even liberal strongholds such as Denver and Boulder.

That said, states that already have same-day registration are often resistant to changing it. In Maine, a Republican legislature passed a law in 2011 preventing people from registering, and then voting, less than two business days before an election. Legislators cited studies that in three of the previous 10 elections, there were more registered voters than voting-age Maine citizens. There were also concerns that 1,452 active registrations were listed as being more than 200 years old, and another 2,200 active registrants had no street address. Nonetheless, proponents led by state Democrats were able to place a "people's veto" referendum on the 2011 ballot, overturning the legislature's action and restoring same-day registration by a 60-to-40 percent margin.

"I wasn't surprised that they won. There was more energy on the 'yes' side; they had a clearer goal in mind," said Jim Melcher, a political scientist at the University of Maine at Farmington. "But I think the vote was less a show of support for the Maine Democratic Party than it was Mainers voting to keep something that they are comfortable with."[16]

At least one state—Connecticut—is moving towards same-day registration. Democratic governor Dan Malloy championed the move, saying his state is "going in a very different direction than 32 other states" across the country that have recently tightened election laws. Connecticut's same-day registration will take effect in 2013, and will allow people to register with as little proof as a utility bill, with proof due no more than 30 days after an election. "There is no verification," warned state representative Tony Hwang, saying that if someone wants the right to vote immediately, better identification verification should be required. "My parents left China as teenagers to escape the tyranny of Communism," he told fellow legislators. "I treasure the opportunities this country offers, and the sanctity of our liberties and freedoms. These should be guaranteed by the power and truth of our votes on Election Day."[17]

Despite many good intentions, same-day registration is a gimmick, dreamed up by people who say they want to boost voter turnout. We've been down this road before. Motor Voter laws allow people to register to vote at the Department of Motor Vehicles and public welfare assistance offices. Liberal absentee voter laws let people cast ballots while on vacation, or from remote locations. And some states allow for early voting, before

Election Day. All these provisions have failed to increase voter turnout. It's about time that someone stepped forward and admitted that the root cause of low turnout isn't restrictive voting laws, but voter apathy. People are fed up with mediocre candidates, gerrymandered districts, and uncompetitive (and possibly illegitimate) elections.

In 2008, the Census Bureau reported that a survey of eligible, nonregistered individuals found that the largest percentage (46 percent) were "[n]ot interested in the election/not involved in politics." Only 4.2 percent reported that they "[d]id not know where or how to register," and only six percent said they had registration problems. Other reported reasons for not participating in the election ranged from not being interested (13.4 percent) to not liking the candidates or campaign issues (12.9 percent). The biggest reason cited was "too busy" (17.5 percent).

VANISHING VOLUNTEERS

America has a vanishing corps of Election Day poll workers, as older workers retire or die, and it becomes ever more difficult to convince younger generations to take on a job that involves 14-hour days without a break, and pays between $65 and $150 for the whole day. The complexity of election laws has made the job increasingly stressful, and holds the possibility of verbal or other abuse from angry voters.

There is also the possibility of election workers being sent on wild-goose chases. Carol Anne Coryell, a member of the election board of Fairfax County, Virginia, recalled that during one election she constantly received unfounded complaints from Democratic lawyers about voters being disenfranchised. "It got to the point where I would almost call it harassment," she said. "I checked with both the Democratic and Republican election official at every precinct where there were reports of people not being able to vote, denied the right to vote, and even people having to recite their Social Security number in public. None, I mean none, checked out. They took me away from real problems I should have dealt with."

"The lack of poll workers is a huge problem across the nation, and it's only going to get worse if states and counties don't act quickly," said Kay Albowicz of the National Association of Secretaries of State. "When the current crop gets to where they can't stand the long days, there's probably not going to be very many people to replace them."

Most of the election officials we spoke with estimated that the average age of their poll workers was the late 60s to early 70s. But with the increasing importance of technology in the election process, there is a greater need than ever for the technical talents of young people. Some efforts are underway that would turn college students and graduating high-school seniors into poll workers. The Help America Vote Foundation is working with states to change laws that require poll workers to be over 18, and registered voters. Their hope is that young people who work at the polls as an understudy to an older poll worker may become engaged enough to want to help out after they leave school.

Students could volunteer in other ways, too. The technologically savvy could explain voting machines to those who need an explanation. They could help new and elderly voters understand the process. They could assist disabled voters who need help getting to the polling place. Some could even serve as translators.

Compounding the challenge of involving young people in the election process is the sad fact that in many schools, civics is no longer part of the curriculum. In his farewell address as he left the presidency in 1989, Ronald Reagan warned of the consequences of not educating Americans in their history. "If we forget what we did, we won't know who we are," he said. "I am warning of an eradication of the American memory that could result, ultimately, in an erosion of the American spirit. Let's start with some basics: more attention to American history and a greater emphasis on civic ritual."

Few would argue that since 1989 we have paid enough attention to Reagan's warning. We may be paying part of the price for that neglect every election cycle, when it becomes harder and harder to find enough poll workers. A shorthanded election process will eventually become a process that shortchanges the people.

"EASIER TO VOTE, HARDER TO STEAL"— CLARIFY PROVISIONAL BALLOTS

When Congress passed the Help America Vote Act in 2002, its lead Democratic sponsor, Senator Chris Dodd of Connecticut, praised it for "making it easier to vote and harder to steal." But clearly HAVA is a first step. "Progress has been inadequate," said Robert Pastor, former executive director of the Commission on Federal Election Reform, the panel co-chaired by Jimmy Carter and James Baker in 2005 to address election issues left unresolved by HAVA.[18]

HAVA's most important reforms require that states meet two "minimum standards" in conducting their elections. One standard mandates that states set up a centralized, statewide voter registration list, to avoid duplications and limit how often a flawed voter list prevents someone from voting.

The other generally positive reform in HAVA is a requirement that every voter in every state be allowed to cast a "provisional" ballot if he or she shows up at a precinct and finds that his or her name is not on the registration list. For example, someone may have registered at a state Department of Motor Vehicles office while renewing a driver's license, but the DMV may not have properly forward the registration application to election officials.

If the authorities determine, after the polls close, that the voter was eligible and had attempted to register, the vote counts. The way the system works now, provisional ballots are held until the polling place is closed on Election Day, and then forwarded to the local election official or board of elections for a determination of whether the individual was really registered, and eligible to vote. Once election officials have decided whether the provisional ballot should be counted, the voter can ascertain, via a toll-free telephone number or website, whether his vote was counted, and if not, the reasons why.

HAVA also requires that any person who votes after the established time for polls to close, due to a court order or other administrative decision to extend polling hours, must use a provisional ballot; those ballots must be kept separate from all other provisional ballots. Thus, if there is a challenge to the extension of polling deadlines, the extra ballots have not disappeared into the anonymity of the ballot box, and can be "uncounted." This actually occurred in St. Louis in 2000, when lawyers for the Democratic Party were able to obtain an order that extended polling hours, based on the claim that there were long lines at polling places. But that ruling was later overturned as invalid, because the named plaintiff in the suit had actually been dead since 1999. Thousands of illegal extra votes were cast—and counted.

Provisional voting can be a real safety net for a victim of a bureaucratic mistake by a local election board, something that happens all too frequently. It alleviates the time that election judges spend during polling hours investigating why someone isn't listed on the rolls. But provisional voting raises some serious concerns, since ordinary safeguards against fraud do not apply. Normally, individuals must be on the voter registration list in order to cast a ballot. Allowing unverified registrants the ability to vote must be accompanied by safeguards ensuring that authorities count only legal votes. Because the federal rules on implementing provisional ballots are general, it has been left up to each state to issue detailed procedures on how to handle them. For that and other reasons, provisional ballots remain one of the most likely issues to spur lawsuits in the next election.

Indeed, thorny legal issues have already cropped up. In 2002, Congress mandated that a provisional ballot must be given to any individual whose name is not on the list of registered voters (or whose right to vote is challenged) if he "declares that such individual is a registered voter in the jurisdiction in which the individual desires to vote." But Congress's use of the word "jurisdiction," without defining it, led quickly to lawsuits trying to overturn the tradition of precinct-based voting and allow voters to cast ballots anywhere in a state.

Organizations ranging from the now-defunct ACORN to the NAACP have claimed that the word "jurisdiction," as used in the HAVA section on provisional ballots, has a much wider meaning than the local precinct where an individual is assigned to vote based on residence. In essence, they claim that Congress had preempted the tradition of precinct-based voting, and that states were required to count provisional ballots that were cast outside the voter's precinct. Thirty states and the District of Columbia require that, to be counted, provisional ballots be cast in the correct *precinct*, while 15 states will count a provisional ballot cast in the correct *jurisdiction*, such as a municipality, county, or state—but in an "incorrect" precinct.

Luckily, the courts have decided in favor of the traditional view, that ballots must be cast in the precinct where the voter lives. The U.S. Court of Appeals for the Sixth Circuit has held that there is no evidence in the statute, or in the legislative history of HAVA, that Congress intended to override the historic tradition of precinct-based voting.

Although HAVA requires states to provide a provisional ballot to an individual trying to vote outside his assigned precinct, states do not have to count that provisional ballot. Litigation against this leads one to speculate on whether the people filing lawsuits really believe that voters are so ill informed that they do not know which precinct they live in, or where they are supposed to vote—information that is contained on every voter's registration card, and on sample ballots mailed before elections. One could, of course, speculate on a more sinister motive, since the Sixth Circuit pointed out that one of the main reasons behind traditional precinct-based voting is that "it makes it easier for election officials to monitor votes and prevent election fraud."

All this means that provisional ballots could become the equivalent of Florida's chads and the infamous punch-card ballots in a future, close presidential race.

During the aftermath of the 2000 presidential election, both political parties and presidential campaigns sent thousands of volunteers and lawyers to Florida to observe the recounting of those punch-card ballots, and to argue and litigate over every ballot as to whether it should count as a vote for their respective candidates. Only about one-third of the country used punch-card ballots in 2000, but HAVA has now ensured that the entire country must use provisional ballots.

A tug of war over provisional ballots may be inevitable in key states where the margin of victory is no greater than the number of provisional ballots cast. Both campaigns would once again send squadrons of lawyers to any closely contested state, to watch and argue as every single provisional ballot in every election jurisdiction in the state is reviewed, and a determination is made by local election officials as to whether it should be counted. Results could once again be delayed for weeks, if not months, after Election Day.

How likely is this to happen? In 2002, there was a 35-day delay in determining the winner of Colorado's Seventh Congressional District, when Republican Bob Beauprez led Democrat Mike Feeley by only 386 votes. But there were 3,800 outstanding provisional ballots to be examined, and each of the three counties in the district had different rules on which ballots should be tossed out, and which ones should be counted.

One county used a provisional ballot that didn't comply with the one provided by the Colorado secretary of state's office. Matters weren't helped when the secretary of state issued six different rule interpretations to the counties on how they should count the ballots. One on November 7 from Bill Compton, director of Colorado's elections division, created more panic than clarity among county election officials. It read:

> We need each of you to read between the lines on the memo regarding provisional ballots. . . . Please remember, SUBSTANTIAL COMPLIANCE is all that is necessary for the conduct of elections under Title One (of the Civil Rights Act). Please use your common sense and best judgment in this process.

Such rule-shifting directives didn't help matters, or inspire confidence in the overall count. The resulting chaos took weeks to resolve. In the end, Beauprez was declared the winner by 121 votes.

In 2008, it took the New Mexico Democratic Party almost 10 days to determine the winner of its presidential primary, because Senator Hillary Clinton's margin of victory was smaller than the number of provisional ballots that had been cast in the race. Out of a total of 149,779 votes cast in the primary, Clinton won by only 1,709 votes, receiving 4,215 provisional ballots to Barack Obama's 3,935. In this election, the campaigns and the Democratic Party had agreed ahead of time on what the rules would be for the counting of provisional ballots—but that is not likely to happen in a combative contest between two presidential campaigns of opposing parties.

Imagine the litigation—similar to the "equal protection" claims raised in the *Bush v. Gore* decision before the Supreme Court—over the different rules that states (or even different counties within states) apply to determine whether a provisional ballot is counted. Claims could be made over how much investigation a local election official must do to determine whether an individual voter's registration paperwork was somehow lost or otherwise not forwarded to election officials by another government agency like the DMV, or even a third-party organization like ACORN that may have conducted a voter registration drive. The fights and legal maneuvering over the counting of provisional ballots in a future election could make the chad fight in Florida in 2000 look like a mere dress rehearsal for a legal meltdown—in several states at the same time.

It doesn't take a visionary to see that, in the absence of clear rules, we can expect campaign lawyers to attempt to turn the most implausible legal theory into a court ruling in their favor. Vague rules on provisional voting could create a nightmare in which the results of a presidential race aren't known for days. Recall the 35 days it took Colorado officials to decide just one congressional race.

ABSENT RULES, ENTER CHAOS

State officials such as secretaries of state should be granted investigative subpoena powers to look into both vote fraud and disenfranchisement issues. Historically, election officials have relied too heavily on candidates to identify election problems. Most election boards do not have the authority to conduct vigorous investigations of fraud, and must rely on local district attorney's offices, which usually are heavily engaged in criminal cases, and not interested in prosecuting election fraud for fear of being labeled partisan or racially motivated. Election officials should have the investigative powers necessary to pursue fraud, and to impose administrative fines on violators. Similarly, state attorneys general should be authorized to use statewide grand juries to investigate election fraud anywhere in a state.

Local registration and election boards should be composed of citizen appointees. All such boards should have equal representation from both major political parties, and at least one independent or third-party member. We've seen over and over, from St. Louis to Palm Beach County, how conflicts of interest are created when election boards are run by those who must run for office themselves.

All county and municipal election authorities should be required to have independent audits conducted of their vote tabulation systems, software, and security procedures on a regular basis. In business, companies undergo outside audits by independent bodies to confirm to their stockholders that the companies are truthfully reporting on their financial condition and status. Election bodies should similarly be required to have such audits, to confirm to their "stockholders," the voting public, that security procedures are sufficient to guarantee free and fair elections.

Independent, nonpartisan groups, as well as candidates and parties, should be authorized to appoint poll watchers to observe an election and the vote tabulation. Poll watchers are essential for running elections that are free of fraud and manipulation. Besides having poll watchers in specific precincts, parties, candidates, and nonpartisan groups should be able to designate statewide poll watchers with the authority to observe activities at any precinct or vote tabulation center.

All vendors who supply voting machines and computer software should be required to undergo investigation for financial solvency, security, and integrity. Most states have no such requirement for such vendors. Only an investigation similar to the one that lottery vendors must undergo in most states can ensure that manufacturers of election machines have established a good track record in other jurisdictions.

Clear and consistent rules for identifying what constitutes a vote, and for the timetables and procedures for contesting an election result, must be developed by each state. Disputes over the vagueness in Florida's election law inflamed the controversial 2000 recount. In *Bush v. Gore*, the Supreme Court held that voters in states should be given "equal protection of the law" by assuring that all votes are counted equally—but also held that its ruling wouldn't be a precedent in other cases. Establishing the legitimacy of a vote is a tricky business. Overvotes, for two or more candidates, and undervotes, for no candidate, can have very different meanings. Overvotes are usually the result of a mistake, but about 70 percent of undervotes are deliberate, because a voter didn't want to make a choice.

WHERE DO WE GO FROM HERE?

Many Americans still smart from a history of discriminatory hurdles to voting, and they instinctively resist anything that smacks of exclusion. That is understandable. We should oppose any attempt to create artificial barriers to voter participation. Discrimination can take many forms: turning away voters already in line when polls close, intimidating or misinforming voters at the polls, using badly flawed or poorly designed ballots, failing to provide bilingual materials, failing to fix problem voting machines. We must guard against all these practices. But we also must recognize that voters have responsibilities to acquaint themselves with the election process, and they cannot expect that their vote will be counted no matter what mistakes they make in casting it.

Better voter education in schools, literacy programs, and public service announcements reminding people what they must do to cast a valid vote can all help reduce the number of spoiled ballots, and ensure that as many valid votes as possible are cast. We also should consider better pay for the people who run our elections, as well as more professional training. Many election officials in some of our rural counties are paid less than janitors at the local school.

But we also must return to the traditional view that citizenship requires orderly, clear, and vigorous procedures to ensure that the integrity of our elections is maintained. An era of rampant egalitarianism has influenced the election process to the point where opportunists or enthusiasts can take advantage of casual "inclusive" rules to alter the course of public affairs.

"The more rules are settled in advance, the better elections we will have," says Brad King, a former state elections director of Minnesota, who is now co-director of Indiana's elections division. "What we don't want is the designed sloppiness that a few politicians allow to seep into our system through ambiguity and vagueness." Ambiguity in election law is a surefire recipe for funny business at the polls, litigation afterward, and a chance that some votes won't be counted properly.

But few in the media or in urban government seem concerned about the designed sloppiness of our election system. Our current "honor" system in voter registration and voting, and the lax enforcement of voting laws (in which prosecutors shy away from bringing election fraud cases unless the evidence is almost literally handed to them on videotape), is analogous to having counterfeit bills circulating and the Treasury Department not wanting to be bothered until the printing press is located.

Should "anything goes" continue to be the standard we often allow, the nation may wake to another crisis far bigger than the 2000 Florida folly. Perhaps then we will demand to know just who subverted the safeguards in our election laws. But wouldn't it be better if—with the lessons of Florida and even more recent election snafus and scandals so obvious—we did something now?

Acknowledgments

Expressing appreciation to those who helped make a book possible is always a tricky endeavor. You are almost certain to forget someone, so apologies are offered in advance to anyone whom I inadvertently pass over.

Books are normally solitary labors. But for me this one had the advantage of a knowledgeable, judicious, and wise coauthor. I couldn't have asked for a better collaborator than Hans von Spakovsky.

I owe my former colleagues at *The Wall Street Journal* a great deal. Paul Gigot, the editor of the editorial page, knows a good story when he sees so much of the media ignoring something. He allowed me to spend a great deal of time on this topic. James

Taranto, Howard Dickman, and Robert Pollock vastly improved many of the articles I wrote for the *Journal*.

I am especially grateful to Roger Kimball of Encounter Books for believing in this project. Encounter's staff pulled off amazing feats in bringing this book to you before the 2012 election. Kacey Chuilli was a wonderful copy editor, and made all the pieces fit just so.

I am also in debt to those in the think-tank and philanthropic worlds who provided helpful advice, including John Samples of the Cato Institute, Ed Feulner of the Heritage Foundation, Brian Anderson of the Manhattan Institute, and Michael Grebe of the Bradley Foundation. I will always be grateful to Clara del Villar for her encouragement.

Many chapters were improved by conversations with Linda Morrison, Marita Noon, Marla Rose, Grover Norquist, Dan Walters, Gia Feistel, Chris Ruddy, Mallory Factory, Jon Caldera, Paul Jacob, Gail Heriot, James and Heather Higgins, and Rich Lowry. And thanks to Marla Rose of *The Columbus Dispatch* for keeping me abreast of all that goes on in Ohio, the swingiest state in the country.

I also owe my father more than I can say.

—John Fund

My mother, Traudel von Spakovsky, grew up in Nazi German and survived some of the worst ravages of World War II. My father, Anatol von Spakovsky, escaped being arrested and killed by the Communists twice; once in Russia, and again in Yugoslavia. As immigrants to this country, they taught me the value of democracy and how lucky we were to be living in the freedom and liberty that is the birthright of every American.

I also could not have worked on this book without the help of my wonderful wife, Susan. Thanks to my coauthor, John Fund, for bringing me into this project, and for his cutting-edge reporting on voter fraud and election reform over the years. And I must express my thanks to the dedicated fighters for clean elections and voting integrity with whom I served at the Justice Department, including Brad Schlozman, Christopher Coates, and Christian Adams. Your bravery in the face of vitriolic, mean, and unfair attacks from the radicals inside and outside the Civil Rights Division is something to be admired, and something that every American voter should know about.

—Hans von Spakovsky

☆ ☆ ☆ ☆ ☆ ☆ ☆ ☆

Endnotes

INTRODUCTION

1.   Testimony of Dr. Larry J. Sabato, Director, University of Virginia Center for Governmental Studies, before the U.S. Senate Committee on Governmental Affairs, May 3, 2001.

2.   Fox News poll, sample of 910 registered voters, April 9 to April 11, 2012. http://www.foxnews.com/politics/2012/04/18/fox-news-poll-most-think-voter-id-laws-are-necessary/#ixzz1t5XKvteb.

3.   Interview with Curtis Gans, October 3, 2009.

4.   Sample of 1,000 likely voters, Rasmussen Reports survey, April 12 to April 13, 2012.

5.   Purcell v. Gonzalez, 549 U.S. 1, 4 (2006).

6.   Peter Baker, *Washington Post*, November 11, 2000.

7.   Luke Broadwater, "City 'free speech' attorney seeks dismissal of charges against Henson," *Baltimore Sun*, February 6, 2012.

8.   Staff writer, *Shreveport Times*, August 31, 2003.

9.   Fox News, "Stealing Your Vote," April 22, 2012.

CHAPTER ONE

1.   Interview with Fox News, "Stealing Your Vote," April 20, 2012.

2.   Interview with Mary Kiffmeyer, former Minnesota secretary of state, April 12, 2012.

3.   Fox News, "Stealing Your Vote," April 20, 2012.

4.   James K. Glassman, "The Felon Vote," *New York Post*, March 1, 2005.

5.   Interview with Dan McGrath, April 27, 2012.

6.   Tim Pugmire, "Photo ID Requirement Would Not Prevent Voter Fraud," Minnesota Public Radio, November 22, 2010.

7.   "Felon Voter Fraud Convictions Stemming From Minnesota's 2008 General Election," MinnesotaMajority.com, October 13, 2011.

8.   In the Matter of the Contest of General Election held on November 4, 2008, for the purpose of electing a United States Senator from the State of Minnesota, Cullen Sheehan and Norm Coleman v. Al Franken, A09-697(Minn. June 30, 2009), slip op. at 3.

9.   Letter from Kenneth E. Raschke Jr., Assistant Attorney General, to Mark Ritchie, Secretary of State, on Canvass of Rejected Absentee Ballots, November 17, 2008.

10. Letter from Alan I. Gilbert, Solicitor General, to the State Canvassing Board, December 10, 2008.

11. Coleman v. Ritchie, No. A08-2169, slip op. at 2 (Minn. December 18, 2008).

12. Minn. Stat. § 204C.38 [emphasis added].

13. *Coleman*, slip op. at 2. "Counting" or "recording" errors are arithmetic errors in the vote totals.

14. Minn. Stat. § 204C.22.

15. Minn. Stat. § 204C.22(11).

16. For the ballots and the decisions of the Minnesota Canvassing Board, *see* "Minnesota Senate Recount: Latest Coleman-Franken Results," StarTribune.com, http://senaterecount.startribune.com/ballots/index.php?review_date=2008-12-18&index=9. *See also* John R. Lott Jr. & Ryan S. Lott, "Ballot Madness: Tipping the Scales in Minnesota's Senate Recount," FoxNews.com, December 22, 2008.

17. Slip op. at 6.

18. Minutes of State Canvassing Board, December 16-19, 2008, page 12.

19. Editorial, "The 'Absentee' Senator," *Wall Street Journal*, July 2, 2009.

20. Interview with John Zogby, July 9, 2004.

21. Letter posted on website of Democratic National Committee's Voting Rights Institute, July 2, 2004.

22. Melissa Bailey, "DeStefano Envisions a New Voting Frontier," *New Haven Independent*, December 14, 2011.

23. Florida Department of Law Enforcement, *Report on Voter Fraud*, January 1998.

24. Interview with Scott Rasmussen, June 1, 2008.

25. Staff writer, *Indian Country Today*, November 4, 2002.

26. Interview with Donna Brazile, September 10, 2003.

CHAPTER TWO

1. The "Now" program, MSNBC Television, April 19, 2012, accessed at Newsbusters.org.

2. Bob Gardiner, "Democrat Admits Role in Voter Fraud Case," *Albany Times-Union*, August 27, 2011.

3. Police briefs, "Voter Fraud Investigators Threatened at Gunpoint," *Charleston Daily Mail*, February 29, 2012.

4. Greg Abbott, "Voter Fraud Abounds," *USA Today*, March 20, 2012.

5. Samantha Berrier, "Sentenced to Jail for Casting Ballots on Behalf of Dead Relatives," *Oregon Capitol News*, January 19, 2011.

6. Associated Press, "Southern Indiana Mayor Faces Voter Fraud Charges," Indystar.com, May 2, 2012.

7. Bill Estep, "Jury Convicts All 8 Defendants in Clay Vote-Buying Case," *Lexington Herald-Leader*, March 26, 2010.

8. Brian Joseph, "Activist Nativo Lopez Pleads Guilty to Voter Fraud," *Orange County Register*, June 22, 2011.

9. Editorial, "Voter Fraud," *Richmond Times-Dispatch*, April 6, 2012.

10. Mark Bowes, "Virginia Investigates Voter Fraud," *Richmond-Times Dispatch*, April 22, 2012.

11. Matthew Vadum, *Subversion Inc.: How Obama's ACORN Red Shirts Are Still Ripping Off American Taxpayers* (WND Books, 2011), pages 285-86.

12. "The Investigators" segment, WBBH-TV, "NBC 2 Investigates Voter Fraud," February 2, 2012.

13. Press release, Florida Department of Law Enforcement, November 1, 2011.

14. Jeff Burlew, "Crump Plans Lawsuit in Madison Voter-Fraud Case," *Tallahassee Democrat*, January 18, 2012.

15. Eric Shawn, Fox News, "Stealing Your Vote," April 22, 2012.

16. Interview with Artur Davis, April 6, 2012.

17. Christopher Bedford, "Voter Fraud Is Common," *Daily Caller*, January 11, 2012.

CHAPTER THREE

1. *See* Ga. Code Ann. §21-2-417 (2011); Ind. Code §3-5-2-40.5 (2011); H.R. 2067 (Kan. 2011); S.B. 14 (Tex. 2011); South Carolina House Bill 3003 (signed on May 18, 2011 by governor).

2. "Rhode Island Governor Signs Voter ID Bill," Reuters, July 6, 2011.

3. Commission on Federal Election Reform, *Building Confidence in U.S. Elections, Report of the Commission on Federal Election Reform* 18, 2005, *available at* http://www1.american.edu/ia/cfer/.

4. James Wooten, *Dasher: The Roots and the Rising of Jimmy Carter* (Summit Book, 1978), page 244.

5. Wooten, page 251.

6. 553 U.S. 181, 128 S.Ct. 1610, 1619 (2008). Indiana's voter ID law has also been upheld by the Indiana Supreme Court. *See* League of Women Voters v. Indiana, 929 N.E.3d 758 (Ind. 2010).

7. Hans A. von Spakovsky, "Where There's Smoke, There's Fire: 100,000 Stolen Votes in Chicago," Legal Memorandum No. 23 (Heritage Foundation, April 16, 2008), *available at* http://www.heritage.org/ Research/Legalissues/lm23.cfm.

8. Crawford v. Marion County Election Board, 472 F.3d 949, 953 (7th Cir. 2007).

9. Press release, Brooklyn, New York District Attorney's Office, "D.A. Holtzman Announces Grand Jury Report Disclosing Systematic Voting Fraud in Brooklyn," September 5, 1984; In the Matter of Confidential Investigation, No. R84-11 (N.Y. Supreme Court, 1984).

10. Frank Lynn, "Boss Tweed Is Gone, But Not His Vote," *New York Times*, September 9, 1984.

11. Alex Pappas, "NH Poll Workers Shown Handing Out Ballots in Dead Peoples' Names," *The Daily Caller*, January 11, 2012.

12. Garry Rayno, "Petitions Urge Probe of O'Keefe in Balloting Case," *Union Leader*, February 3, 2012.

13. Transcript, *Briefing on Voter Fraud and Voter Intimidation*, United States Commission on Civil Rights, October 13, 2006, at 185.

14. Letter from John Branciforte to Senator Robert Bennett, June 8, 2008.

15. *See* Madeline Friedman, "Anatomy of Voter Fraud: Will Officials Follow Up on Alleged $10 Vote Payoff?" *Hudson Reporter*, July 1, 2007; "Unclear Which Agency Will Investigate Voter Fraud: Prosecutor's Office Waiting for Referral," *Hudson Reporter*, July 8, 2007.

16. Friedman, "Anatomy of Voter Fraud: Will Officials Follow Up on Alleged $10 Vote Payoff?"

17. U.S. v. Brown, 494 F. Supp. 2d 440 (S.D. Miss. 2007). The lawsuit was filed under Sections 2 and 11 of the Voting Rights Act, and led to the first judgment finding racial discrimination in voting by black officials against white voters. The court said that it had "not had to look far to find ample direct and circumstantial evidence of an intent to discriminate against white voters which has manifested itself through practices designed to deny and/or dilute the voting rights of white voters in Noxubee." *Id.* at 449.

18. *Brown*, 494 F. Supp. 2d at 486, n. 73. According to news accounts and sources in the Justice Department, in an apparent attempt to intimidate this witness, a Noxubee deputy sheriff and political ally of Brown arrested the witness for disorderly conduct and reckless driving only days after the government named him as a witness in a filing with the federal court. In an unprecedented move, the federal judge stayed the county prosecution. *See* John Mott Coffey, "Noxubee Voting Rights Trial to Begin Tuesday," *Commercial Dispatch*, January 13, 2007; Bill Nichols, "Voting Rights Act Pointed in a New Direction," *USA Today*, April 3, 2006.

19. Although the Help America Vote Act of 2002 requires states to implement "a single, uniform, official, centralized, interactive computerized statewide voter registration list," there is no national voter registration database that would allow states to compare their voter registration lists to detect individuals registered in more than one state. 42 U.S.C. §15483(a)(1) (2002).

20. Scott Dodd and Ted Mellnik, "Voters Found on Both N.C., S.C. Rolls," *The Charlotte Observer*, October 24, 2004.

21. Russ Buettner, "Exposed: Scandal of Double Voters—46,000 Registered to Vote in City & Fla," *New York Daily News*, August 22, 2004.

22. Russ Buettner, "Parties Can Count on 'Em—Twice," *New York Daily News*, August 22, 2004.

23. U.S. v. McIntosh, Case No. 04-CR-20142 (D.KS 2004); U.S. v. Scherzer, Case No. 04-CR-00401 (W.D. MO 2005), U.S. v.

Goodrich, No. 04-CR 00402 (W.D. MO 2005), U.S. v. Jones, No. 05-CR-0257 (W.D. MO 2004).

24. Cindy Bevington, "Voter Cited by Opponents of Indiana's ID Law Registered in Two States," *Evening Star,* January 9, 2008.

25. *Crawford,* 128 S.Ct. at 1612.

26. "Rhode Island Governor Signs Voter ID Bill," Reuters, July 6, 2011.

27. Jeffrey Milyo, *The Effects of Photographic Identification on Voter Turnout: A County Level Analysis,* Institute of Public Policy Report 10-2007, Truman School of Public Affairs, University of Missouri (November 10, 2007), *available at* http://munews.missouri.edu/news-releases/2008/0102-voter-id.php.

28. David B. Muhlhausen and Keri Weber Sikich, *New Analysis Shows Voter Identification Laws Do Not Reduce Turnout,* The Heritage Foundation, September 10, 2007, *available at* http://s3.amazonaws.com/thf_media/2007/pdf/cda07-04.pdf.

29. Jason D. Mycoff, Michael W. Wagner, and David C. Wilson, *The Empirical Effects of Voter ID Laws: Present or Absent,* PS: Political Science & Politics, 42 (2009), 121–126. An earlier version of this paper appeared as Jason D. Mycoff, Michael W. Wagner, and David C. Wilson, *Do Voter Identification Laws Affect Voter Turnout?* Working Paper, Department of Political Science and International Relations, University of Delaware (2007).

30. *Voter IDs Are Not the Problem: A Survey of Three States,* Center for Democracy & Election Management, American University 37 (January 2008), *available at* http://www.american.edu/spa/cdem/upload/VoterIDFinalReport1-9-08.pdf. This article criticized a widely cited study in Wisconsin by John Pawasarat that reported that 20 percent of the state's population lacked a driver's license and that minorities, youth, and elderly residents were less likely to have ID cards. It overstated the percentage of residents without a driver's license by oversampling African Americans and low-income people and failing to adjust estimates.

31. Michael Alvarez, Stephen Ansolabehere, et al., *2008 Survey of the Performance of American Elections, Final Report*, 20 (2006).

32. Stephen Ansolabehere, "Ballot Bonanza," *Slate*, March 16, 2007.

33. "82% Say Voters Should Be Required to Show Photo ID," Rasmussen Reports, August 19, 2010, http://www.rasmussenreports. com/public_content/politics/general_politics/august_2010/82_say_ voters_should_be_required_to_show_photo_id.

34. John Lott, *Evidence of Voter Fraud and the Impact That Regulations to Reduce Fraud Have on Voter Participation Rates*, University of Maryland Foundation (August 18, 2006), *available at* http://papers.ssrn. com/sol3/papers.cfm?abstract_id=925611.

35. Press release, American University, "Much-Hyped Turnout Record Fails to Materialize—Convenience Voting Fails to Boost Turnout," November 6, 2008.

36. David Bositis, *Blacks and the 2008 Election, A Preliminary Analysis*, Joint Center for Political and Economic Studies, November 2008.

37. U.S. Census Bureau, *Voting and Registration in the Election of November 2004* (May 25, 2005), http://www.census.gov/hhes/www/ socdemo/voting/publications/p20/2004/tab04a.xls; U.S. Census Bureau, *Voting and Registration in the Election of November 2008* (February 2009), http://www.census.gov/hhes/www/socdemo/voting/publications/ p20/2008/Table%2004b.xls.

38. *See* Georgia Secretary of State, *Voter Registration System, Active Voters by Race/Gender, General Election Voting History* (November 2, 2010), *available at* http://www.sos.georgia.gov/elections/ voter_registration/2010%20Stats/By%20Age,%20Race,%20&%20 Gender_2010_General%20Election.pdf;http://www.sos.georgia.gov/ elections/voter_registration/11-7-06_precinct.pdf.

39. Brian Kemp, letter to the editor, *Washington Post*, June 25, 2011.

40. Common Cause of Georgia v. Billups, 554 F.3d 1340 (11th Cir. 2009); *cert. denied*, 129 S.Ct. 2770 (U.S. 2009).

41. Democratic Party of Georgia v. Perdue, 288 Ga. 720, 707 S.E.2d 67 (Ga. 2011).

42. At the time one of the authors, Hans von Spakovsky, was the counsel to the Assistant Attorney General for Civil Rights at the Justice Department, and helped review the information submitted by Georgia.

43. www.youtube.com/watch?v=BZf25pmgR4c.

44. Common Cause of Georgia v. Billups, 504 F.Supp.2d 1333, 1380 (N.D. Ga. 2007).

45. David A. Bositis, *Blacks and the 2010 Midterms: A Preliminary Analysis*, Joint Center for Political and Economic Studies, November 16, 2010, page 3.

46. Bositis, *Blacks and the 2010 Midterms: A Preliminary Analysis*, page 12.

47. Editorial, "GOP's Anti-Fraud Regulations Smack of Vote Suppression," *USA Today*, June 13, 2011.

48. Provisional ballots are required by 42 U.S.C. §15482(a) and Indiana Code §3-11.7-2-1.

49. Indiana Democratic Party v. Rokita, 458 F.Supp.2d 775, 822–823 (S.D. Ind. 2006).

50. Common Cause of Georgia v. Billups, 439 F.Supp.2d 1294, 1354 (N.D. Ga. 2006).

CHAPTER FOUR

1. Artur Davis, "I've Changed My Mind on Voter ID Laws," *Montgomery Advertiser*, October 17, 2011.

2. Steven T. Dennis, "Emanuel Cleaver and Artur Davis Spar Over Voter ID Laws," *Roll Call*, October 25, 2011.

3. Speech, True the Vote conference, April 27, 2012.

4. Editorial, "Bill Clinton Does 'Jim Crow'," *Wall Street Journal*, August 3, 2011.

5. Louis Jacobsen, "Rhode Island's Voter ID Law: Oddity or Game Changer," *Governing* magazine, July 28, 2011.

6.   Phil Marcelo and Karen Lee Ziner, "Liberals, Democrats Stunned by RI Passage of Voter ID," *Providence Journal*, July 11, 2011.

7.   David Klepper, "Few Reports of Problems With Rhode Island's New Voter ID Law," *Providence Journal*, April 24, 2012.

8.   Simon van Zuylen-Wood, "Why Did Liberal African-Americans in Rhode Island Help Pass a Voter ID Law?," *New Republic*, February 7, 2012.

9.   Staff writer, "Voter ID Critics Express Distaste in Letter to Chafee," *Providence Journal*, July 16, 2011.

10. John Gramlich, "Angering Their Own Party, Rhode Island Democrats Approve Voter ID," Stateline.org, July 20, 2011.

CHAPTER FIVE

1.   *In the Matter of Anailin Reyes*, A 097-952-267, U.S. Department of Justice, Executive Office for Immigration Review, Immigration Court, Orlando, Florida.

2.   *In the Matter of Anailin Reyes.*

3.   Government Accountability Office, *Elections: Additional Data Could Help State and Local Election Officials Maintain Accurate Voter Registration Lists* 42 (2005).

4.   Criminal Division, Public Integrity Section, U.S. Department of Justice, *Election Fraud Prosecutions & Convictions: October 2002–September 2005* (2006). DOJ also prosecuted noncitizens for registering and voting in Alaska, Colorado, and North Carolina.

5.   U.S. v. Velasquez, Case No. 03-CR-20233 (So. D. Fla 2003).

6.   Andy Pierrotti, *NBC Investigates: Voter Fraud*, February 2, 2012, available at www.nbe-2/story/16662854/2012/02/02/nbc2-investigates-voter-fraud?clienttype=printable.

7.   *See* U.S. Department of Justice, *Federal Prosecution of Election Offenses* 66 (7th ed. 2007), 18 U.S.C. §611.

8.   *See* Robert Redding Jr., "Purging Illegal Aliens From Voter Rolls Not Easy; Maryland Thwarted in Tries So Far," *Washington Times*, August 23, 2004.

9. Ricci v. DeStefano, 129 S. Ct. 2658, 174 L. Ed. 2d 490 (2009).

10. Justin Levitt, Brennan Center for Justice, *The Truth About Voter Fraud* 18 (2007).

11. Daren Briscoe, "Non-Citizens Testify They Voted in Compton Elections," *Los Angeles Times*, January 23, 2002.

12. A judge's removal of the mayor from office was later overturned, but the removal of a councilwoman who participated in noncitizen voter fraud was upheld. *See* Bradley v. Perrodin, 106 Cal. App. 4th 1153 (2003), *review denied*, 2003 Cal. LEXIS 3586 (Cal. 2003); Robert Greene, "Court of Appeal Upholds Perrodin Victory Over Bradley in Compton," *Metropolitan News-Enterprise*, March 11, 2003; Daren Briscoe, Bob Pool, and Nancy Wride, "Judge Voids Compton Vote, Reinstalls Defeated Mayor," *Los Angeles Times*, February 9, 2002.

13. *See* H.R. Doc. No. 105-416 (1998).

14. Press release, California Secretary of State, "Jones Releases Report on Orange County Voter Fraud Investigation," February 3, 1998.

15. Jessica Rocha, "Voter Rolls Risky for Aliens: Non-Citizens' Registering Is a Crime; 4 Cases Turn up in N.C.," *News & Observer*, December 7, 2006.

16. Government Accountability Office, *Elections: Additional Data Could Help State and Local Election Officials Maintain Accurate Voter Registration Lists* 60.

17. In a typical example, voter registration cards are listed as an acceptable secondary source document to prove Maryland residency when obtaining a driver's license in Maryland. *See* Maryland Motor Vehicle Administration, Sources of Proof, http://www.marylandmva.com/DriverServ/Apply/proof.htm.

18. 8 U.S.C. § 1324a (2008).

19. See *In Re Report of the Special January 1982 Grand Jury 1*, No. 82 GJ 1909 (N.D. Ill. December 14, 1984), at 8-9.

20. *See* Douglas Frantz, "Vote Fraud in City Outlined at Hearing," *Chicago Tribune*, September 20, 1983; Hans A. von Spakovsky,

"Where There's Smoke, There's Fire: 100,000 Stolen Votes in Chicago," Legal Memorandum No. 23 (Heritage Foundation, April 16, 2008), *available at* http://www.heritage.org/Research/Legalissues/lm23.cfm.

21. Desiree F. Hicks, "Foreigners Landing on Voter Rolls," *Chicago Tribune*, October 2, 1985.

22. 8 U.S.C. §§ 1373(a), (c). Given the requirements of this statute, the initial refusal of the Justice Department and the INS to comply with "numerous requests from the Committee and California election officials to provide citizenship data on individuals" in the Dornan-Sanchez investigation was inexplicable; the Attorney General either made a basic legal error, or decided, for political reasons, not to cooperate in an investigation that could have thrown out the Democratic winner of a congressional race. *See* H.R. Doc. No. 105-416, at 13 (1998).

23. Robert Redding, "Purging Illegal Aliens from Voter Rolls Not Easy; Maryland Thwarted in Tries So Far," *Washington Times*, August 23, 2004.

24. *See* letter from Sam Reed to Robert S. Coleman, Director, Seattle District Office, USCIS, March 22, 2005.

25. "INS Hampers Probe of Voting by Foreigners, Prosecutor Says," *Houston Chronicle*, September 20, 1997. *See* Frank Trejo, "Internal Strife Embroils Dallas INS Office—Local Agents' Whistle-Blowing Leads to Far-Flung Controversy," *Dallas Morning News*, March 8, 1998; Dena Bunis, "Dallas INS' Probe of Electorate Echoes Here: Fallout from the Dornan-Sanchez Inquiry Sparks an Internal INS Debate Over a Texas Computer-Match Investigation," *Orange County Register*, June 5, 1997.

26. Ruth Larson, "Voter-Fraud Probe in Dallas Runs into INS Roadblock: Agency Denies It Should Have Further Aided U.S. Attorney," *Washington Times*, September 25, 1997.

27. Christina Bellantoni, "Little to Stop Illegal Aliens from Voting," *Washington Times*, September 24, 2004.

28. *The 2010 Election: A Look Back at What Went Right and Wrong*, statement of Colorado Secretary of State Scott Gessler before the Committee on House Administration, 112th Congress (2011).

29. Milan Simonich, "Secretary of State Says Voter Fraud Probably Uncovered," *Alamogordo Daily News*, March 15, 2011.

30. Karen Saranita, "The Motor Voter Myth," *National Review*, November 11, 1996, at 42.

31. Saranita, "Motor Voter," at 42.

32. Affidavit of Nelson Molina, H.R. Doc. No. 105-416, at 181 (1998). Molina's wife was in the meeting with the field director and filed a supporting affidavit.

33. Martin Wisckol, "Activist Nativo Lopez Pleads Guilty to Voter Fraud," *Orange County Register*, June 22, 2011.

34. *Non-Citizen Voting and ID Requirements in U.S. Elections: Hearing Before the Committee on House Administration*, 109th Congress (2006) (statement of Paul Bettencourt, Harris County Tax Assessor–Collector and Voter Registrar).

35. Joe Stinebaker, "Loophole Lets Foreigners Illegally Vote; 'Honor System' in Applying Means the County Can't Easily Track Fraud," *Houston Chronicle*, January 16, 2005.

36. Guillermo Garcia, "Voter Fraud Case Takes a New Twist," *Express-News*, September 12, 2007; Jim Forsyth, "Hundreds of Non Citizens Have Registered to Vote in Bexar County," 1200 WOAI, May 16, 2007.

37. "Immigrant Who Voted Illegally on Road to Becoming a U.S. Citizen," Fox News, August 26, 2010.

38. Gonzalez v. Arizona, No. 08-17094 (9th Cir. April 17, 2012).

39. Georgia v. Holder, Case No. 1:10-CV-1970 (D. D.C); letter from T. Christian Herren, Chief, Voting Section, U.S. Department of Justice, to Anne Lewis, March 31, 2011. The proof-of-citizenship bill was Act No. 143 (S.B. 86) 2009.

40. *Securing the Vote: Arizona: Hearing Before the Committee on House Administration*, 109th Congress (2006) (statement of Andrew

P. Thomas, Maricopa County District Attorney); *see also* transcript of Southwest Conference on Illegal Immigration, Border Security and Crime, May 16, 2006.

41. Press release, California Secretary of State, "Official Status Report on Orange County Voter Fraud Investigation," February 3, 1998.

42. Letter from Joseph D. Rich, Chief, Voting Section, Civil Rights Division, U.S. Department of Justice, to Donald H. Dwyer Jr., August 24, 2004.

43. Office of the Legislative Auditor General, State of Utah, ILR 2005-B, February 8, 2005; Deborah Bulkeley, "State Says 14 Illegals May Have Cast Ballots," *Deseret Morning News*, August 8, 2005. At least 20 of the registered voters were under deportation orders.

44. "Bill Would Change Voter Registration Rolls," Associated Press, February 7, 2006.

45. *See* Ohio Secretary of State, Directive No. 2004-31, September 7, 2004; letter from Chris Nelson, South Dakota Secretary of State, to County Auditors, October 25, 2004; letter from Thomas J. Miller, Iowa Attorney General, to Chester J. Culver, Iowa Secretary of State, October 20, 2004.

CHAPTER SIX

1. Florida Department of Law Enforcement, *Florida Voter Fraud Issues: Report And Observations* 7 (1998).

2. The *Miami Herald* used innovative computer technology from SAS to assist its reporters in tracking down illegal votes through software comparisons of voter rolls with property records, city personnel files, absentee witness lists, death certificates, and felony conviction records. This is a lesson for election officials on how they should be using technology and software to maintain clean voter rolls, deter fraud, and check the validity and authenticity of voter registration applications. *See* "Miami Herald Wins Pulitzer Prize," http://www.sas.com/news/success/miamiherald.html.

3.   Roger Thurow, "Southern Cross: A Place Much Revered in Civil-Rights Lore Is Still Much Divided," *Wall Street Journal*, July 20, 1998.

4.   U.S. Census Bureau, Greene County MapStats, http://quickfacts.census.gov/qfd/states/01/01063.html. *See* Magistrate Judge's Report and Recommendation, U.S. v. Smith, No. CR-97-S-45-W, at 1, 2 (N.D. Ala. 1997) (stating that Greene County had "a 92% African American population") [hereinafter Magistrate's Report].

5.   U.S. Census Bureau, Greene County MapStats.

6.   Robert DeWitt, "Greene County Out of Bankruptcy," *Tuscaloosa News*, October 22, 2006.

7.   The Assistant U.S. Attorney assigned to the case was Pat Meadows, a career prosecutor with more than 25 years of experience as a federal prosecutor and a local assistant district attorney; Alabama Assistant Attorney General Gregory Biggs was designated as a Special Assistant U.S. Attorney to assist with the case. The primary FBI agent leading the investigation was Marshall Ridlehoover. *See* Magistrate's Report at 9.

8.   Leewanna Parker, "Absentee Ballot the Trump Card," *Greene County Independent*, November 3, 1994.

9.   *Id.*

10. Leewanna Parker, "Questions Remain About Election," *Greene County Independent*, November 10, 1994; Leewanna Parker, "Federal, State Absentee Ballot Probe May Continue Many Months," *Greene County Independent*, April 3, 1996. County tax assessor John Kennard actually called the FBI in September 1994 to complain that "a significant number of absentee ballots had been mailed to addresses that were not the voters' addresses." Magistrate's Report at 7, 8.

11. *See* U.S. v. Gordon, 836 F.2d 1312 (11 Cir. 1988), *cert. denied*, 487 U.S. 1265 (1988); McNally v. U.S., 483 U.S. 350 (1987) (holding that 18 U.S.C. § 1341 does not proscribe a scheme or artifice to defraud the citizenry of the intangible right to honest government). In 1988, Congress enacted 18 U.S.C. § 1346 in response to the McNally

decision to prohibit schemes meant to deprive citizens of the "intangible right of honest services." *See* U.S. Department of Justice, Criminal Division, Public Integrity Section, *Federal Prosecution of Election Offenses* 74 (2007). Having gotten away with absentee-ballot fraud in 1985 on technical grounds, Gordon was clearly not deterred from engaging in fraud once again in the 1994 election.

12. Leewanna Parker, "Election 1994: Hot Local Races Decided at Polls, Absentee Boxes," *Greene County Independent*, November 10, 1994.

13. Exactly 1,429 absentee ballots were cast, representing 37 percent of all votes cast in the county. Fewer than 40 absentee ballots were cast by white voters. Magistrate's Report at 3, 4.

14 Leewanna Parker, "Six to Face Voter Fraud Charges in Federal Court," *Greene County Independent*, February 18, 1998.

15. Parker, "Absentee Ballot the Trump Card."

16. Magistrate's Report at 6.

17. Parker, "Election 1994: Hot Local Races Decided at Polls, Absentee Boxes," *supra* note 13. Johnson filed suit to contest the results of the election. Leewanna Parker, "Bill Johnson Files Election Contest Against Roberson," *Greene County Independent*, December 1, 1994.

18. Parker, "Questions Remain About Election." In 1978, Kennard was the first black elected to be the Tax Assessor.

19. Leewanna Parker, "Spencer Says He's Fielding Complaints from Worried Voters," *Greene County Independent*, March 13, 1996.

20. *Id*. *See also* Leewanna Parker, "Voters Calling Agents 'Polite'," *Greene County Independent*, March 13, 1996.

21. Citizens for a Better Greene County had about 600 members, and its bylaws mandated that its board of directors be composed of four individuals: a black man and woman and a white man and woman. Magistrate's Report at 5; DeWitt, "Greene County Out of Bankruptcy."

22. Leewanna Parker, "More Indictments to Come, Locals Say," *Greene County Independent*, February 1, 1997. The Greene County case demonstrates the importance of state challenge laws, which have been attacked (unsuccessfully) in litigation in Ohio as "unconstitutional."

23. Rich Lowry, "Early and Often—Absentee Voting Fraud," *National Review*, June 17, 1996.

24. Parker, "Federal, State Absentee Ballot Probe May Continue Many Months."

25. Magistrate's Report at 11.

26. Leewanna Parker, "Probe Reactivates Black Belt Committee," *Greene County Independent*, March 20, 1996.

27. See U.S. v. Smith, 231 F.3d 800, 804 (11th Cir. 2000), *cert. denied*, 532 U.S. 1019 (2001). NAACP officials and other civil rights leaders also met with Attorney General Janet Reno protesting the vote fraud investigation. *See* Thurow, "Southern Cross: A Place Much Revered in Civil-Rights Lore Is Still Much Divided."

28. Susan Lamont, "Black Voting Rights Activists in Alabama Fight Frame-Up by Federal, State Officials," *The Militant*, June 8, 1998, *available at* http://www.themilitant.com/1998/6222/6222_29.html.

29. "Civil Rights Leader Gets Jail Term for Voter Fraud," *New York Times*, June 6, 1999.

30. Leewanna Parker, "Democrats Appeal to State Party Chairman for Relief," *Greene County Independent*, May 1, 1996. One of the candidates had opposed commission chairman Garria Spencer in the 1994 election. The Alabama Democratic Party overruled the local Greene County Democratic Party and reinstated the candidates on the ballot. Leewanna Parker, "Ruling Spurs Reordering of Ballots," *Greene County Independent*, May 22, 1996.

31. Interview with Pam Montgomery, July 28, 2008. When commission chairman Garria Spencer was first indicted, Montgomery overheard Spencer tell a federal prosecutor during court proceedings that "you ain't going to get us—we are untouchable."

32. Tyree was a deputy registrar as well as the mother of one of Smith's children. *Government's Sentencing Memorandum*, U.S. v. Smith, No. CR-97-S-0045-W, at 1, 12, 14 (N.D. Ala. 1997).

33. Tyree's signature appeared as a witness on 166 absentee ballots—more than any other person. Magistrate's Report at 6. *See*

Indictment, U.S. v. Smith, No. CR-97-S-0045-W, at 3-5 (N.D. Ala. 1997); Parker, "More Indictments to Come, Locals Say."

34. Government's Sentencing Memorandum, U.S. v. Smith, No. CR-97-S-0045-W, at 11 (N.D. Ala. 1997). County Commission chairman Garria Spencer and Eutaw City councilman Spiver Gordon were among the persons present. Transcript of Trial, U.S. v. Smith, No. CR-97-S-0045-W, at 1200 (N.D. Ala. 1997).

35. Parker, "Election 1994."

36. *Id. See also* press release, G. Douglas Jones, U.S. Attorney, Northern District of Alabama, "6 Greene County Residents Plead Guilty to Federal Voter Fraud," February 26, 1999; Leewanna Parker, "Six Admit Guilt in '94 Vote Fraud Conspiracy," *Greene County Independent*, March 3, 1999.

37. U.S. v. Smith, 231 F.3d 800 (11 Cir. 2000), *cert. denied*, 532 U.S. 1019 (2001).

38. *Id.* Additional unindicted conspirators aided and abetted the voter fraud, including Cora Stewart, Jennifer Watkins, and Burnette Hutton. *See Government's Sentencing Memorandum*, U.S. v. Smith, No. CR-97-S-0045-W, at 3-7 (N.D. Ala. 1997).

39. Leewanna Parker, "Gestapo Was Vote Thieves," *Greene County Independent*, June 3, 1998.

40. Thurow, "Southern Cross: A Place Much Revered in Civil-Rights Lore Is Still Much Divided."

41. Parker, "Gestapo Was Vote Thieves."

42. *Id.*

43. Leewanna Parker, "Voters Showed No Hesitation in Casting Ballots," *Greene County Independent*, June 10, 1998. Some officials said the 57-percent figure was too low because they believed the voter registration list had between 600 and 1,000 persons listed who were not eligible to vote in Greene County.

44. Gita M. Smith, "Alabama County Votes for Change: Fund Misuse, Fraud Targeted in Election," *Atlanta Journal Constitution*, June 6, 1998.

45. Leewanna Parker, "Voter Fraud Trial Begins Mar. 1," *Greene County Independent*, February 24, 1999.

46. Leewanna Parker, "NAACP to Hear Another Side of County's Voter Fraud Story," *Greene County Independent*, July 29, 1998.

47. *Id.*

48. Leewanna Parker, "Bond Reaffirms Alignment to Local Voter Fraud Defendants," *Greene County Independent*, August 19, 1998.

49. Press release, G. Douglas Jones, at 4.

50. Tommy Stevenson, "Greene SCLC Head Calls Charges 'Baseless'," *Tuscaloosa News*, February 14, 2010, http://www.tuscaloosanews.com/article/20100214/news/100219776?p=1&tc=pg.

51. Interview with Elizabeth George, July 19, 2008.

52. Interview with Pam Montgomery, July 28, 2008.

53. Pabey v. Pastrick, 816 N.E.2d 1138, 1140 (Ind. 2004).

54. Pabey, 816 N.E.2d at 1146.

55. Andy Grimm, "Ex-Mayor Upholds East Chicago Tradition: Corruption," *Chicago Tribune*, May 5, 2011.

56. Pabey, 816 N.E.2d at 1146, 1147.

57. Matthew Vadum, "Mississippi NAACP Leader Sent to Prison for 10 Counts of Voter Fraud," *The Daily Caller*, July 29, 2011; Meg Coker, "Sowers Guilty on Ten Voter Fraud Counts," *Tunica Times*, April 21, 2011.

58. "Madison County Officials Arrested for Voter Fraud," WCTV News, November 1, 2011.

59. Dana Beyerle, "Absentee Ballots in Bullock Stir Suspicions," *Tuscaloosa News*, August 16, 2002.

60. Jason Morton, "Ex-Clerk Guilty in Voter Fraud Case," *Tuscaloosa News*, September 1, 2010.

61. Interview with Greg Biggs, April 22, 2008; see also Dana Beyerle, "Alabama Not Rid of Voter Fraud," *Tuscaloosa News*, October 20, 2002.

62. Matt Elofson, "Woman Faces Felony Absentee Ballot Fraud Charge," *Dothan Eagle*, October 20, 2010; "Former Pike County

Commissioner Pleads Guilty to Voter Fraud," Associated Press, October 27, 2010.

63. U.S. v. Boards, 10 F.3d 587 (8th Cir. 1993).

64. U.S. v. Townsley, 843 F.2d 1070 (8th Cir. 1988).

65. U.S. v. Odom, 736 F.2d 104 (4th Cir. 1984).

66. U.S. v. Girdner, 754 F.2d 877 (10th Cir. 1985).

67. U.S. v. Clapps, 732 F.2d 1148 (3rd Cir. 1984).

68. U.S. v. Mason, 673 F.2d 737 (4th Cir. 1982).

69. U.S. v. Morado, 454 F.2d 167 (5th Cir. 1972).

70. Neil Munro, "12 Charged With Voter Fraud in Georgia Election," *The Daily Caller*, November 24, 2011; Stephen Abel, "12 Former Officials Indicted for Voter Fraud," WALB 10, November 22, 2011.

71. Eric Shawn, "Officials Plead Guilty in New York Voter Fraud Case," Fox News, December 21, 2001; Bob Gardinier, "Vote-Probe Arrests Include Councilmen," *Times Union*, December 21, 2011. The plea offer made to the city clerk was based in part on information showing he may have helped forge absentee ballots in campaigns dating back to at least 2007. Brendan J. Lyons, "Troy Clerk Resigns After Plea Offer," *Times Union*, July 25, 2011.

72. Neil Munro, "12 Charged With Voter Fraud in Georgia Election," *The Daily Caller*, November 24, 2011.

73. "Light, Not Heat, in Hale County," *Tuscaloosa News*, October 9, 2007.

74. Editorial, "Turn the Page," *Greene County Independent*, March 3, 1999.

CHAPTER SEVEN

1. Letter from William E. Moschella, Assistant Attorney General of Legislative Affairs, U.S. Department of Justice, to F. James Sensenbrenner, Chairman, Committee on the Judiciary, U.S. House of Representatives, April 12, 2006.

2. U.S. v. Jones, 125 F.3d 1418, 1431 (11th Cir. 1997).

3. Johnson v. Miller, 864 F.Supp. 1354 (S.D. Ga. 1994).

4.   Johnson v. Miller, 864 F.Supp. at 1368.

5.   Miller v. Johnson, 515 U.S. 900, 924-925 (1995).

6.   Hays v. State of Louisiana, 839 F.Supp. 1188, 1196 (1993).

7.   Hays v. State of Louisiana, 936 F.Supp. 360, 369, 372 (W.D. La. 1996).

8.   http://pjmedia.com/tatler/2011/10/03/photos-barack-obama-appeared-and-marched-with-new-black-panthers-in-2007/.

9.   Testimony before the U.S. Commission on Civil Rights, April 23, 2010.

10. Declaration of Bartle Bull, U.S. v. New Black Panther Party for Self-Defense, Case No. 09-0065 (E.D. PA).

11. Letter from Loretta King, Acting Assistant Attorney General of Civil Rights, U.S. Department of Justice, to James P. Cauley III, August 17, 2009.

12. Northwest Austin Municipal Utility District Number One v. Holder, 557 U.S. 193 (2009).

13. Letter from Thomas E. Perez, Assistant Attorney General for Civil Rights, U.S. Department of Justice, to James P. Cauley III, February 10, 2012.

CHAPTER EIGHT

1.   Associated Press, "Former Tenn. Lawmaker John Ford Convicted of Taking Bribes," *Washington Post*, April 28, 2007.

2.   Office of the Attorney General, State of Tennessee, Op. No. 06-005 (January 9, 2006).

3.   Marc Perrusquia, "Judge: Let's Air Details of Fraud—Public Has Rights, Colton Says in Ophelia Ford Election Case," *The Commercial Appeal*, May 22, 2007.

4.   Affidavit of John Harvey, Terry Roland v. Ophelia Ford, in the Tennessee State Senate, December 11, 2005.

5.   Marc Perrusquia, "Did a Dead Man Vote in Ford-Roland Contest?" *The Commercial Appeal*, December 11, 2005.

6.   Perrusquia, "Did a Dead Man Vote in Ford-Roland Contest?"

7.   *Report of Ad Hoc Committee on District No. 29 Election Contest,* Tennessee Senate, April 17, 2006, page 5.

8.   *See* Tennessee Code § 2-7-112. This section was amended effective January 1, 2012, to change the ID provision from one allowing non-photo IDs such as a social security card, credit card, or voter registration card, to requiring photo IDs such as a driver's license, a passport, a government employee ID card, or a military ID card.

9.   Ford v. The Tennessee Senate, Case No. 06-2031 (W.D. TN. 2006).

10.   Ford v. The Tennessee Senate, slip op. February 1, 2006, page 15-17, 30.

11.   *Report of Ad Hoc Committee on District No. 29 Election Contest,* Tennessee Senate, April 17, 2006, page 3.

12.   Travis Loller, "Senate Votes Ford Out," *The Tennessean,* April 20, 2006.

13.   Ford v. Wilder, 469 F.3d 500, 502-503 (6th Cir. 2006).

14.   Loller, "Senate Votes Ford Out."

15.   "Disputed Memphis Precinct Poll Worker Scrutinized," Associated Press, February 1, 2006.

16.   Perrusquia, "Judge: Let's Air Details of Fraud."

17.   Marc Perrusquia, "Dead-Voter Scandal Rears Its Ugly Head," *The Commercial Appeal,* November 7, 2006.

18.   Perrusquia, "Judge: Let's Air Details of Fraud."

CHAPTER NINE

1.   *Frequently Asked Questions,* U.S. Electoral College, http://www.archives.gov/federal-register/electoral-college/faq.html. From 1889 to 2004, 595 amendments were introduced in Congress to amend the Electoral College. Congressional Research Service, *The Electoral College: An Overview and Analysis of Reform Proposals* 17 (2004).

2.   U.S. Constitution, art. II, § 1, cl. 2.

3.   McPherson v. Blacker, 146 U.S. 1, 29 (1892).

4.   Congressional Research Service, *The Electoral College:1–2.*

5.   U.S. Constitution, amend. XII; 3 U.S.C. §§ 1–21. Congress meets in joint session to count the electoral votes in January. If no candidate wins a majority of the electoral votes, the House selects the president and the Senate selects the vice president, with each state delegation in the House having only one vote.

6.   Nebraska and Maine provide for allocation of their electoral vote by congressional districts with two electors awarded to the state-wide winner.

7.   U.S. Constitution, art. V.

8.   *See* National Popular Vote, www.nationalpopularvote.com. For a justification for this change in extensive detail, *see also* John R. Koza, et al., *Every Vote Equal: A State-Based Plan for Electing the President by National Popular Vote* (2011).

9.   Letter from John Boehner, House of Representatives Speaker; Mitch McConnell, Senate Republican Leader; and Rick Perry, Governor of Texas; to Governors of the Fifty States, June 29, 2011 [hereinafter Boehner Letter], *available at* http://www.flashreport.org/blog/wp-content/uploads/2011/08/Letter-Boehner.McConnell.Perry-1.pdf.

10.   Tara Ross and Trent England, "George Soros Supports the Tea Party? What the National Popular Vote Wants You to Believe," *The Weekly Standard*, August 16, 2011.

11.   *See* Tara Ross, "The Electoral College: Enlightened Democracy," Legal Memorandum No. 15 (Heritage Foundation, November 1, 2004), *available at* http://www.heritage.org/research/reports/2004/11/the-electoral-college-enlightened-democracy.

12.   James Madison, *Notes of Debates in the Federal Convention of 1787* (W.W. Norton & Co., 1987), pages 573-575.

13.   Boehner Letter.

14.   John Samples, "A Critique of the National Popular Vote Plan for Electing the President," Cato Institute Policy Analysis No. 622, October 13, 2008, *available at* http://www.cato.org/pubs/pas/pa-622.pdf.

15.   Tara Ross, at 6.

16. Bradley A. Smith, "Vanity of Vanities: National Popular Vote and the Electoral College," 7 *Election Law Journal* 3, 198–199 (2008).

17. http://www.nationalpopularvote.com/pages/answers/m15. php#m15_4.

18. John Samples, at 9.

19. U.S. Constitution, art. I, § 10, cl. 3.

20. Edwin Meese III et al. eds., *The Heritage Guide to the Constitution* 178 (2005).

21. Matthew Pincus, "When Should Interstate Compacts Require Congressional Consent?" 42 *Columbia Journal of Law and Social Problems* 511, 516 (2009).

22. *Id.*

23. John Samples, at 9.

24. 434 U.S. 452 (U.S. 1978); *see also* Virginia v. Tennessee, 148 U.S. 503 (1893).

25. *The Heritage Guide to the Constitution, supra* note 17.

26. U.S. Steel Corp., 434 U.S. at 473.

27. *Id.*

28. Tara Ross, "Federalism & Separation of Powers—Legal and Logistical Ramifications of the National Popular Vote Plan," 11 *Engage* 2, 40 (September 2010).

29. 524 U.S. 417, 439–440 (1998).

30. 514 U.S. 779 (1995).

31. *Id.* at 831.

32. *Id.* at 831 (citing Gomillion v. Lightfoot, 364 U.S. 339, 345 (1960), quoting Frost & Frost Trucking Co. v. Railroad Commission of California, 271 U.S. 583, 594 (1926).

33. Boehner Letter.

34. *Id.*

35. National Popular Vote, *Agreement Among the States to Elect the President by National Popular Vote*, Art. III, *available at* http://www. nationalpopularvote.com/resources/43-Compact-TAATS-V43.pdf.

36. *Id.* at Art. IV.

37. Some might argue that the NPV compacts have no formal enforcement mechanism, and therefore states maintain their right to withdraw as they see fit. *See* James Taranto, "Faithless Lawmakers," *Wall Street Journal*, July 29, 2010, *available at* http://online.wsj.com/article/SB10001424052748703578104575397100729241576.html?mod=WSJ_Opinion_MIDDLETopOpinion. Nevertheless, this scenario creates a constitutional catch-22: Either the states have created an unconstitutional compact that can be enforced, or the compact could cause an electoral crisis should a state withdraw from the compact during or immediately before an election.

38. Bradley A. Smith, "Vanity of Vanities: National Popular Vote and the Electoral College," 7 *Election Law Journal* 3, 198, 210 (2008).

39. Boehner Letter.

40. John Samples, at 3–4.

41. *Id*. at 6. The states that lose influence under the NPV are California, Oklahoma, Minnesota, Louisiana, Oregon, Mississippi, Connecticut, Colorado, Arizona, Kansas, Arkansas, Iowa, Utah, West Virginia, Nevada, New Mexico, Nebraska, Maine, Montana, New Hampshire, Idaho, Hawaii, Rhode Island, Delaware, South Dakota, North Dakota, Vermont, Alaska, Wyoming, and the District of Columbia. *Id*. at 4, Table 1.

42. Ross, "Federalism & Separation of Powers," 38 (citations omitted).

43. Gary Gregg, "Electoral College Watch," National Review Online, October 25, 2004, http://old.nationalreview.com/gregg/gregg200410270939.asp.

44. Testimony of Tara Ross, *Enacting the Agreement Among the States to Elect the President by National Popular Vote*, Hearing on SB 344 Before the Senate Committee on Legislative Operations and Elections, 2011 Legislature, 76th Session (November 2011).

45. Brad Smith, at 207.

46. 531 U.S. 98 (2000).

47. Gary Gregg.

48. Tara Ross, at 38.

49. Brad Smith, at 203.

50. Provisional ballots are required by the Help America Vote Act, 42 U.S.C. § 15482 (2002).

51. Brad Smith, at 213. Some NPV supporters also point erroneously to the election of 1824, in which the House of Representatives selected John Quincy Adams over Andrew Jackson; however, since some state legislatures still selected electors, there was no actual popular vote total.

52. *Id.* at 213. Smith also points out that the national popular vote margin of 540,000 votes between Gore and Bush in 2000 was within the margin of error, so "one cannot say with any confidence that Gore [or Bush] clearly represented the popular majority."

53. Tara Ross, at 13.

CHAPTER TEN

1. U.S. v. Brown, 494 F.Supp.2d 440 (S.D. Miss. 2007), *aff'd* 6561 F.3d 420 (5th Cir. 2009).

2. U.S. v. Brown, 494 F.Supp.2d at 443.

3. J. Christian Adams, *Injustice: Exposing the Racial Agenda of the Obama Justice Department*, (Regnery Publishing, Inc., 2011), page 47.

4. Submitted written testimony of Christopher Coates, U.S. Commission on Civil Rights, September 24, 2010, page 5.

5. Testimony of Christopher Coates, page 3.

6. Testimony of Christopher Coates, page 4.

7. U.S. v. Brown, 494 F.Supp.2d at 450.

8. U.S. v. Brown, 494 F.Supp.2d at 449.

9. U.S. v. Brown, 494 F.Supp.2d at 485.

10. U.S. v. Brown, 494 F.Supp.2d at 457.

11. U.S. v. Brown, 494 F.Supp.2d at 464.

12. U.S. v. Brown, 494 F.Supp.2d at 486, footnote 73.

13. U.S. v. Brown, 494 F.Supp.2d at 460, footnote 34.

14. John Coffey, "Judge Delays Ruling on Witness Intimidation Ban," *Columbus Commercial Dispatch*, November 8, 2005.

15. U.S. v. Brown, 494 F.Supp.2d at 464.

16. U.S. v. Brown, 494 F.Supp.2d at 472, footnote 51.

17. U.S. v. Brown, 494 F.Supp.2d at 456.

18. U.S. v. Brown, 561 F.3d 420, 429 (5th Cir. 2009).

19. Adam Nossiter, "U.S. Says Blacks in Mississippi Suppress White Vote," *New York Times*, October 11, 2006.

20. "Voting Rights Act Pointed in a New Direction," *USA Today*, April 3, 2006.

21. U.S. v. Brown, 494 F.Supp.2d at 480.

22. U.S. v. Brown, 494 F.Supp.2d at 444.

23. U.S. v. Brown, 561 F.3d at 431.

24. U.S. v. Brown, 494 F.Supp.2d at 479.

25. Jack Elliott Jr., "Noxubee's Brown Unshaken By Court Ruling," Associated Press, March 9, 2009.

CHAPTER ELEVEN

1. Interview with James O'Keefe, January 13, 2012.

2. Staff writers, "Fraud Worries Prompt Guide for Voter Lists," *New Hampshire Union Leader*, January 22, 2012.

3. Staff writers, "Hidden Video Renews NJEA, Gov. Christie Dispute," *Newark Star-Ledger*, October 27, 2010.

4. Terry Hurlbut, "O'Keefe 'Wild Teacher' Videos Claim First Casualty," November 11, 2010.

5. *Jersey Journal*, June 30, 1997.

6. Interview with Bret Schundler, January 20, 2012.

7. Jonathan Miller, "You Throw Mud, He'll Throw a Mountain," *New York Times*, May 27, 2007.

CHAPTER TWELVE

1. Due to lax enforcement by the Justice Department, many states failed to accurately report absentee military voting data as required by federal law. While there have been significant improvements in recent years in the quality of this data, data from the earlier

elections are general estimates based on a variety of sources. This 30 percent estimate is courtesy of the Military Voter Protection Project and AMVETS Clinic at Chapman University School of Law, M. Eric Eversole, "Military Voting in 2010: A Step Forward, But a Long Way to Go," at 2 n.7 (*MVP Project's 2010 Military Voting Report*, 2011).

2.   M. Eric Eversole and Hans A. von Spakovsky, "A President's Opportunity: Making Military Voters a Priority," Legal Memorandum No. 71 (Heritage Foundation, July 19, 2011).

3.   *Uniformed and Overseas Citizens Absentee Voting Act Survey Report Findings, September 2007*, U.S. Election Assistance Commission, at 1, Tables 21c and 22, *available at* www.eac.gov.

4.   Overseas Vote Foundation, *2008 OVF Post Election UOCAVA Survey Report and Analysis*, at 20 (Arlington, VA: February 2009).

5.   Kurt Erickson, "Regulators Examine Illinois' Military Ballots," Stltoday.com, October 13, 2010, *available at* http://www.stltoday.com/news/local/govt-and-politics/regulators-examine-illinois-military-ballots/article_08eefef6-d732-11df-89a0-00127992bc8b.html.

6.   *See* letter from Clifford L. Stanley, Under Secretary of Defense, Personnel and Readiness, to President Barack Obama and Congress, March 17, 2011, at 11–14, *available at* http://www.fvap.gov/resources/media/2010_180_day_report.pdf.

7.   *2010 Post Election Survey Report to Congress*, Federal Voting Assistance Program, September 2011.

CHAPTER THIRTEEN

1.   Interview with Catherine Englebrecht, January 12, 2012.

2.   Press release, office of Leo Vasquez, Harris County Tax Assessor–Collector, August 25, 2010.

3.   Chris Moran, "Vasquez, Group Hurl Voter Registration Accusations," *Houston Chronicle*, August 25, 2010.

4.   "Houston Politics" blog, *Houston Chronicle*, August 26, 2010.

5.   "Is the SEIU Connected to Voter Fraud in Harris County, Texas?," *The Blaze*, September 27, 2010.

6.   Press release, Liberty Institute, "Citizen-Volunteers Attacked by Political Machine Strike Back," October 25, 2010.

7.   Interview with Kelly Shackleford, January 23, 2012.

8.   Interview with Catherine Englebrecht.

9.   Editorial, "Picture This Contradiction," *Wall Street Journal*, March 13, 1997.

10. 42 U.S.C. § 1973gg-6(g).

11. Russ Buettner, "City Mulls Action Against Two-Timing Voters," *New York Daily News*, August 24, 2004.

12. Interview with Donetta Davidson, former Colorado Secretary of State, December 11, 2002.

13. Interview with Donetta Davidson.

14. Interview with Mary Kiffmeyer, former Minnesota Secretary of State, October 11, 2006.

15. Interview with Donetta Davidson.

16. Eric Russell, "Same Day Registration Buoys Democrats, But They May Be Reading Too Much Into Results," *Bangor Daily News*, November 9, 2011.

17. Christopher Keating and Jon Lender, "Martin Luther King III Hails Election Changes," *Hartford Courant*, April 24, 2012.

18. Interview with Robert Pastor of American University, September 14, 2011.

Index

U.S. Postal Service: absentee ballots
and military voters, 221; voter
registration validation process, 51
*U.S. Steel Corp. v. Multistate Tax
Commission*, 175–177
U.S. Term Limits, Inc. v. Thornton, 176
Utah, noncitizen voting in, 99, 130

van Zuylen-Wood, Simon, 81
Vasquez, Leo, 229
Velasquez, Rafael, 87
Vermont: National Popular Vote
plan, 170, 179; O'Keefe's filming
of ease of impersonation fraud, 211
Virginia, voter fraud examples, 38–39
von Spakovsky, Hans, 126, 127, 131,
133–135, 138, 189, 191–193
voter fraud: denials of, 33–34, 43–44;
encouraged by National Popular
Vote plan, 168, 183–184; examples
of, 34–43, 227–232; influence
in close elections, 157–165;
partisanship and, 8–10; public
opinion about, 4–6; state-level
steps needed to prevent, 232–254
voter ID laws, 18–19, 45–73;
disenfranchised voter myth and,
58–71; examples of need for,
47–58; identification required
elsewhere, 60, 64, 71–72, 232–233;
opposition to, 39, 46; public
opinion about, 3, 4, 71; steps
needed to prevent fraud, 232–233
voter registrations: conflicting
goals of electoral participation
and system integrity, 2, 25–32;
duplicate, in Minnesota, 16–17;
steps needed to prevent fraud,
236–237; voting age, in Minnesota
and, 18
voting machines, Jersey City's
delivery of already voted machines,
215

Voting Rights Act (VRA): Justice
Department hierarchy and,
124; Noxubee, Mississippi and,
138–139, 144–146, 151–155,
187–193, 203–209; Obama Justice
Department's refusal to enforce
in race-neutral manner, 132–151;
Section 5, 62, 125, 148–151
*Voting Rights—And Wrongs: The
Elusive Quest for Racially Fair
Elections* (Thernstrom), 134
vouching, for voters, 19

Wagner, Alex, 34
Walker, Albert, 199–200, 202
Washington, D.C.: National Popular
Vote plan and, 170, 179; O'Keefe's
filming of ease of impersonation
fraud, 209–211
Washington, Donald, 10
Washington State: National Popular
Vote plan and, 170; noncitizen
voting, 92, 99
West Virginia, voter fraud examples,
35
White, Charlie, 36
Whitten, Donald, 35
Wiggins, Marvin, 119
Wigglesworth, Yvonne, 87
Wilder, John, 158
Williams, Anastasia, 80, 81–82
Williams, Jada Woods, 40–41
Williams, Michael, 158
Winn, Nat, 111–112
Wisconsin, same-day registration in,
240–241
Wolf, Frank, 145–146
Working Family Party, 119–120

Yeomans, Bill, 129

Zogby, John, 24–25